MW00757147

HISTORY OF
United States Naval Operations
IN WORLD WAR II

*

VOLUME FOURTEEN

Victory in the Pacific

1945

HISTORY OF UNITED STATES NAVAL OPERATIONS
IN WORLD WAR II

By Samuel Eliot Morison

I *The Battle of the Atlantic*, September 1939 – May 1943
II *Operations in North African Waters*, October 1942 – June 1943
III *The Rising Sun in the Pacific*, 1931 – April 1942
IV *Coral Sea, Midway and Submarine Actions*, May 1942 – August 1942
V *The Struggle for Guadalcanal*, August 1942 – February 1943
VI *Breaking the Bismarcks Barrier*, 22 July 1942 – 1 May 1944
VII *Aleutians, Gilberts and Marshalls*, June 1942 – April 1944
VIII *New Guinea and the Marianas*, March 1944 – August 1944
IX *Sicily – Salerno – Anzio*, January 1943 – June 1944
X *The Atlantic Battle Won*, May 1943 – May 1945
XI *The Invasion of France and Germany*, 1944 – 1945
XII *Leyte*, June 1944 – January 1945
XIII *The Liberation of the Philippines: Luzon, Mindanao, the Visayas*, 1944 – 1945
XIV *Victory in the Pacific*, 1945
XV *Supplement and General Index*

Also
Strategy and Compromise

Photo by TSgt. Louis R. Lowery USMC

The Marine Corps men grasping the pole are Sgt. H. O. Hansen, Pl. Sgt. E. I. Thomas and 1st Lt. H. G. Schrier. Pfc. J. R. Michaels holds the carbine, Cpl. C. W. Lindberg stands behind

The First Flag-raising on Mount Suribachi, Iwo Jima

HISTORY OF UNITED STATES NAVAL OPERATIONS IN WORLD WAR II

VOLUME XIV

Victory in the Pacific

1945

BY SAMUEL ELIOT MORISON

With Illustrations

LITTLE, BROWN AND COMPANY
BOSTON • NEW YORK • TORONTO • LONDON

LIBRARY OF CONGRESS CATALOG CARD NO. 47-1571

10 9

KP

Published simultaneously in Canada
by Little, Brown & Company (Canada) Limited

PRINTED IN THE UNITED STATES OF AMERICA

To

The Memory of

WILLIAM FREDERICK HALSEY

1882–1959

Fleet Admiral, United States Navy

This was the greatest of all the achievements of the war and I think also of all the events known to us in history, the most decisive for the victor, the most ruinous for the conquered. They were utterly defeated at all points and endured no small sufferings, to no end.

— THUCYDIDES: *Peloponnesian War*, Book VII

Preface

I NOW DISCHARGE MY PROMISE, and complete my design, of writing the *History of United States Naval Operations in World War II.* Eighteen years have elapsed since I was commissioned in the Navy by President Franklin D. Roosevelt to do this task; thirteen years since the first volume came off the press. Fortunately good health, excellent assistance and the constant support and encouragement of my beloved wife, Priscilla Barton Morison, have enabled me to keep up a rate of production better than one volume a year.

A complete list of my assistants, with the exception of those who were given short temporary assignments, follows: –

Captain Bern Anderson USN, May 1952 to June 1960 [1]
Specialist 1st class Elinor M. Ball, April 1946 to April 1947
Dr. K. Jack Bauer, May 1957 to present
Commander Alexander C. Brown USNR, March 1945 to June 1946
Yeoman 1st class Antha E. Card W-USNR, March 1944 to September 1956 [2]
Yeoman 1st class Herbert M. Donaldson USNR, February 1946 to August 1948
Specialist 1st class Jane M. Donnelly, W-USNR, May 1946 to April 1947
Seaman 1st class Lawrence O. Donovan USNR, August 1945 to April 1946
Lieutenant Richard E. Downs USNR, May 1946 to April 1947
Commander George M. Elsey USNR, March to July 1944, and February to August 1949

[1] Retired as Rear Admiral 30 June 1960.
[2] Miss Card was separated from the Navy in Jan. 1946 but shortly after resumed work for the History as my personal secretary and continued to Sept. 1956.

Lieutenant Albert Harkness Jr. USNR, January 1946 to April 1947
Yeoman 3rd class Alexander D. Henderson USNR, August 1945 to May 1946
Yeoman 2nd class Edward Ledford USN, November 1956 to July 1958
Lieutenant Philip K. Lundeberg USNR, June 1948 and January to June 1950 [3]
Chief Yeoman Donald R. Martin USNR, February 1943 to present [4]
Ensign Richard S. Pattee USNR, June 1948 to June 1952
Lieutenant Commander Roger Pineau USNR, July 1947 to August 1957 [5]
Lieutenant Commander Henry D. Reck USNR, February 1944 to September 1948
Lieutenant Commander Henry Salomon Jr. USNR, February 1943 to December 1947 [6]
Yeoman 1st class Roger F. Schofield USN, September 1953 to November 1956
Commander James C. Shaw USN, November 1947 to June 1950 [7]

I also owe a debt of gratitude to Rear Admiral John B. Heffernan and Rear Admiral Ernest M. Eller, Directors of Naval History, under whom this History has been written. Fortunate indeed for an historian to have, as Directors, naval officers who are scholars themselves, and with whom he enjoyed the intimate relations of shipmate and friend during the period of hostilities.

The Naval War College at Newport, Rhode Island, under its successive presidents from Admiral Raymond A. Spruance (1945) to Vice Admiral Stuart H. Ingersoll (1960), has allotted office space for Captain Anderson and myself. The facilities of the drafting

[3] Lt. Lundeberg also did research on Volume X between and subsequent to his actual tours of duty, so that his total length of service to this History exceeded three years.

[4] Mr. Martin was separated from the Navy in Mar. 1947 but is still working for this History as a civilian.

[5] Lt. Cdr. Pineau was separated from the Navy in 1950 but continued working for this History as a civilian to Aug. 1957.

[6] Lt. Cdr. Salomon died 1 Feb. 1958.

[7] Now Rear Admiral USN retired.

room and cartographers, including Mr. Richard A. Gould, who did the maps for this volume, have also been available and extensively used. This association with the War College and its excellent library and staff has been a very pleasant and valuable experience.

Mr. Vernon E. Davis of the J. C. S. Historical Division helped me to unravel the tangle of events leading to the surrender of Japan.

Captain E. John Long USNR procured many of the illustrations.

Mr. Dean C. Allard, head of the Historical Records Branch of the Division of Naval History, has been most patient and helpful under my repeated requests.

Almost as important as those who actually worked on the research has been Miss Elizabeth Humphreys of Little, Brown and Company. She has copy-read the manuscript of each volume, and greatly improved it through her unerring scent for solecisms, contradictions and lack of uniformity in typographical style.

Writing the present volume began off Okinawa, an operation in which I participated on board Admiral Deyo's flagship *Tennessee*, as a member of the staff of her C.O., Captain John B. Heffernan. Before that operation was over I visited Iwo Jima, and spent some time at Fleet Admiral Nimitz's headquarters at Guam, reading action reports and talking with participants. After the end of the war I concentrated on the earlier years, and only returned to the subject matter of this volume in 1959. In it I have been particularly helped by Captain Bern Anderson, Dr. K. Jack Bauer and Mr. Donald R. Martin. Captain (now Rear Admiral) Anderson did much of the research for the text. Mr. Martin prepared Appendix I, and Dr. Bauer, Appendix II.

It must be repeated that this is not in the usual sense of the word an "official history," nor am I an "official historian." I was commissioned in the Naval Reserve in 1942 with the special mission to write it and have continued so to do as a civilian since my retirement from active duty in 1946. The Navy has given me every facility, but has not attempted to prejudice my conclusions or set the pattern of my writing. Little, Brown and Company of Boston, publishers of the classic works of Alfred Thayer Mahan, accepted this series as a regular publishing venture. The royalties are paid to the Navy, which has set them aside in a special capital fund which will be used to promote research and writing in United States Naval History.

This is the final narrative volume of the series. It will be followed by Volume XV, *General Index and Supplement*, which will contain (1) a general index of the entire series, including the task organizations which were not indexed in the separate volumes, (2) a description of different types of combatant ships, auxiliaries and naval airplanes used in World War II, (3) a summary of post-surrender operations in the Pacific, and (4) a cumulative list of errata, which will enable possessors of first editions to bring them up to date. So I make a special request to readers to send in promptly any additional errata that they may discover.

All times in this volume are of zone "Item" (Greenwich minus 9) and dates are east longitude dates, except where I am describing events in the United States itself.

Sources generally used without specific citation are the Action Reports and War Diaries of individual ships and commands, and the Cincpac Monthly Intelligence Summary, which was prepared by a staff under Captain Ralph C. Parker.

* * *

Every sailor must have a shore base whence he shoves off and whither, from time to time, he returns. From my base in Boston, where "every street leads down to the sea," I set sail in U.S.S. *Buck* in 1942 on the first leg of a long voyage. She went down in 1944; many of my old shipmates have departed; but I have been allowed to complete my voyage and my mission. So, thankful for past favors and hopeful for the future, I pick up my old mooring buoy and row ashore, happy to have reached home safely.

SAMUEL E. MORISON

44 BRIMMER STREET
BOSTON, MASSACHUSETTS
February, 1960

Contents

Preface ix
Abbreviations xxiii

PART I

IWO JIMA

I Decisions, Plans and Preparations, *October 1944–February 1945* 3
1. The Bonins and Ryukyus in Pacific Strategy 3
2. Planning for Iwo Jima 5
3. Air Bombing and Naval Bombardment 9
4. Japanese Preparations 13

II Preliminary Poundings, *10–18 February 1945* 20
1. Carrier Wings Over Japan 20
2. Two Days' Pounding, 16–17 February 25
3. D-day minus 1, 18 February 30

III D-day at Iwo Jima, *19 February 1945* 33
1. Pre-landing Bombardment 33
2. H-hour, 0900 35
3. Build-up and Support 40
4. Air Operations 44

IV The Conquest of Iwo Jima, *19 February–16 March 1945* 47
1. The Struggle Ashore, 20–21 February 47
2. Carrier Strikes and Air Support, 21 February–1 March 52
3. The Land Battle, 22 February–16 March 59

V Securing the Island, *17 March–1 June 1945* 67
1. The Mopping-up Process 67
2. Air Base and Conclusion 70

PART II

OKINAWA

VI Preparing for the Ryukyus, *October 1944–March 1945* 79
1. Okinawa and the Okinawans 79
2. Planning Operation ICEBERG 86
3. Japanese Preparations 92
4. The Fast Carriers' Contribution, 18–31 March 94
5. The Royal Navy's Participation 102

VII Moving In on the Ryukyus, *18 March–1 April* 108
1. Sorties from Ulithi and Carrier Support 108
2. The Minesweepers 113
3. Kerama Retto Occupied 117

VIII More Preliminaries, *25–31 March* 130
1. The Fire Support Group 130
2. Air Support, Naval Bombardment and UDTs 132
3. L-day minus One, 31 March 138

IX The Landings, *1 April 1945* 140
1. Organization of One Attack Group 140
2. A Landing on the Southern Beaches 146

X ICEBERG Logistics, *March–June 1945* 156
1. The Logistic Support Group 156
2. The Provisions Problem 163
3. Ammunition – and Conclusion 165

XI Feeling Each Other Out, *2–5 April 1945* 170
1. Where Is the Enemy? 170

2. Unloading 172
3. Retirement and Retaliation 175

XII TEN-GO Gets Going, *6–8 April* 181
1. The Gallant Fight of *Newcomb* and *Leutze* 181
2. Radar Pickets Blooded 186
3. Attacks on Antisubmarine Screen and Minecraft 191
4. Raid on Kerama 195

XIII Fast Carrier Support, *1–12 April 1945* 199
1. The End of *Yamato*, 7 April 199
2. Task Force 58 Operations, 11 April 209
3. Royal Navy off Sakishima Gunto, 1–12 April 211

XIV The Second Week at Okinawa, *7–13 April 1945* 215
1. The Situation Ashore, 8–11 April 215
2. East Side 218
3. Air Battles of 9 and 12 April 221
4. The Death of President Roosevelt 230

XV The Crucial Fortnight, *14–30 April* 233
1. The Radar Pickets' Ordeal 233
2. Progress Ashore; Ie Shima; Naval Gunfire Support 239
3. Fast Carriers of the United States Navy and Royal Navy 247

XVI May Days at Okinawa 251
1. The Radar Picket Line 251
2. The Fast Carrier Force 262
3. Operations on and near Okinawa 266

XVII Okinawa Secured, *June–September 1945* 273
1. The Last Month of Battle, 3 June–2 July 273
2. The Air and Naval Base 276

PART III

MISCELLANEOUS OPERATIONS

XVIII Pacific Fleet Submarines, *December 1944–August 1945* 285
1. Offensive Operations 285
2. Lifeguard Service 294

XIX Third Fleet in Japanese Waters, *June–July 1945* 298
1. June Typhoon 298
2. Honshu and Hokkaido Bombed and Bombarded 309

XX Parthian Shots and Final Passes, *24 July–15 August 1945* 317
1. The *Kaitens* Score 317
2. The Loss of *Indianapolis* 319
3. Last Swipes at Japan 330

XXI Victory and Peace 336
1. The Approach to Peace, January–August 1945 336
2. Allied Plans for the Occupation 353
3. Japan Surrenders, 15 August–2 September 358

Appendix I Task Organization for the Capture of Okinawa 371

Appendix II United States Ships Sunk or Badly Damaged by Enemy Action in the Iwo Jima and Okinawa Operations 389

Index 393

List of Illustrations

(Illustrations appear between pages 198 and 199)

The First Flag-raising on Mount Suribachi, Iwo Jima *Frontispiece*

The Invasion of Iwo Jima:
- Liberator over Iwo Jima, 15 December 1944
- Planning for Invasion
- LCIs Moving In, 17 February 1945
- One of the Damaged LCIs
- H-hour, D-day
- Boat Waves Forming
- Fifth Marine Division Advancing near Mount Suribachi
- Fourth Marine Division Moving up the Beach

The Battle for Iwo Jima:
- Marines Moving In on a Cave
- Fifth Division Command Post

Beaching Craft Unloading under Mount Suribachi, 24 February

On Iwo Jima:
- A Marine-Navy JASCO in Position
- Effect of Naval Gunfire on a Japanese Pillbox

Views from Mount Suribachi, 21 April 1945

Spring Bombing by U.S.S. *Essex* Planes:
- Kure, 19 March
- Midget Submarine Pen, Okinawa, 27 March

The Ordeal of U.S.S. *Franklin*, 19 March

Kerama Retto:
- General View of the Roadstead
- Landing on Aka Shima, 26 March

Deadly Japanese Midgets:
Baka Bomb
Suicide Boat, Zamami Jima

L-day at Okinawa:
Avengers over the Beaches
LVTs Passing U.S.S. *Tennessee*
LVT(A)s of First Wave with Control Craft
LSMs Going In

Okinawa and Off Shore:
Unloading on Beach Yellow 3
Destroyer *Ault* Fueling in Heavy Weather

Commodore Augustine H. Gray USN

Rear Admiral Bertram J. Rodgers USN

CTF 38 and CTF 58:
Vice Admiral John S. McCain USN
Vice Admiral Marc A. Mitscher USN in U.S.S. *Randolph*

Rear Admiral C. Turner Joy USN

Rear Admiral Donald B. Beary USN

Commander Leon Grabowsky USN

Commander I. E. McMillian USN

Operation TEN-GO Gets Going:
Twilight Air Attack on Transport Area
U.S.S. *Newcomb* after Kamikaze Crash

The Air Attack of 12 April:
U.S.S. *Zellars* after Kamikaze Crash
U.S.S. *Tennessee* after Splashing One on Each Bow
U.S.S. *Tennessee* Fighting Fires

The Last of Battleship *Yamato*

Going, Going, Gone! (The Last of Light Cruiser *Yahagi*)

Kamikaze Victims off Okinawa:
U.S.S. *Laffey*, after Hits on 16 April
U.S.S. *Aaron Ward*, after Hits on 3 May

A Kamikaze Victim Survives:
U.S.S. *Hazelwood*, after Hits on 29 April
Hazelwood Restored, with Helicopter Deck, 1959

Aircraft Carriers:
U.S.S. *Enterprise* Crashed off Kyushu, 14 May
Deck Scene

June Typhoon:
The Angry Sea
U.S.S. *Pittsburgh* minus her Bow

Victory:
Congratulations
Ships of Third Fleet in Sagami Wan, 27 August

The Surrender on board U.S.S. *Missouri*, 2 September 1945:
Mr. Shigemitsu Signs
General MacArthur Signs

Immediately after the Surrender:
The Japanese Delegation Departs
Wings over U.S.S. *Iowa*

Homeward Bound

(*All photographs not otherwise described are Official United States Navy*)

List of Maps and Charts

Carrier Operations in Support of Iwo Jima 23

Iwo Jima, 19 February 1945 36

Iwo Jima, Progress of the Battle 60

Iwo Jima as a Developed United States Air Base 71

Okinawa Gunto 84

The Kerama Retto 123

Japanese Suicide Boat Operations Chart 125

Hagushi Beaches, Okinawa 142

Okinawa Landings 1 April 1945 – on Purple and Orange Beaches 150

Major Air Attacks 6 April 183

Radar Picket Stations off Okinawa 189

Track of the *Yamato* Task Force, 6–7 April 201

Action of 7 April and End of *Yamato* 207

Progress on Okinawa 1–11 April 219

Major Air Attacks 12 April 228

Attacks on U.S.S. *Laffey* 16 April 234

Track of Typhoon and of U.S.S. *Hornet*, 5 June 302

Plot of Typhoon Center, 5 June 303

Track Chart of Task Force 38, 1 July–15 August 315

The Sinking of U.S.S. *Indianapolis*, 29 July 323

The Northwest Pacific, 1945 *At End*

Abbreviations

Officers' ranks and bluejackets' ratings are those contemporaneous with the event. Officers and men named will be presumed to be of the United States Navy unless it is otherwise stated; officers of the Naval Reserve are designated USNR. Other service abbreviations are USA, United States Army; USCG, United States Coast Guard; USCGR, Reserve of same; USMC, United States Marine Corps; USMCR, Reserve of same; RAN, Royal Australian Navy; RN, Royal Navy; RCN, Royal Canadian Navy; IJN, Imperial Japanese Navy.

A.A.F. – United States Army Air Forces
AK – Navy Cargo ship; AKA – Attack cargo
AP – Transport; APA – Attack transport; APD – destroyer transport
A/S – Antisubmarine
Batdiv – Battleship division
BB – Battleship
BLT – Battalion Landing Team
Bu – Bureau; Buord – Bureau of Ordnance; Bupers – Bureau of Naval Personnel; Buships – Bureau of Ships, etc.
CA – Heavy cruiser
C.A.P. – Combat Air Patrol
Cardiv – Carrier division
C.I.C. – Combat Information Center
Cincpac – Commander in Chief, Pacific Fleet (Admiral Nimitz)
CL – Light Cruiser
C.O. – Commanding Officer
C.N.O. – Chief of Naval Operations
Com – before cardiv, desdiv, etc., means Commander Carrier Division, Commander Destroyer Division, etc.
Cominch – Commander in Chief, United States Fleet (Admiral King)
CTF – Commander Task Force; CTG – Commander Task Group
CV – Aircraft Carrier; CVE – Escort Carrier; CVL – Light Carrier
DD – Destroyer; DE – Destroyer Escort
H.M.A.S. – His Majesty's Australian Ship; H.M.S. – His Majesty's Ship; H.M.N.Z.S. – His Majesty's New Zealand Ship; H.M.C.S. – His Majesty's Canadian Ship

H.Q. — Headquarters
IFF — Identification, Friend or Foe
JASCO — Joint Assault Signal Company
J.C.S. — Joint Chiefs of Staff
LC — Landing craft; LCI — Landing craft, infantry; LCM — Landing craft, mechanized; LCS — Landing craft, support; LCT — Landing craft, tank; LCVP — Landing craft, vehicles and personnel; LSD — Landing ship, dock; LSI — Landing ship, infantry; LSM — Landing ship, medium; LST — Landing ship, tank; LSV — Landing ship, vehicle; LVT — Landing vehicle tracked (or Amphtrac). (A), (G), (L), (M) and (R) added to above types mean armored, gunboat, large, mortar and rocket.
Op — Operation; Opnav — Chief of Naval Operations; op plan — Operation Plan
O.N.I. — Office of Naval Intelligence
O.S.S. — Office of Strategic Services
O.T.C. — Officer in Tactical Command
PC — Patrol craft; PCE — Patrol craft, escort
P.O.W. — Prisoner of war
RCT — Regimental Combat Team
s.f.c.p — Shore fire control party
S.O.P.A. — Senior Officer Present Afloat
SS — Submarine
TF — Task Force; TG — Task Group; TU — Task Unit
UDT — Underwater Demolition Team
U.S.C.G.C. — United States Coast Guard Cutter
USSBS — United States Strategic Bombing Survey
VB; VC; VF; VT; VOS — Bomber; Composite; Fighter; Torpedo Observation-Scout plane or squadron
YMS — Motor minesweeper; YP — Patrol vessel

Aircraft Designations

(Numerals in parentheses indicate number of engines)

United States

B-24 — Liberator, Army (4) heavy bomber; B-26 — Marauder, Army (2) medium bomber; B-29 — Superfortress, Army (4) heavy bomber
F4F — Wildcat; F6F — Hellcat; F4U — Corsair; Navy (1) fighters

OS2U – Kingfisher, Navy (1) scout-observation float plane
P-38 – Lightning, Army (2); P-47 – Thunderbolt, Army (1); P-51 – Mustang, Army (1) fighters
PBJ – Navy Mitchell (2) medium bomber
PBM-3 – Mariner, Navy (2) patrol bomber (flying boat)
PBY – Catalina, Navy (2) patrol bomber; PBY-5A, amphibian Catalina; PB4Y-1 – Navy Liberator bomber (4); PB4Y-2 – Navy Privateer bomber (4)
PV-1 – Ventura, Navy (2) medium bomber
SB2C, SBW – Helldivers; SBD – Dauntless, Navy (1) dive-bombers
TBF, TBM – Avenger, Navy (1) torpedo-bombers

Japanese

Betty – Mitsubishi Zero-1, Navy (2) high-level or torpedo-bomber
Fran – Nakajima, Navy (2) all-purpose bomber
Frances – Nakajima, Navy (2) bomber
Frank – Nakajima, Army (1) fighter
Jake – Aichi or Watanabe, Navy (1) reconnaissance bomber
Jill – Nakajima, Navy (1) torpedo-bomber
Judy – Aichi, Navy (1) dive-bomber
Kate – Nakajima, Navy (1) torpedo-bomber
Nate & Oscar – Nakajima, Army (1) fighters
Nick – Kawasaki or Nakajima Zero-2, Army (2) fighter
Sally – Mitsubishi, Army (2) medium bomber
Tojo – Nakajima Zero-2, Army (1) fighter
Tony – Zero-3, Army or Navy (1) fighter
Val – Aichi 99, Navy (1) dive-bomber
Zeke – Mitsubishi Zero-3, Navy (1) fighter

PART 1

Iwo Jima

CHAPTER I

Decisions, Plans and Preparations[1]

October 1944–February 1945

1. *The Bonins and Ryukyus in Pacific Strategy*

IT WAS a long, hard pull for the Navy across the Pacific to within striking distance of Japan; but, by the time Saipan in the Marianas had been conquered (August 1944) and the major part of Luzon liberated (February 1945), two practicable routes were open to the ultimate objective – the Nanpo Shoto and the Nansei Shoto island chains. The first, better known to Americans and Europeans as the Bonins,[2] begins not far off Tokyo Bay and continues southerly for some 700 miles to Minami Shima, which is 290 miles northwest of the northernmost Marianas, and 615 miles north of Saipan. Most of these islands are tiny volcanic cones, too small for an airfield. But Chichi Jima and Iwo Jima had distinct possibilities.

The other island chain, the Nansei Shoto (better known to Americans and Europeans as the Ryukyus), forms a great arc some 600 miles long, from Honshu, southernmost of the Japanese home is-

[1] This subject is also covered to some extent in Vols. XII Chap. I and XIII Chap. I. To the sources mentioned there add J. A. Isely and P. A. Crowl *The U.S. Marines and Amphibious War* (1951) chap. x, Lt. Col. Whitman S. Bartley USMC *Iwo Jima: Amphibious Epic*, published by Marine Corps Historical Branch 1954. In addition the writer discussed the strategic questions affecting the operations in this volume with Rear Admiral Forrest Sherman in May 1945, and profited by a perusal of his personal compilation, "Future Operations Recommendations to Cominch."

[2] The Bonin Islands (Ogasawara Gunto to the Japanese) properly are the central group of Nanpo Shoto comprising Muko, Chichi, and Haha. The southern group, which includes Iwo Jima, is called the Volcano Islands, but Bonins is often used for the entire chain. *Jima* or *Shima* means an island, *Shoto* an archipelago, *Gunto* an island group.

lands, to Formosa, making the eastern border of the East China Sea. This chain contains five or six islands suitable for air bases, the best and largest being Okinawa.

The spokesmen for taking Luzon (led by General MacArthur) and for taking Formosa (led by Admiral King) had held long discussions at Cincpac headquarters, at San Francisco, and with the Joint Chiefs of Staff at Washington. The Luzonites won because the Army estimated that securing Formosa would require nine combat divisions and more service troops than were likely to be available before the surrender of Germany. This was practically decided at the San Francisco Conference of 29 September – 1 October 1944, between Admirals King, Nimitz and Spruance and Generals Harmon and Buckner. Admiral Nimitz there submitted a carefully written memorandum, which not only urged that Luzon be the target but gave his opinion as to what should follow. He recommended a staggered, two-pronged advance, as follows. The first – target date 20 January 1945 – should thrust "up the ladder of the Bonins" to Chichi Jima or Iwo Jima; the second – target date 1 March – along the arc of the Ryukyus to one or more positions such as Okinawa or Amami O Shima. The purpose of the one would be to obtain emergency landing facilities for Saipan-based B–29s and a base for their fighter escorts in bombing Japan proper; and of the other, to secure and develop a sound air and naval base for the invasion of the Japanese home islands.

Admiral Spruance, who seems to have been the first high-ranking naval officer to appreciate the possibilities of Okinawa, observed with pleasure at San Francisco that Admiral King, who hitherto had been insistent on taking Formosa, had been reluctantly won over by Admiral Nimitz's logic. At this point in the discussion King turned to Spruance and remarked, "Haven't you something to say? I understand that Okinawa is your baby." To which Spruance, a man of deep thought but few words, replied that Nimitz had put the case so well that he had nothing to add.

From San Francisco Admiral King brought the word to the Joint Chiefs of Staff, who on 3 October issued the directive to General MacArthur and Admiral Nimitz, in pursuance of which the operations described in this volume were carried out: —

1. General MacArthur will seize and occupy Luzon, target date 20 December, and provide support for subsequent occupation of the Ryukyus by Admiral Nimitz's forces.
2. Admiral Nimitz, after providing covering and support forces for the liberation of Luzon, will occupy one or more positions in the Bonins-Volcano Group, target date 20 January 1945, and one or more positions in the Ryukyus, target date 1 March 1945.
3. Both C. in C.'s will arrange for coördination of forces and resources between themselves and with the Commanding Generals of XX Army Air Force,[8] and of the China-Burma-India area.

So there it was, on the line. The eastern (Iwo Jima) operation was placed first after Luzon because it was expected to be easier than the western (Okinawa) one. It was never anticipated that the same troops would be used for both operations, but the same Pacific Fleet would have to cover and support both, while the Seventh Fleet and Amphibious Force were engaged in covering and liberating the Southern Philippines, as described in our previous volume. It was necessary that Fast Carrier Forces (TF 38 or 58) be detached from supporting these Philippines operations in time to cover both the Bonins and the Ryukyus invasions.

2. *Planning for Iwo Jima*

Postponing consideration of the Okinawa plans to Part II, we shall explain why Iwo Jima of glorious though gory memory was chosen as the Bonins objective. The only alternative was the more northerly and larger Chichi Jima, which had a good protected harbor, Port Lloyd. But that island is too rugged for quick airfield

[8] XX A.A.F. included XX Bomber Command in China and XXI Bomber Command in Marianas.

construction, and air reconnaissance showed that it was more heavily fortified than Iwo.

The Bonin Islands might have been an American possession if President Franklin Pierce's administration had backed up Commodore Matthew Calbraith Perry. Chichi Jima was first settled from Honolulu in 1830 by two New Englanders – Aldin B. Chapin and Nathaniel Savory – a Genoese, and 25 Hawaiians, who made a living raising provisions for sale to passing whalers. Commodore Perry called at Port Lloyd on 14 June 1853, next day purchased for fifty dollars a plot of land on the harbor, stocked it with cattle brought over in U.S.S. *Susquehanna*, set up a local government under Savory, promulgated a code of laws, and took possession for the United States. He intended to make Chichi Jima a provisioning station for the United States Navy and American mail steamers. But this action was repudiated by the Pierce administration in Washington. Thus, in 1861 Japan was able to annex the Bonin Islands without opposition. The government did not disturb the American colony, and serious colonization of the group by Japanese did not start until 1887.[4]

Iwo Jima, central island of the Volcano group, had great value as a strategic outpost, but for nothing else. Situated in lat. 24° 45′ N, long. 141°20′ E, shaped like a bloated pear or a lopsided pork chop, Iwo is only 4½ miles long and 2½ miles wide. The volcanic crater of Mount Suribachi, 550 feet above sea level, at the stem of the pear, remained inactive during World War II, but numerous jets of steam and sulphur all over the island suggested that an eruption might take place at any moment. The northern part of the island is a plateau with rocky and inaccessible shores, but beaches extended from the base of Mount Suribachi for more than two miles north and east. These beaches, the land between them, and a good part of the terrain are deeply covered with brown volcanic ash and black cinders which look like sand, but are so much lighter than sand that walking is difficult and running impossible. Marston mat had to be laid to accommodate wheeled and even tracked ve-

[4] Lionel B. Cholmondeley *History of the Bonin Islands* (London 1915).

hicles. Up to 1944 the island was inhabited by about 1100 Japanese civilians who raised sugar and pineapples, extracted sulphur and ran a crude sugar mill; but all were evacuated before this operation began.

The unique importance of Iwo Jima for warlike purposes was derived from its location and topography. It lies almost midway between Honshu and the Marianas, 625 miles north of Saipan and 660 miles south of Tokyo. The Japanese constructed two airfields on the island, and a third had been started. On 14 July 1944 General "Hap" Arnold, head of the Army Air Forces, recommended to the Joint Planners that Iwo be seized to provide for emergency landings of the B–29 Superforts, and to base P–51 fighter planes to escort them in raids on Tokyo. The Joint Planners agreed, provided that the seizure of Iwo would not interfere with other and more important operations.[5]

As soon as the 3 October 1944 directive arrived at Cincpac headquarters, Admiral Nimitz's staff planners, presided over by Rear Admiral Forrest Sherman, moved fast. On 7 October they produced a staff study which became the basis for the plan and outlined the Iwo operation very much as it was carried out.[6]

Admiral Raymond A. Spruance, Commander Fifth Fleet, had the over-all command at Iwo Jima. Under him Vice Admiral Richmond K. Turner commanded the Joint Expeditionary Force (TF 51). As this was to be a Marine Corps landing, Lieutenant General Holland M. Smith USMC was made Commander Expeditionary Troops (TF 56), which consisted of the V Amphibious Corps, Major General Harry Schmidt USMC. Also under Turner were Rear Admiral Harry W. Hill, Commander Attack Force (TF 53), and Rear Admiral W. H. P. Blandy, Commander Amphibious Support Force (TF 52). Also in support of the operation were Vice Admiral Marc A. Mitscher's Fast Carrier Force (TF 58), an expanded Logistic Support Group commanded by Rear Admiral Donald B.

[5] Craven & Cate V 586–587.

[6] Cincpac-Cincpoa "Joint Staff Study DETACHMENT" 7 Oct. 1944. Operation DETACHMENT was the code name for the capture of Iwo, but it was little used.

Beary, and a Search and Reconnaissance Group (TG 50.5) under Commodore Dixwell Ketcham.

The landing force, the V 'Phib Corps, comprised the 3rd Marine Division (Major General Graves B. Erskine USMC), which had recently liberated Guam; the 4th Marine Division (Major General Clifton B. Cates USMC), then at Maui; and the new 5th Marine Division (Major General Keller E. Rockey USMC), then on the island of Hawaii. General Schmidt's headquarters were on Guam, but to plan for Iwo he moved to Pearl Harbor on 13 October. When General MacArthur was persuaded to postpone the Lingayen landings to 9 January, the two operations coming up were postponed for a full month – Iwo Jima to 19 February, and Okinawa to 1 April 1945.

There also had to be keen planning on the logistics end.[7] In operations for the liberation of the Philippines, a seagoing logistics group was set up in order to bring oil, replacement planes, spare parts and fleet tugs to the fast carrier forces at sea. This procedure proved so successful that the group was now enlarged and extended by adding ammunition ships and other auxiliaries, redesignating the group Service Squadron 6, and placing it under the command of Rear Admiral Beary, who had been head of Training Command Atlantic Fleet at Norfolk.[8] *Detroit*, one of the old light cruisers, was allotted to him as flagship. The Iwo operation, comparatively short, gave the new method of issue and transfer a good tryout. Twenty-seven fleet oilers were employed. Between 8 February and 5 March 1945 they delivered at sea 2,787,000 barrels of fuel oil (1,702,000 of them to Fast Carrier Force), 7,126,000 gallons of aviation gas (3,378,000 to the fast carriers), and 105,000 barrels of diesel oil. Ulithi, the headquarters of Commodore Carter's Servron 10, was the terminus of merchant tankers that supplied fleet oilers or floating storage.

Shasta and *Wrangell* on 19 February made the first successful

[7] Worrall R. Carter *Beans, Bullets, and Black Oil* (1953) chap. xxii; Comservron 6 (Rear Adm. Beary) "Logistic Analysis Iwo Operation" 8 Mar. 1956. For Leyte logistics see Vol. XII Chap. V.

[8] For brief biography see Vol. X 47*n*.

experiment in alongside transfer of ammunition at sea.[9] Three escort carriers, recently modified to carry replacement planes, and two of the older CVEs operated with oiler groups. By 1 March they had delivered 254 new planes and 65 pilots and crewmen to fleet, light and escort carriers. *Virgo*, fitted as a mobile general stores ship, made the first successful experiment in transferring by line packages of dry stores, small stores and clothing.

A valuable innovation was the conversion of two LSTs to be mother ships to landing craft.[10] Each had bunks, cooking and mess facilities for 40 officers and 300 men, 20 reefer boxes carrying 160,000 rations of fresh and frozen provisions, space for the same number of dry rations, and large evaporators. Now, at last, boat crews, left on the beach when transports retired for the night, had a chance for a shower bath, a hot meal and a "sack." During the first two weeks of the Iwo operation these mother ships also refueled and watered 54 small vessels such as PCEs and LCTs, and reprovisioned an additional 76.

3. *Air Bombing and Naval Bombardment* [11]

The Army Air Force setup in the Pacific was modified in August 1944 when Lieutenant General Millard F. Harmon assumed command of the newly formed Army Air Forces, Pacific Ocean Areas. General Harmon was also deputy commander to "Hap" Arnold of XX Air Force, which included the B–29s operating from Chinese bases, and of XXI Bomber Command of B–29s in the Marianas. In December 1944, Admiral Nimitz named him Commander Strategic Air Force, Pacific Ocean Areas, with control over all land-based aviation in the Pacific.

[9] *Serpens,* a Coast-Guard-manned cargo ship of Servron 8 refitted as ammunition carrier, blew up in Lunga Roads, Guadalcanal, on 29 Jan. 1945 with the loss of all hands but three.

[10] Commo. Carter (p. 290) credits this type to "Admiral Turner's ingenuity and initiative."

[11] Comcrudiv 5 (Rear Adm. Allan E. Smith) Action Reports of 17 Dec. 1944 and 21 Jan. 1945; Craven & Cate V chap. xix.

As air bases became available in the Marianas the VII Army Air Force (Major General Willis H. Hale) began to subject Iwo Jima to one of the longest sustained air bombardments of the war. This air force, widely scattered over the Pacific, was mainly engaged in keeping bypassed islands neutralized. Truk was the main target, but others – such as Ponape, Wotje, Marcus and Wake – were given attention from time to time. As new bases in the Marianas were developed, General Hale's fighters and bombers moved forward to attack the Bonins chain. On 10 August the first B–24s based on Saipan bombed Iwo Jima. Thereafter that island and others nearby were hit whenever the weather permitted. There were 10 such raids on the island in August, 22 in September, and 16 in October. Most of them were aimed at cratering the airfields, but some were anti-shipping strikes on harbors in Chichi Jima and Haha Jima. These were laid on to oblige the Navy, which was concerned over the extensive reinforcement of Iwo Jima that was being staged through Port Lloyd and other island harbors. General Hale protested that his B–24 pilots were not trained for anti-shipping attacks, but not until the B–29s began operating from Saipan were these strikes called off.

The first B–29 from the United States landed on Saipan on 12 October, and by the end of November there were enough to launch the first strike against Japan.[12] Before that happened the Japanese, realizing what they were in for, counterattacked the Saipan fields twice, and ineffectively; but after the first B–29 raid against the Japanese homeland, on 24 November, they hit back hard. Early on the 27th, as the Superforts were loading bombs for a second strike, two twin-engined Japanese bombers came in low, destroyed one B–29 and damaged eleven others. Around noon the same day 10 to 15 single-engined fighters evaded the radar screen, destroyed three more B–29s and severely damaged two. These raids, which continued intermittently until 2 January, succeeded in damaging six and destroying eleven B–29s.

Since the loss of a B–29 was serious, strenuous efforts were made

[12] For description of the Superfortress, see Vol. XIII 162.

to intercept or stop these raids. Vice Admiral John H. Hoover, Commander Forward Area, stationed two destroyers 100 miles northwest of Saipan as early warning pickets. They detected some raids, but not all. Since it was rightly suspected that the Japanese bombers staged through Iwo Jima, Admiral Nimitz gave that island top priority on 24 November. He ordered the curtailment of VII A.A.F. strikes on bypassed islands and shipping in order to concentrate a joint aërial bombing and naval bombardment on Iwo, 8 December.

A fighter sweep by 28 P–38s opened the attack at 0945; 62 B–29s bombed at 1100 and 102 B–24s at noon; Crudiv 5 (Rear Admiral Allan E. Smith), comprising heavy cruisers *Chester*, *Pensacola* and *Salt Lake City* with six destroyers, arrived off Iwo at 1330 and opened bombardment at 1347. "Hoke" Smith approached the island from the west, rounded Mount Suribachi and then reversed track in a half-circle. Unfortunately the sky was so heavily overcast as to force the planes to bomb by radar and to hamper ships' spotting. Surface visibility was good enough to enable the island to be well covered by a naval bombardment, which lasted for 70 minutes and expended 1500 rounds of 8-inch and 5334 rounds of 5-inch shell. The bombers dropped 814 tons of bombs. Photographs, taken three days later, showed that both airfields on Iwo were wholly or in part operational, but no more enemy air raids hit the Marianas until Christmas Day.

The job of keeping Iwo airfields neutralized was now turned over to B–24s of VII A.A.F. Between 8 December 1944 and 15 February 1945 they flew at least one strike daily over the island. The day before Christmas, Rear Admiral Smith's heavy cruisers, together with five destroyers, delivered a second bombardment, coördinated with a B–24 strike. This strike was slightly more eventful than the initial one in December, but even less effective. The bombardment, which expended 1500 rounds of 8-inch, provoked return fire from a 6-inch coast defense battery (designated "Kitty" on the target maps) in the northeast part of the island, but "Kitty's" claws managed to strike no closer than 200 yards. As proof of the slight damage inflicted by this bombardment, the Japanese were able to pay a vicious return visit to Saipan on Christmas Eve, a raid of 25 planes which destroyed one B–29 and damaged three more beyond repair.

Crudiv 5 returned 27 December for a repeat performance, lighter than the others; and a fourth bombardment was set up for 5 January 1945. While fighter planes and B–24s hit Iwo Jima the same cruisers and six destroyers bombarded Chichi Jima, 145 miles northward, and the slightly nearer Haha Jima. Their hope was to catch a convoy bringing Japanese supplies to these islands, whence they were forwarded to Iwo by small craft at night. Destroyer *Fanning*, steaming ahead of the group as radar picket, encountered at 0206 a surface target, later identified as *LSV–102*, which she sank. At 0700 Admiral Smith's group opened a one hour and 49 minutes' bombardment of Chichi Jima. During it, destroyer *David W Taylor* suffered an underwater explosion, probably from a mine, which flooded her forward magazine. The Haha Jima bombardment by *Salt Lake City* and two destroyers lasted for an hour. Crudiv 5 then pounded Iwo Jima for another hour and three quarters. The reply was negligible, and a few aircraft which made passes at the cruisers were easily driven off.

The next bombardment came on 25 January, following a three-hour forenoon bombing by VII A.A.F. B–24s, escorted by P–38s. Rear Admiral Oscar C. Badger was now O.T.C., wearing his flag in battleship *Indiana*, and he brought along two more destroyers as well as Crudiv 5. The bombardment opened at 1400 and lasted for two hours. *Indiana* planted 203 rounds of 16-inch on the island and Crudiv 5 added 1354 rounds of 8-inch.

Beginning the last day of January, and for two weeks, VII A.A.F bombed the island night and day. The Superforts also got in a few licks on 24 and 29 January and 12 February, adding 367 tons of bombs to the impressive total that hit, or at least were aimed at, the island.[13]

Probably no island in World War II received as much pre-

[13] "Analysis of Air Operations Pacific Ocean Areas and B–29 Operations," Nov.–Dec. 1944.

liminary pounding as did Iwo Jima. For ten weeks, until 16 February when the intensive pre-landing bombardment began, the island was hit by land-based aircraft almost every day, and the total tonnage of bombs dropped was not far from 6800.[14] In addition, 203 rounds of 16-inch, 6472 rounds of 8-inch and 15,251 rounds of 5-inch shell were fired in the five naval bombardments. Under ordinary circumstances, so heavy and prolonged a bombardment would have been more than sufficient to pulverize everything on an island of that size. Yet the Japanese restored the airfields on Iwo Jima to operation a few hours after each attack, and continued to fortify the island.

Staff planners and Admiral Nimitz himself anticipated no unusual difficulty in taking Iwo Jima. Pacific Fleet technique for wresting islands from the enemy had been worked out as the result of abundant experience at Tarawa, Kwajalein, Eniwetok, Saipan, Guam and Peleliu. Yet when the Marines landed on the island 19 February, after three more days of intensive bombardment, expecting to secure it in a few days, they were forced to fight for it bitterly almost yard by yard over a period of one month and to lose 6137 of their number. How that could happen becomes apparent when we examine the Japanese defense system on Iwo Jima.

4. *Japanese Preparations* [15]

Until after the American seizure of the Marshall Islands in February 1944, Iwo Jima was simply a whistle stop on the air line from Japan to the Marianas and Carolines. Chichi Jima had been a small naval base since 1914, and most of the Japanese armed forces in the Nanpo Shoto were there; Iwo Jima had only a single airstrip capable of accommodating about 20 planes and a garrison of about 1500 men. After losing the Marshalls, Imperial General Headquarters

[14] Comairpac "Analysis of Air Operations – Iwo Jima" 21 June 1945.

[15] Cincpac-Cincpoa Bulletin No. 136–145 *Defense Installations on Iwo Jima* 10 June 1945, Bartley *Iwo Jima,* MacArthur *Historical Report* II.

realized that the Marianas and Carolines were threatened and began to strengthen their next line of defense. In March 1944 the build-up of Iwo began in earnest. By the end of May there were over 5000 Army troops with artillery and machine guns, and a Navy guard force with a dozen coast defense guns of 120-mm caliber and upward, 12 heavy antiaircraft guns and thirty 25-mm twin-mount antiaircraft guns, manned by about 2000 men. The naval commander on the island was an airman, Rear Admiral Toshinosuke Ichimaru. By D-day the total strength of the island garrison was about 21,000 officers and men.

When the Americans invaded Saipan in June, Imperial General Headquarters placed the defense of the Volcano group directly under Tokyo, organized the 109th Infantry Division, and sent it to Iwo under the command of Lieutenant General Tadamichi Kuribayashi. Tokyo strategists correctly estimated that Iwo Jima would be the choice for an Allied landing and they set about to make it impregnable. Thanks to the energy and skill of General Kuribayashi, they almost did.

Troops originally intended to reinforce the Marianas were now diverted to Iwo Jima. Because the island had no harbor, and attack by United States submarines was feared, reinforcements were unloaded at Chichi Jima, whence they were sent on to Iwo by small craft. This procedure did not save them from loss. On 18 July 1944, for example, U. S. submarine *Cobia* sank *Nisshu Maru*, transporting a tank regiment from Japan to Iwo, about 180 miles northwest of Chichi. Most of the troops were rescued but 28 tanks were lost. In six months, the Japanese lost about 1500 men en route to Iwo by surface and submarine attacks on their vessels.

Occasional sinkings of transports did little to check the build-up. Now relieved of arming Marianas and Marshalls, Japan had plenty of steel, concrete and other material to spare. Keen-eyed aërial photo interpreters working for Admiral Turner watched prepared positions on Iwo grow in strength and intensity from day to day. Owing to cliffs on the bulgy northeastern part of the pear-shaped island, the only places possible to land on were the beaches north and east of Mount Suribachi, between which lay No. 1 Motoyama airfield with No. 2 not far north. General Kuribayashi figured out that the beaches and No. 1 airfield would be untenable in face of the naval and air strength which probably would be applied against them, and so decided to concentrate his defenses in and about Mount Suribachi in the south, and on the plateau around Motoyama village on the bulge. His naval advisers, on the other hand, insisted that the attack must be stopped at the water's edge. A compromise was made whereby the Navy constructed a series of pillboxes and strongpoints covering the beaches, and Kuribayashi assigned the troops to man them. Thus, Iwo had the benefit of the older technique for repelling an amphibious attack ("annihilate it at the water's edge") plus the new technique, tried at Peleliu, Leyte and Lingayen, of a desperate defense in depth.

The Japanese naval coast defense guns of 120-mm (4.7-inch) and 155-mm (6-inch) caliber were so sited as to enfilade the beaches and approaches to them in a narrow arc of fire. Casemated behind four to six feet of concrete, they were so located as to have maximum protection from naval gunfire. Behind the beaches on both sides was a system of concrete pillboxes so placed as to be mutually supporting. Large concrete blockhouses were also built in this part of the island. Antiaircraft guns were placed in pits so that a direct hit was required to knock them out. A system of tunnels connected the various positions, in each of which a deep cave shelter was provided for the troops.

On the slopes of Mount Suribachi was a labyrinth of dug-in gun positions for coast defense artillery, mortars and machine guns. These were accompanied by elaborate cave and tunnel systems providing living quarters and storage space for servicing the weapons. From the volcano's rim, everything that went on at both sets of beaches, or on most of the island, could be observed.

General Kuribayashi's one main line of defense crossed the island between Nos. 1 and 2 airfields, taking full advantage of the terrain features. Here was a network of dug-in positions for artillery, mortars, machine guns and infantry weapons. These were in a system of caves connected by underground tunnels. A second line of defense ran between No. 2 airfield and the central Motoyama sector. Accurate range and firing data were provided at each weapon position, so that high accuracy could be obtained with minimum exposure. But the main feature of the bulbous part of the island was an intricate network of caves and excavated rooms, all connected by deep tunnels. In some places there were five levels of these caves, and few were less than thirty feet underground. One cave might have several entrances, and most served the double purpose of protection to men and a position for weapons. A mortar could be set up at a cave or tunnel mouth, fired and then withdrawn. Even tanks were emplaced in pits or narrow ravines with only the turret exposed. Added to the natural strength of the underground system was the use of camouflage with materials blending into the surrounding terrain and vegetation. Many of these positions were so cleverly prepared that they were not spotted until they opened fire, or the protective camouflage was blown away by our gunfire. Later, when the Marines were fighting ashore, a camouflaged rifle pit or machine-gun position might be exposed only when the troops were taken under fire from the rear.

All this followed the battle plan drawn up by General Kuribayashi in September 1944. He was to "transform the central island into a fortress." When the landings took place, the garrison must aim at "gradual depletion of enemy attack forces, and, even if the situation gets out of hand, defend a corner of the island to the death." "All forces will prevent losses during enemy bombing and shelling by dispersing, concealing and camouflaging personnel, weapons and matériel." The password for this operation meant "desperation," or "desperate battle."

Following the successful Allied landings on Luzon in January 1945 the Japanese high command was forced to take a new look at the strategic situation. In an atmosphere of pessimism and mutual suspicion it was difficult to reach any but the most general agreements on policy. But the need was urgent, and on 20 January 1945 an "Outline of Army and Navy Operations" was promulgated.[16] This new policy predicted that the final battle of the war would be fought in Japan itself. The outline attempted to provide a strategic defense in depth by prescribing an inner defense line running from the Bonins through Formosa to the coast of China and southern Korea. Key strongpoints to be developed on this defense perimeter were Iwo Jima, Okinawa, Formosa, the Shanghai area and the South Korea coast. China and Southeast Asia were classed as secondary theaters. When United States forces, the principal enemy, penetrated this inner defense perimeter, an intense war of attrition was to be waged against them in order to reduce their preponderance, shatter their morale and delay the invasion of the home islands. Air forces were to exert themselves fully over the perimeter defense zone, but air strength in general was to be conserved until a landing was under way, then concentrate on the invasion fleet, with emphasis on the use of the Kamikaze Corps. The planes themselves were to be concentrated in Kyushu, the Ryukyus, Formosa and Eastern China. Ground forces were to hold out as long as possible without reinforcement.

General Kuribayashi did his best to implement this directive, and his best was very good indeed. During the long series of air attacks and bombardments the garrison holed up, then came out to repair damage. Reinforcements and new guns and matériel were brought in at night and improvement of all defenses continued. If, as the Japanese expected, the assault could have been made shortly after the Marianas were secured in the fall of 1944, the island would have been ill prepared to meet it, but the postponement to February 1945 gave Kuribayashi his opportunity to sell the island at the highest price. Subsequent complaints by General Holland Smith and others about the amount and quality of naval bombardment and air bombing were completely off the beam: Iwo's defenses were of a nature that neither could possibly neutralize them. The only way to knock out most of the positions was for ships to close to point-

[16] MacArthur *Historical Report* II 542 ff.

blank range, 2000 yards or less, and blast them out. This could not be done until the attack force was ashore, and one knew the location of the strongpoints.

Intelligence of Japanese defenses through aërial photographs was helped by submarine *Spearfish*, which snooped Iwo in early December and took photographs of the beaches through her periscope. The nature of the soil was correctly estimated, and the number of defensive positions seen was not far short of the truth. But she could not spot the caves and tunnels, and nobody in Marine headquarters seems to have put together the experience at Biak and Peleliu to anticipate the new Japanese tactics of defense in depth, which were to cost the Marine Corps dear.

The Japanese Navy's only contribution to the defense of Iwo Jima was in the form of submarines bearing the human torpedoes that they called *kaiten*, but the initial success of this gimmick, sinking a fleet oiler in Ulithi lagoon on 20 November, was not repeated.[17] A *kaiten* unit composed of *I-370*, *I-368* and *I-44* sailed for Iwo Jima 22–23 February 1945. The first-named ran afoul of destroyer escort *Finnegan* (Lieutenant Commander H. Huffman USNR), escorting a convoy from Iwo Jima to Saipan, on 26 February. She made a surface radar contact distant seven miles at 0555, sound contact at 0630, delivered three depth-charge and hedgehog attacks and hung on until 1034 when a very deep underwater explosion was heard and debris with Japanese markings rose to the surface. That marked the end of *I-370*.

Before the Iwo operation began, escort carriers *Anzio* (Captain G. C. Montgomery) and *Tulagi* (Captain J. C. Cronin) were made nuclei of hunter-killer antisubmarine units. A fighter plane from *Anzio*, flying a ten-mile-square search in the early hours of 26 February, at the request of destroyer *Bennion*, which had made and lost contact, sighted *RO-43* (not a *kaiten* submarine) and destroyed it west of Chichi Jima by a depth-bomb drop from 150 feet. Next day *Tulagi* sent planes after two submarines reported to be southeast of Iwo Jima but apparently missed them; *Anzio* planes, however,

[17] See Vol. XII 51.

flew a repeat performance on the 27th and sank *I–368*, a few miles west of Iwo Jima.[18]

I–44 reached Iwo waters, but was kept down by destroyers for over 48 hours, almost suffocating the crew, and then returned to base. Vice Admiral S. Miwa, commanding Sixth Fleet (the submarines), was furious, and relieved the skipper of his command. A second *kaiten* unit of *I–36* and *I–58* (the boat that later sank *Indianapolis*) was then formed, and departed Kure 1 March. The first had to turn back shortly after its sortie, and *I–58*, after a frustrating cruise around Iwo, constantly harassed by antisubmarine craft, was recalled on 9 March.[19]

[18] CTG 52.2 (Rear Adm. Durgin) Action Report of 21 April 1945, Enclosure A, p. 8.

[19] M. Hashimoto *Sunk* (1954) pp. 139–143.

CHAPTER II

Preliminary Poundings

10–18 February 1945

1. *Carrier Wings over Japan* [1]

DURING the last three days before Iwo D-day, every effort was intensified, the most intense being a series of carrier-borne air strikes over and around Tokyo. These were laid on not only as a diversion – a shield, as it were, for Iwo Jima – but to destroy enemy planes and reduce Japanese capability for launching air attacks.

Admiral Halsey had been eager to hit Japan since October, but the support of Task Force 38 was urgently needed in the Philippines; and by the time this opportunity came, in February 1945, Halsey was no longer in command. Third Fleet completed its Luzon missions in late January and made for Ulithi, where the new "backfield" was waiting to take over. At midnight 26 January, Admiral Raymond A. Spruance relieved Admiral William F. Halsey, and Third Fleet again became Fifth Fleet. At the same time, Vice Admiral Marc A. Mitscher relieved Vice Admiral John S. McCain as Commander Fast Carrier Force, and TF 38 became TF 58. As the carriers would not have to depart in support of Iwo until 10 February, their fagged-out sailors and airmen enjoyed a welcome two weeks of upkeep and rest, swimming, playing softball and

[1] Action Report of Com Fifth Fleet (Admiral Spruance) 14 June, CTF 58 (Vice Adm. Mitscher) for 10 Feb.–4 Mar. 1945, 13 Mar., and of his task group commanders for the same period: CTG 58.1 (Rear Adm. Clark) 15 Mar.; CTG 58.2 (Rear Adm. Davison) 12 Mar.; CTG 58.3 (Rear Adm. F. C. Sherman) 28 Mar.; CTG 58.4 (Rear Adm. Radford) 1 Mar.; CTG 58.5 (the night carrier group, Rear Adm. Gardner) 12 Mar.

drinking beer on Mogmog. At the same time changes in the composition of Task Force 58 were made, partly owing to battle and storm damage to *Franklin* and *Monterey*, partly because new *Essex*-class carriers (*Bennington*, *Randolph* and *Bunker Hill*) joined the Fleet. And a new night-flying carrier group, TG 58.5, was formed around veterans *Enterprise* and *Saratoga*.

For the first carrier strike against the heart of Japan, Task Force 58 was organized as follows: —[2]

Fifth Fleet, Admiral Spruance in INDIANAPOLIS

TF 58, Vice Admiral Mitscher in BUNKER HILL

	TG 58.1 Clark	TG 58.2 Davison	TG 58.3 F. C. Sherman	TG 58.4 Radford	TG 58.5 Gardner
CV	HORNET WASP BENNINGTON	LEXINGTON HANCOCK	ESSEX BUNKER HILL	YORKTOWN RANDOLPH	ENTERPRISE SARATOGA
CVL	BELL. WOOD	SAN JACINTO	COWPENS	LANGLEY CABOT	
BB	MASS'TS INDIANA	WISCONSIN MISSOURI	S. DAKOTA NEW JERSEY	WASHINGTON N. CAROLINA	
CB			ALASKA		
CA	VINCENNES	S. FRANCISCO BOSTON	INDIANAPOLIS		BALTIMORE
CL	MIAMI SAN JUAN		PASADENA WILKES BARRE ASTORIA	SANTA FE BILOXI SAN DIEGO	FLINT
	15 DD	19 DD	14 DD	17 DD	12 DD

This first carrier strike against Japan proper since the Halsey-Doolittle raid of 1942 was regarded with some apprehension by Task Force 58, as almost half the air groups would be on their first combat mission. To meet expected counterattacks, especially those from the Kamikaze Corps, each air group on a big carrier now comprised at least 73 fighter planes (Corsairs and Hellcats), leaving only 30 units to be divided between dive- and torpedo-bombers.

Task Force 58 sortied from Ulithi 10 February and shaped a course eastward of the Marianas and Bonins. On the 12th, the air

[2] See Appendix I for complete task organization and C.O.'s.

groups rehearsed with the 3rd Marine Division on Tinian. Two days later the task force fueled at sea from one of Admiral Beary's replenishment groups. Everything possible was done to guard against detection. Measures included radio deception, scouting by Pacific Fleet submarines to dispose of any picket vessels there might be en route, scouting by B–29s and Navy Liberators from the Marianas to clear the air. On the 15th a scouting line of five destroyers ranged ahead of the carriers, and antisubmarine air patrol was set up. At 1900 a high-speed run-in began towards launching positions, where the carriers arrived at dawn 16 February. Thanks to these precautions, and to thick weather most of the way, they arrived undetected.

The launching position lay about 125 miles SE of Tokyo but only 60 miles off the coast of Honshu. Flying conditions were very bad – ceiling of 4000 feet, broken clouds at 1000 feet, rain and snow squalls, NE wind force 6 to 7. But, having come so far for what Admiral Mitscher predicted would be "the greatest air victory of the war for carrier aviation," [8] foul weather could not stop him. Heavy fighter sweeps were launched promptly on 16 February, to cover the airfields around Tokyo Bay.

Low overcast also hampered the Japanese, and the only offensive sweep to meet sizable opposition was the first from TG 58.2 over the Chiba Peninsula on the east side of Tokyo Bay. About 100 Japanese fighters attacked Admiral Davison's planes as they crossed the coast and about 40 of them were shot down. American pilots found the Japanese on the whole reluctant to engage; Admiral Mitscher had correctly told his pilots, "He is probably more afraid of you than you are of him." The fifth sweep, by TG 58.3 whose targets were to the westward, managed to find clear weather and had the honor to be the first Navy fighter planes to arrive over Tokyo. These initial sweeps, intended to clear the air of enemy fighters for bombing runs, found little opposition. Before return-

[8] CTF 58 Action Report, Encl. C, the Admiral's "Air Combat Notes for Pilots" posted in every ready room. For anyone wishing to know fighter-plane tactics at this stage of the war, this is an excellent source; so large a proportion of the VF pilots had had no combat experience that Mitscher took nothing for granted.

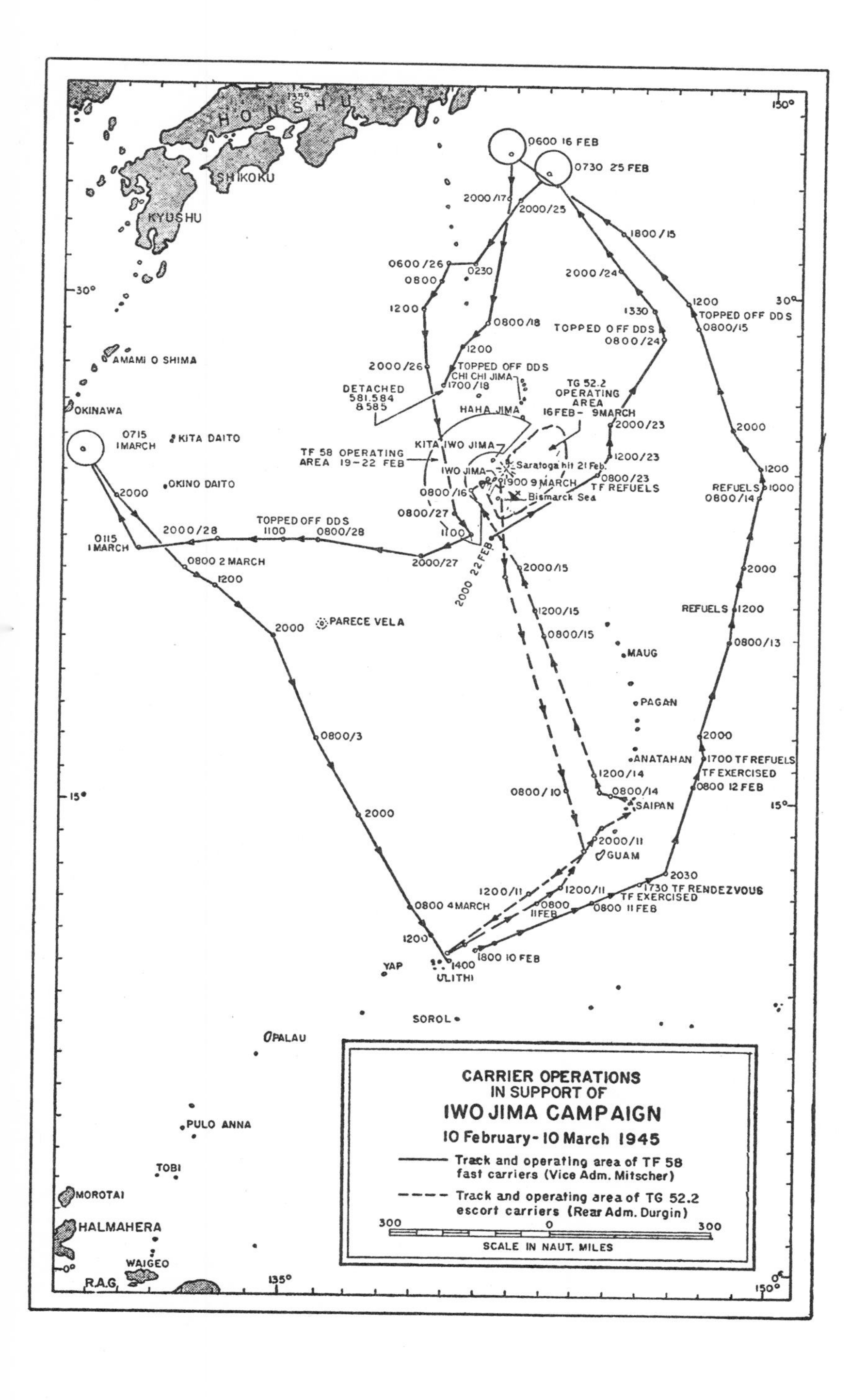

HONSHU
SHIKOKU
KYUSHU
AMAMI O SHIMA
OKINAWA
KITA DAITO
OKINO DAITO
PARECE VELA
CHI CHI JIMA
HAHA JIMA
KITA IWO JIMA
IWO JIMA
MAUG
PAGAN
ANATAHAN
SAIPAN
GUAM
YAP
ULITHI
SOROL
PALAU
PULO ANNA
TOBI
MOROTAI
HALMAHERA
WAIGEO
0600 16 FEB
0730 25 FEB
0715 1MARCH
TF 58 OPERATING AREA 19 - 22 FEB
TG 52.2 OPERATING AREA 16 FEB - 9 MARCH
DETACHED 581.584 & 585
Saratoga hit 21 Feb.
Bismarck Sea
1900 9 MARCH
TF REFUELS
TOPPED OFF DDS
REFUELS
1700 TF REFUELS
TF EXERCISED
1730 TF RENDEZVOUS
0800 12 FEB
0800 11 FEB
1800 10 FEB
0800 4 MARCH
0800 2 MARCH
2000 22 FEB.
CARRIER OPERATIONS IN SUPPORT OF
IWO JIMA CAMPAIGN
10 February - 10 March 1945
Track and operating area of TF 58 fast carriers (Vice Adm. Mitscher)
Track and operating area of TG 52.2 escort carriers (Rear Adm. Durgin)
SCALE IN NAUT. MILES
R.A.G.

ing to their ships the planes swept across the designated airfields, strafing planes that they caught grounded. Succeeding sweeps by Hellcats and Corsairs kept these fields covered throughout the day.

Admiral Mitscher, fearing that more targets would be weathered in during the afternoon, ordered bombing attacks against aircraft frame and engine plants in the Tokyo area at 1130, earlier than he intended. The first was directed against the Ota and Koizumi plants northwest of Tokyo. The Ota plant, previously damaged by B–29s, was almost completely destroyed in this and the next attack on 25 February, when Koizumi was first hit, as the aviators were unable to find it on the 16th.[4] Many planes that could not get through to their assigned target expended their bombs on airfields.

During the afternoon three Japanese picket boats that had evaded detection in the thick weather were spotted by destroyer *Haynsworth* and promptly sunk.[5] At sunset, after the daytime fighters had been recovered, TG 58.5 launched a sweep of night fighters to cover the enemy airfields at dusk. The task force was not disturbed during the night.

Before dawn 17 February, TG 58.5 sent off planes in search of shipping, and at dawn the other groups launched fighter sweeps. These were followed by bombing strikes on the Musashimo, Tama and Tachikawa plants near Tokyo. At about 1115, with weather growing steadily worse, Admiral Mitscher canceled further strikes. After recovering planes the task force retired towards Iwo Jima.

The results of these first carrier strikes at the heart of Japan were substantial but not spectacular. In addition to damaging aircraft frame and engine plants, a number of ships and small craft were attacked and sunk in Tokyo Bay, the biggest prize being *Yamashiro*

[4] USSBS "Report on Nakajima Aircraft Ltd." (June 1946) which does not distinguish between damage inflicted by the different attacks.

[5] *Haynsworth* recovered several survivors, who were transferred to *Essex* and placed in the brig under Marine guard. The prisoners became objects of considerable interest to the carrier's crew, who clustered around the cell doors, plied the prisoners with candy bars and cigarettes, and gave them their first lessons in Navy English. Thus, when Admiral Sherman came below to take a look at them, he was startled by the Japanese politely folding arms across stomach, bowing from the waist, and remarking what they had been told was the proper greeting to a flag officer, "F— you, Joe!"

Maru of 10,600 tons. Best results were obtained against enemy aircraft, although the temperature was so low that a considerable number of our aircraft guns froze. TF 58 claimed 341 enemy planes shot down in the air and 190 destroyed on the ground, but this cannot be checked from enemy sources. Our losses were 60 planes in combat and 28 operationally out of 738 sorties which engaged the enemy, and a grand total of 2761 sorties, which included those for C.A.P.[6]

During the night of 17–18 February, en route to Iwo Jima, destroyers *Barton*, *Ingraham* and *Moale* destroyed three small Japanese picket boats. *Dortch* encountered a fourth, a PC type which fought back with 3-inch guns and killed three of the destroyer's sailors. This target was finally rammed and sunk by *Waldron*.

In passing Chichi and Haha Jima, Admiral Radford's TG 58.4 launched fighter sweeps and strikes which destroyed several small craft and cratered the airfield on Chichi Jima. During the afternoon of 18 February TGs 58.2 and 58.3 took stations west of Iwo Jima for direct support of the landings next day and the other three task groups made rendezvous with oilers south of that island.

2. *Two Days' Pounding, 16–17 February* [7]

Sunrise 16 February	0644
Sunset 17 February	1720

For the first time in a Central Pacific amphibious operation all pre-landing activities at the objective were under an amphibious group commander, Rear Admiral William H. P. Blandy.[8] "Spike"

[6] Vice Adm. Mitscher Action Report; cf. Comairpac "Analysis of Air Operations, Tokyo Carrier Strikes, Feb. 1945," 28 Apr.

[7] CTF 51 (Vice Adm. Turner) "Report on the Capture of Iwo Jima" 19 May 1945; CTF 52 (Rear Adm. Blandy) Action Report 22 Feb.; CTF 54 (Rear Adm. Rodgers) Action Report 10 Mar.; CTG 52.2 (Rear Adm. Durgin) Action Report 21 Apr.; CTG 52.3 (Com Minecraft, Rear Adm. Alexander Sharp) Report on Minesweeping Operations 6 Mar. 1945.

[8] Born N.Y.C. 1890, honor man of Class of 1913 Naval Academy, service in *Florida* during Vera Cruz landing and World War I; specialized in ordnance

Blandy was the sanguine Celtic type, with a humorous Irish mouth overhung by a large red nose. His quick mind, grasp of essentials and driving energy had served the Navy well during the first two years of the war, as Chief of the Bureau of Ordnance, especially in developing, adapting and manufacturing the Swedish Bofors and the Swiss Oerlikon as the indispensable 40-mm and 20-mm antiaircraft weapons. That signal service, though deeply appreciated throughout the Fleet, exposed him to good-natured gibes whenever a gun jammed or a shell failed to explode, which he accepted with good humor. He had taken part in the Kwajalein operation, commanded an amphibious group at Saipan, and now had the assignment to command and coördinate all pre-landing activities.

Directly under Admiral Blandy were an air support control unit commanded by Captain Elton C. Parker, a support carrier group of a dozen CVEs under Rear Admiral Calvin T. Durgin, minecraft under Rear Admiral Alexander Sharp, underwater demolition teams under Captain Byron H. Hanlon, and three groups of LCI(L) gunboats, mortar boats and rocket support boats under Commander Michael J. Malanaphy. The Gunfire and Covering Force (TF 54), consisting of six battleships, four heavy cruisers, a light cruiser and 16 destroyers under Rear Admiral Bertram J. Rodgers,[9] also came under Admiral Blandy until D-day.

Task Force 54, as finally constituted, included *Idaho* and *Tennessee*, freshly returned from overhaul at West Coast navy yards; *Nevada*, *Texas* and *Arkansas*, veterans of Operations OVERLORD and DRAGOON, which reached the Pacific in November; and 30-year-old *New York*, taking part in an amphibious operation for the first

engineering and developed formulas used for gun manufacture by autofrettage, asst. fire control officer *New Mexico* 1921, exec. *Vega* 1922, duty ashore at Cavite; squadron gunnery and torpedo officer for destroyers Asiatic Fleet in *Stewart* 1923; duty in Buord 1924; gunnery officer *New Mexico* 1927, and staff gunnery officer *West Virginia* 1929; U.S. Naval Mission to Brazil 1931; C.O. *Simpson* 1933; Comdesdiv 10, 1935; C.O. *Utah* 1938; Chief of Buord 1941–1943; Com 'Phib Group 1 at Kwajalein, Marianas and Peleliu; after Iwo Jima commanded the assault on Kerama Retto. Com Cruisers and Destroyers Pacific Fleet July 1945 and Com Joint Army–Navy TF 1 in the Bikini atomic tests. Cinclant Feb. 1947, retired 1950, died 12 Jan. 1954.

[9] For brief biographies of Admirals Rodgers and Durgin see Vol. XI 237 and 279.

time since TORCH in 1942. Heavy cruisers *Chester, Pensacola, Salt Lake City* and *Tuscaloosa* (also a European veteran) and the new light cruiser *Vicksburg*, with assigned destroyers, completed the gunfire support force. Admiral Spruance's flagship *Indianapolis*, together with battleships *North Carolina* and *Washington*, would join on 19 February, D-day.

The combined task forces under Admiral Blandy arrived off Iwo Jima at 0600 February 16. The destroyers and APDs formed a screen seaward of the bombardment ships, and the escort carriers, operating about 50 miles south of the island, provided combat air and antisubmarine patrols. Embarked in *Wake Island* was VOC–1, a group of pilots trained as gunfire spotters, flying fighter planes designated VOFs. This unit, now making its début in the Pacific, had performed the same function successfully in Operation DRAGOON in 1944.[10] The weather at the target was poor. A low ceiling and intermittent rain squalls hampered the spotters. A sweep against airfield and shipping at Chichi Jima launched at 0643 was unable to get through.[11] Minesweeping off Iwo began at 0645 and the bombardment at 0707, but ten minutes later Admiral Blandy ordered the ships to fire only when efficient air spot was available so as not to waste ammunition.

Iwo Jima was subjected to bombardment throughout the day whenever spotting planes could observe the fall of shot. The highlight occurred at 1413 when an OS2U from *Pensacola*, piloted by Lieutenant (jg) D. W. Gandy USNR, first reported a Zeke on his tail; then that he was going after him; and, a split second later, "I got him, I got him!" It was amazing for a slow, flimsy Kingfisher to get a Zeke, but apparently this one did; the victim was sighted falling in flames. Shortly after, the UDT "frogmen," when setting up a navigational light on Higashi Rock a mile and a half east of the island, were fired on from Iwo Jima by small-caliber weapons. *Pensacola* noticed this and opened up on the weapons with her 5-inch guns, and within five minutes had silenced the enemy fire.

[10] See Vol. XI 280.
[11] CTG 52.2 (Rear Adm. Durgin) Action Report.

By 1800 the day's work was finished, and the results were disappointing. As Admiral Rodgers reported, "Little damage was apparent."

D-day minus 2, 17 February, gave a different story. The weather improved, with good visibility. On the day's program were fighter sweeps against Chichi Jima, minesweeping, and beach reconnaissance by UDTs, closely supported by the heavy ships, destroyers and LCI gunboats. Sandwiched between these activities was a bombing by B-24s at 1330.

Bombardment ships were in position off Iwo by 0700. Minesweeping began promptly and at 0803 the heavy vessels were ordered to close the beaches for destructive bombardment. *Pensacola* observed the sweepers being fired on, laid her secondary battery on the firing positions and silenced them within five minutes. But coastal batteries in the northeastern part of Iwo had their revenge. *Pensacola* around 0935 received six hits from 4.7- or 6-inch shells that wrecked her C.I.C., set fire to a plane on her starboard catapult, punctured her hull on the starboard side forward, killed 17 men and wounded 98. She withdrew temporarily to fight fires and treat casualties, but later returned to station and concluded her mission.

By 0911 *Idaho*, *Nevada* and *Tennessee* were 3000 yards off the beaches sending heavy direct fire at assigned targets. At 1025 Admiral Blandy ordered them to retire in order to clear the UDT operations, set for 1100. By that time the minesweepers were clear, having swept up to 750 yards of the shore in precise formation, banging away with their own weapons and occasionally coming under fire from the island.

So far, everything had gone almost "according to plan," but the attempt of the LCI(G) flotilla to cover UDT reconnaissance provoked an unexpected reply from the enemy. The four UDTs were embarked in destroyer transports *Bull*, *Bates*, *Barr* and *Blessman*. Seven destroyers provided cover at the 3000-yard line where the APDs launched their LCP(R)s carrying the swimmers. As the landing craft headed for the 500-yard line, where the swimmers would make the plunge, they were followed by seven LCI gunboats under Lieutenant Commander Williard V. Nash USNR, firing 20-mm and 40-mm guns at the beaches and preparing to launch 4.5-inch rockets. Soon after these gunboats passed the 1500-yard line, mortar shells began falling among them; and a little later, as they were beginning to launch rockets, they came under intense fire from the flanks of the beaches. A heavy battery casemated at the foot of Mount Suribachi joined in with mortars, automatic weapons and small arms, all aimed at the swimmers and LCI(G)s, but the heaviest fire came from a hitherto unrevealed battery in the high ground just north of the beaches. As Admiral Rodgers reported, "These batteries had remained concealed through over two months of softening preparation. . . . Because of their peculiar nature they could be neutralized only by point-blank fire." Around 1100 the seven LCI(G)s, advancing in line abreast, began to take hits, but pressed on to support the swimmers until forced out by damage and casualties. Others dashed in to replace them, to be hit in turn, time after time. "*LCI(G)–471, –438, –441* and several others, although hit several times, gallantly returned to the fray after retiring just long enough to extinguish their fires and plug holes in the hull."[12] *LCI(G)–474,* after closing destroyer *Capps,* had to be abandoned and went down. *LCI(G)–409,* after going in twice and sustaining 60 per cent casualties, closed *Terror,* removed wounded, and took on board officers and men to help damage control. In all, 12 LCI(G)s took part and all were hit, but they stuck to it until the swimmers were recovered and clear. Everyone who watched these vessels was inspired by their courage and persistence.

John P. Marquand, the novelist, who was gathering material in *Tennessee,* thus describes *LCI(G)–466* coming alongside: "There was blood on the main deck, making widening pools as she rolled in the sluggish sea. A dead man on a gun platform was covered by a blanket. The decks were littered with wounded. They were being strapped on wire stretchers and passed up to us over the side. . . .

[12] CTU 52.5.1 (Com LCI(G) Flot. 3, Cdr. M. J. Malanaphy) Action Report 24 Feb. 1945.

The commanding officer was tall, bare-headed and blond, and he looked very young. . . . There was a call from our bridge, 'Can you proceed under your own power?' . . . 'We can't proceed anywhere for three days,' the C.O. said. They had passed up the wounded — seventeen of them — and then they passed up five stretchers with the dead. . . ."[18]

Forty-four men in all were killed or missing and 152 wounded.

Heavy support for the gunboats quickly developed. *Nevada*, being close inshore (Captain H. L. Grosskopf having turned a Nelsonian blind eye to Admiral Blandy's order to withdraw), was in the right position to silence the battery to the north, and concentrated on it for two hours. Captain Hanlon, in general charge of the reconnaissance, asked for an air strike at the base of Mount Suribachi and for the heavy ships to increase their rate of fire on known targets. At 1121, destroyer *Leutze* was hit, severely injuring the C.O., Commander B. A. Robbins, and 33 others, besides seven killed or missing.

By 1240 all swimmers but one had been recovered. The "frogmen" found no obstacles at the beaches and were able to produce accurate gradient maps of the approaches.

With every one of the eleven remaining LCI(G)s damaged, none were available for the afternoon reconnaissance of the western beaches. Hanlon asked for smoke planes, for the destroyers to fire white phosphorus shells, and for close gunfire support from heavy ships and destroyers. Blandy accordingly directed *Tennessee*, *Arkansas*, *Texas* and *Tuscaloosa* to cover the reconnaissance in that order, from south to north. Thus assisted, the UDTs made their reconnaissance and were back in their ships by 1755, with no casualties.

3. *D-day minus 1, 18 February*

Since the last two days of bombardment blasted away camouflage from batteries not previously known to exist, the island's defenses

[18] *Harper's* (May 1945) pp. 497–498.

were for the first time properly revealed; and formidable they were indeed. Fortunately for us, the support of UDTs with LCI(G)s had convinced General Kuribayashi that the main landing had started, and to repel it he unmasked batteries that would have caused very heavy casualties on D-day had they not been discovered two days before. This was the only serious mistake made by the Japanese general in his defensive tactics, which won the rueful admiration of his enemies.

These revelations on 17 February brought about a quick revision of the bombardment pattern for D-day minus 1, 18 February. Orders were issued to concentrate on the immediate vicinity and flanks of the eastern beaches, and for heavy ships to close to 2500 yards or less and deliver concentrated direct fire on all targets. At 0745 February 18 Admiral Rodgers ordered his gunfire ships to "close beach and get going." Each had her assigned target aiming to destroy as many as possible in the landing area and the nearby ground commanding the beaches. Bombardment ships delivered direct fire all day long. Both *Tennessee* and *Idaho* demolished their targets, literally blasting blockhouses and pillboxes out of the ground. The results of the bombardment, which ceased at 1821, were very gratifying. It was worth more than all the previous "softenings" by air bombing and naval gunfire, and was largely responsible for the assault teams' being able to touch down on D-day with few casualties. The sacrifice of brave sailors in the LCI gunboats was well rewarded.

A small enemy air raid developed about 2130 as the amphibious groups were retiring for the night. Destroyer minesweeper *Gamble* was hit by two 250-pound bombs amidships, one of which exploded in the after fireroom, causing extensive damage, and blowing two holes near the keel. Five men were killed or missing and nine wounded. *Hamilton* stood by to assist and remove casualties and *Dorsey* took *Gamble* in tow until she could be turned over to a salvage tug. *Blessman*, making 20 knots to close Admiral Rodgers's group, and carrying a UDT unit, was hit in the forward fireroom and troop spaces by a bomb dropped from a plane which approached from astern. She suffered extensive damage, lost 42 men killed or missing and 29 wounded.

Admiral Turner arrived off Iwo Jima at 0600 February 19 with the main body of the expeditionary force and assumed the duties of CTF 52, relieving Admiral Blandy, whose conduct during those three critical days had been characterized by keen intelligence in the face of unexpected situations.

February 18 (D-day minus 1) was Sunday. The chaplain on one of the transports had printed on cards, and distributed to each Marine, the words of Sir Jacob Astley's famous prayer before the Battle of Edgehill, in 1642: —

> O Lord! Thou knowest how busy I must be this day:
> If I forget Thee, do not Thou forget me.[14]

This well fitted the mood of United States Marines three centuries later.

[14] H. M. Smith *Coral and Brass* p. 254; but "Howlin' Mad" named the wrong author and garbled the prayer.

CHAPTER III

D-day at Iwo Jima[1]

19 February 1945

Sunrise	0641
Sunset	1725

1. *Pre-landing Bombardment*

D–DAY, observed Admiral Turner, opened with weather ideal for an amphibious landing – he had never seen it so good at Guadalcanal, the Gilberts, the Marshalls or Saipan. A light northerly wind floated fleecy clouds lazily over the island. A calm sea raised no surf on the beaches – a wonderful break for the assault, as beach gradients were so steep that even a low surf would embarrass landing craft. The island, wrote John P. Marquand, "never looked more aesthetically ugly than on D-day morning, or more completely Japanese. . . . It also had the minute, fussy compactness of those miniature Japanese gardens. Its stones and rocks were like those contorted, wind-scoured, water-worn boulders which the Japanese love to collect as landscape decorations. 'I hope to God,' a wounded Marine said later, 'that we don't have to go on any more of those screwy islands!' "[2] Only one more, Marine – the even screwier Okinawa – and the war would be almost over.

[1] CTF 51 (Vice Admiral Turner) Action Report; Action Reports mentioned in Chap. II, note 1 above; and those of Com Transgrp B (Commo. H. C. Flanagan); Com Transgrp A (Commo. J. B. McGovern), and C. G.'s V Phib Corps (Maj. Gen. Harry Schmidt USMC), 4th Marine Div. (Maj. Gen. Clifton B. B. Cates), 5th Marine Div. (Maj. Gen. Keller E. Rockey); Bartley *Iwo Jima;* Carl W. Proehl *Fourth Marine Division in World War II* (1946); Howard W. Conner *The Spearhead* (5th Marine Division) 1950; Robert Sherrod *On to Westward, War in the Central Pacific* (1945). The Navy has two excellent movies taken during the action, MN-5562 "Naval Guns at Iwo" and MN-5124 "To the Shore of Iwo Jima."

[2] "Iwo Jima before H-hour" *Harper's* (May 1945) p. 499.

Shortly after daylight 19 February there opened the heaviest pre-H-hour bombardment of World War II. Ships taking part were those of Task Force 54,[8] together with *North Carolina, Washington, Indianapolis, Santa Fe* and *Biloxi* lent by Task Force 58. This made a grand total of eight battleships, five heavy cruisers, three light cruisers and (during the last half hour) ten destroyers.

It began at 0640, two hours and twenty minutes before H-hour. Off the eastern shore were stationed *North Carolina* and *Washington,* whose assigned targets were in the bulbous part of the island. A line of four battleships and four cruisers, with eight destroyers between them, covered the southeastern coast from off the quarry overlooking the northernmost beach, to a point south of Mount Suribachi. Two battleships, five cruisers and one destroyer took care of the western beaches. Targets selected for this phase of bombardment were on and flanking the landing beaches, both airfields and the lower slopes of Suribachi. For the first 85 minutes fire was deliberate: 75 rounds each for the battleships, 100 rounds each for the heavy cruisers. At 0803 gunfire was lifted to permit air strikes to be made by planes from Task Groups 58.2 and 58.3.

These fast carrier groups were operating about 65 miles northwest of Iwo Jima, under the tactical command of Rear Admiral Frederick C. Sherman. At 0805 and 0815 their rockets, bombs, and napalm struck targets on the eastern slope of Suribachi, on high ground north of the landing beaches, and on the airfield in the center of the island. At 0825 the bombardment ships resumed with vastly increased tempo. For the next half hour shells literally rained on Iwo. Battleships fired 155 rounds each, the cruisers 150 rounds each, and the ten destroyers 500 rounds each.

Beginning at 0850 naval gunfire was adjusted, in a complicated and nicely timed pattern, so that the carrier planes could strafe the beaches during the last seven minutes before H-hour.

[8] Less *New York. Chester,* while approaching her firing station, was struck a glancing blow by *Estes,* but carried out her assigned bombardment.

It is impossible to assess the effect of this tremendous concentration of air bombing and gunfire, as distinct from what had been done on the three previous days. Undoubtedly a number of gun positions were damaged, but the Japanese garrison cozily sat it out in their deep underground shelters.

At one minute short of H-hour naval gunfire shifted to targets about 200 yards inland, at 0902 it moved another 200 yards inland and thereafter formed a modified rolling barrage ahead of the troops, constantly adjusted to conform to their actual rate of advance. This barrage was fired by the secondary batteries of the heavy ships, to each of which was assigned a shore fire control party with the troops. S.f.c.p. had the privilege of cutting in to request a special shoot on some just-discovered target before the scheduled fire of its ship was completed.[4]

2. *H-hour, 0900*

Admiral Turner ordered "Land the Landing Force" at 0645. It was obvious that 0900 (H-hour) could easily be met. Iwo was shrouded in the dust and smoke created by the bombardment, but weather conditions were almost perfect. The operation looked like a pushover. Optimists predicted that the island would be secured in four days.

The assault troops were transported and landed by TF 53, the Attack Force, commanded by Rear Admiral Harry W. Hill. The

[4] Comparative ammunition expenditure in D-day bombardments at Iwo Jima 19 Feb. and Okinawa 1 April 1945: –

No. Rounds	*16-inch*	*14-inch*	*12-inch*	*8-inch*	*6-inch*	*5-inch*
Okinawa	475	1325	175	2100	3000	36,260
Iwo Jima	1950	1500	400	1700	2000	31,000

Adm. Turner's Report for the two operations. See Col. Donald C. Weller USMC, "Salvo-Splash!" U.S. Naval Institute *Proceedings* LXXX (1954) 1018–1021, for technical aspects of the naval bombardment.

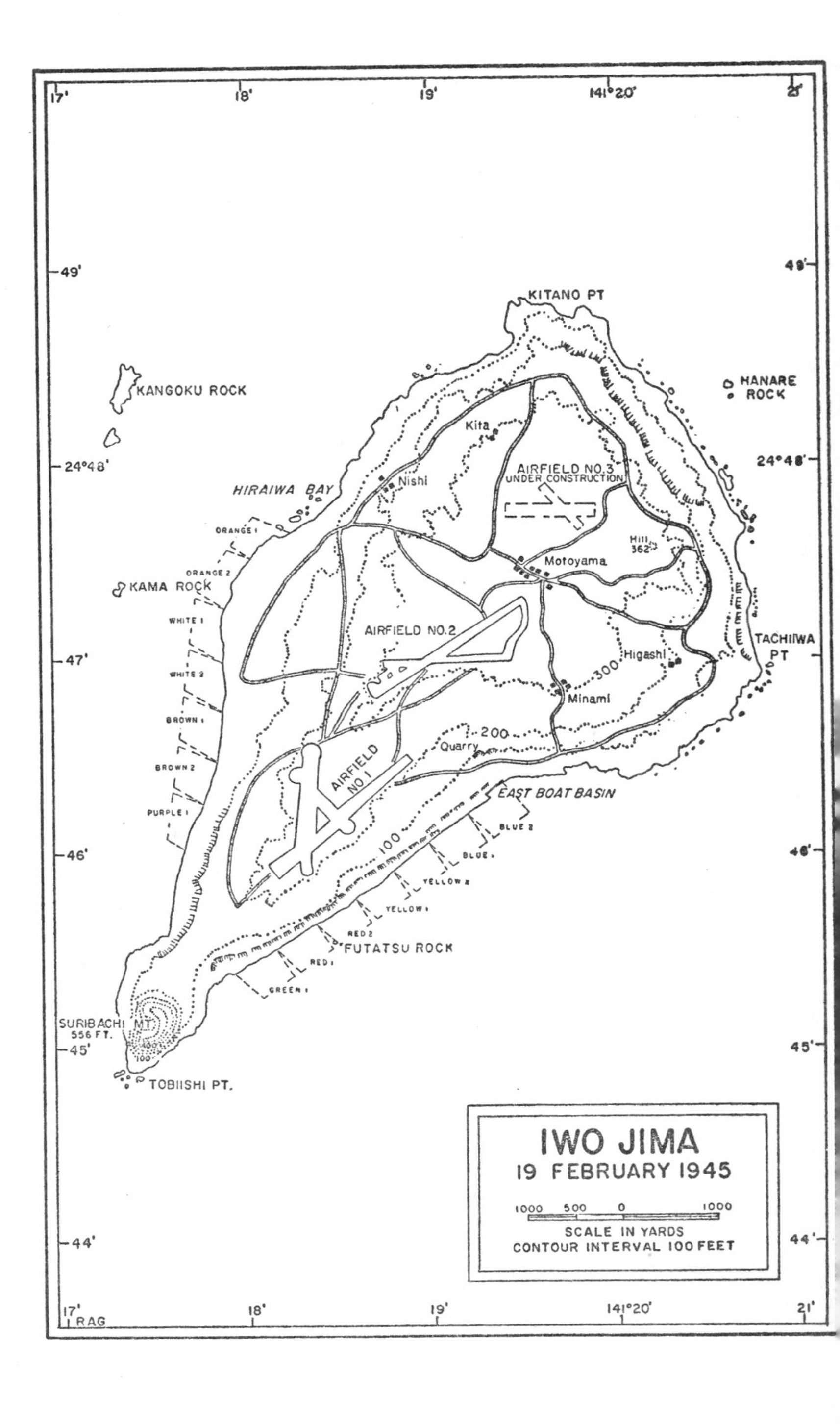

IWO JIMA
19 FEBRUARY 1945
1000 500 0 1000
SCALE IN YARDS
CONTOUR INTERVAL 100 FEET
17'
18'
19'
141°20'
21'
49'
24°48'
47'
46'
45'
44'
KITANO PT
KANGOKU ROCK
HANARE ROCK
Kita
Nishi
AIRFIELD NO.3
UNDER CONSTRUCTION
HIRAIWA BAY
ORANGE 1
ORANGE 2
Hill 362
Motoyama
KAMA ROCK
WHITE 1
AIRFIELD NO.2
TACHIIWA PT
WHITE 2
Higashi
300
Minami
BROWN 1
200
Quarry
AIRFIELD NO.1
BROWN 2
EAST BOAT BASIN
PURPLE 1
BLUE 2
100
BLUE 1
YELLOW 2
YELLOW 1
RED 2
FUTATSU ROCK
RED 1
GREEN 1
SURIBACHI MT.
556 FT.
TOBIISHI PT.
RAG

5th Marine Division was embarked in the 22 transports of Commodore John B. McGovern's transport group; the 4th Marine Division in the 24 transports of Commodore Henry C. Flanagan's transport group. The first five assault waves were landed from LVTs,[5] which, with their troops, were embarked in LSTs of Captain Wilkie H. Brereton's Tractor Group.

The shore from the base of Mount Suribachi to the high broken ground 3500 yards northeastward had been divided on maps gridded for the assault into seven beaches, each 500 yards long, indicated by colors: one Green, two Red, two Yellow, and two Blue. The northeastern part of Blue 2 had been developed by the Japanese into a small boat harbor, which the Marines called the East Boat Basin. Their scheme of maneuver was relatively simple: — the 5th Division to land on the Green and Red beaches and drive across the island, a part to capture or isolate Mount Suribachi, the rest to deploy northward and advance up the island parallel to the 4th Division. The 4th would land on Beaches Yellow 1 and 2 and Blue 1 and drive inland to No. 1 airfield and to the north to protect their right flank.

In the midst of the thunder of bombardment the amphibious forces calmly took their positions. By 0730 the control parties had established line of departure 4000 yards off the beaches. LSTs of the tractor groups took station at the 5500-yard line, dropped ramps and began to discharge LVTs filled with troops, "like all the cats in the world having kittens," as John P. Marquand remarked. It was now time for the newest type of boat, the Landing Craft Support Craft, Large — designated LCS(L) — to do its stuff. Twelve of these 160-foot craft, each capable of firing a salvo of 120 4.5-inch rockets, and bristling with 40-mm and 20-mm and 50-caliber machine guns as well, were present. They headed for the beach at 0740, line abreast, launched their rockets aimed at positions 20 to 50 yards behind the beaches, turned 90 degrees to parallel the shore,

[5] The Marines' LVT amphibians again proved themselves at Iwo. Their low speed was no handicap since the equally slow LVT(A)s spearheaded the landings. But the LVTs could land their troops and supplies on dry land despite surf, steep beaches and soft sand.

firing everything they had, ceased fire at 0854, and withdrew to the line of departure just as the final air strike came in.[6]

At 0830 the first assault wave, consisting of 68 LVT(A), the amphtrac tanks, left the line of departure. It hit the beach almost precisely at H-hour, 0900. Within the next twenty-three minutes the remaining assault waves landed on schedule, and at 0944 twelve LSM, carrying medium tanks, beached.

Up to the point of actually touching land, this operation went off like a parade. Then trouble started. The LVT(A)s found their way blocked by the first terrace, which rose to as high as fifteen feet. The volcanic ash and cinders afforded poor traction, and as the men of the first wave left their vehicles on the run, they were slowed down to a walk. A few amphtracs reached the first terrace through breaches blasted by naval gunfire; some backed into the water and fired their turrets at inland targets; but many bogged down on the beach.

For a few minutes everywhere, and at some spots for as much as half an hour, only scattered small-arm, mortar and artillery fire fell along the beaches. Then both the volume and the accuracy of enemy resistance, mainly mortar fire, increased heavily. A situation developed somewhat similar to the one on Omaha Beach, Normandy, on 6 June 1944, with the important difference that here there was not even a sea wall for protection to the troops, who found it virtually impossible to advance in the face of withering fire. Enemy reaction developed earliest in the 4th Division sector Colonel Walter Wensinger's 23rd Marine Regiment landed on Beaches Yellow; Colonel John R. Lanigan's 25th Marine Regiment on Blue 1. The Japanese had excellent observation posts on high ground north of these beaches. Four of the tank-carrying LSM which beached at 0944 were hit by mortar shells and suffered extensive damage.

General Kuribayashi's static defense now began to show itself

[6] Lt.Cdr. H. D. Chickering USNR Action Report of *LCS(L)51* and letter of 4 Mar. 1945; Bartley p. 49. The LCI gunboats were to have gone in with the LCS(L) but were too badly shot up on D-day minus 2 to participate.

During the naval bombardment his troops retired deep into the ground and waited. As soon as gunfire lifted, they returned to their covered and protected positions and opened up on the advancing Marines. Their cleverly constructed pillboxes and larger gun and mortar positions could not be knocked out except by direct hit. Some of them, the "flush deckers," were built underground with only the firing slit uncovered, and the entire installation concealed from the view of ships or approaching troops by a sand bank. These were almost impossible to spot until they opened up. Gunports for the mortars were often only a couple of feet wide. Only a soldier on the spot could knock out positions such as these, with rifle fire, hand grenades, flame-throwers and demolitions. Aërial bombing, naval gunfire and artillery could contribute little to relieve this situation, which became hideously obvious within an hour of the landings.

As the Marines piled ashore they inched forward and took what shelter they could on the terraces, holding some momentum even though slowed to a crawl. On the left flank, the 5th Marine Division was going into action for the first time. On the extreme left, the 28th Marine Regiment (Colonel Harry B. Liversedge) landed two battalions in column on Beach Green while the 27th Regiment landed on Red 1 and 2. Opposition here was somewhat lighter than the 4th Division encountered, and heavy enemy fire developed more slowly, but within twenty minutes well-directed, accurate artillery, mortar and machine-gun fire began falling all along the 5th Division beaches. On the left, the 1st Battalion, 28th Marines, was to drive straight across the island at its narrowest point — 700 yards wide — while the 2nd Battalion, landing after the first, was to turn left towards Mount Suribachi. The 27th Marines had the job of driving straight inland and linking up with the 4th Division on their right. Having a little more breathing time than their comrades on the right flank, the 5th Division had a chance to get organized and start moving inland. Progress was slow owing to soft footing, heavy enemy fire, and occasional land mines, but never completely halted.

3. *Build-up and Support*

As the volume of enemy fire on the advancing Marines increased, the gunfire of supporting ships off shore stepped up. Prior to noon, most of the gunfire ships were busy delivering a rolling barrage with 5-inch shell. Fortunately, it had been arranged to repeat a scheduled shoot if progress ashore turned out to be slower than anticipated. This was done frequently. In addition, ships were instructed, whenever they observed fire coming from an enemy position, to lay on main batteries immediately and shoot it out. Other gun or mortar positions were spotted by planes, which called up ships' gunfire. The spotting was good and the shooting silenced many enemy positions, but they refused to stay silenced. A direct hit was the only certain way to silence a gun for good.

In no previous operation in the Pacific had naval gunfire support been so effective as at Iwo Jima. This was due in great measure to Lieutenant Colonel D. M. Weller USMC, V 'Phib Corps naval gunfire officer, who helped V 'Phib staff prepare the naval gunfire plan and had been beside Admiral Blandy during the preliminary bombardment. *Santa Fe* was the star of the fire support cruisers. She laid almost continuous 5-inch and 6-inch shell fire within 200 yards of the BLT on the left flank of 5th Division, with the result that hardly a shot was fired by the enemy from the base of Mount Suribachi, which commanded their line of advance. Battleship *Nevada* became the sweetheart of the Marine Corps. Her skipper, Captain H. L. ("Pop") Grosskopf, an old gunnery officer and a ruthless driver, had set out to make his battleship the best fire support ship in the Fleet, and did. *Nevada,* when firing her assigned rolling barrage about 0925, found that her secondary battery could not penetrate a concrete blockhouse and turned over the job to her main battery. This damaged a hitherto undisclosed blockhouse behind Beach Red 1, blasting away its sand cover and leaving it naked and exposed. At 1100 this blockhouse again became troublesome; the battleship then used armor-piercing shells, which took the position completely apart. At 1512 *Nevada* observed a gun firing from a cave in the high broken ground east of the beaches. Using direct fire, she shot two rounds of 14-inch, scoring a direct hit in the mouth of the cave, blowing out the side of the cliff and completely destroying the gun. One could see it drooping over the cliff edge "like a half-extracted tooth hanging on a man's jaw." [7]

An excellent illustration of the high state of training and versatility that existed in the Pacific Fleet at this stage of the war is shown by the experience of *West Virginia*, Captain Herbert V. Wiley. After outstanding performances at Leyte Gulf and Lingayen, she arrived at Ulithi 16 February to replenish from Service Squadron 10. At 0300 next morning Captain Wiley received orders from Admiral Nimitz to proceed immediately to Iwo Jima at best speed. Completing replenishment shortly after daylight, she began the 900-mile run to Iwo. At 1045 D-day, she arrived in the bombardment area, reported to Admiral Rodgers, received copies of all orders, charts, gridded maps, and an assigned firing position. Less than two hours after her arrival she was shooting at targets near Mount Suribachi.

A shore fire control party was assigned to each Marine battalion that landed. These parties suffered many casualties from enemy fire and lost much equipment but established communications with their assigned ships unusually early.

The Marines inched their way inland from the beaches preceded by heavy and continuous naval gunfire. At 1035 a small party of the 5th Division succeeded in making its way across the narrowest part of the island to the western beaches. But no continuous line of communications could be established as the troops which followed were forced to mop up Japanese positions that had inadvertently been bypassed; the defenders had held fire until they could shoot at the rear of the assault echelon.

Tanks began landing in the 5th Division sector at 0930. After considerable difficulty getting off the beaches they moved inland to support the troops. Some were disabled by land mines, but all be-

[7] Col. R. D. Heinl USMC, letter to writer 4 Dec. 1959.

came high priority targets for the enemy's antitank weapons and many were knocked out. In the final analysis it was the flame-thrower teams, riflemen with hand grenades, and engineers with demolition charges, blowing up pillboxes or sealing off cave entrances, that secured ground.

On the right of the 5th Division sector, resistance was heavy and progress was slow; yet, by 1130, RCT 28 was on and across the southern end of No. 1 airfield and, by 1500, RCT 27 had reached the cliffs overlooking the western beaches. Mount Suribachi was now cut off from the rest of the island's defenses.

The 4th Division on the right found the going very tough indeed. RCT 23, on the left flank, had gained only 500 yards by noon; it reached the edge of No. 1 airfield by 1405 but was unable to cross it or gain more ground. Tanks which landed in support at 1000 were slow in surmounting the beaches and some were knocked out by land mines. *LSM–216* beached four times under fire before she could find firm enough footing for her tanks to roll off.[8] RCT 25, on the right, attacked in two directions, inland towards the airfield and north against high broken ground. Here they were much distressed by fire coming from pillboxes located in the cliffs of the old quarry above East Boat Basin. To eliminate them, a new kind of spotting was tried. *LCS(L)–51* moved in to 650 yards off the boat basin and spotted for cruiser *Vicksburg*, gunfire support for that sector. Lieutenant J. J. Sweeney USMC, embarked in the LCS, directed her tracer fire to the hot spots, and the cruiser, following the tracers with her 6-inch guns, smashed them. This went on from 0910 to 1030. The LCS, followed by four more of the same class, fired both guns and rockets at spots indicated by troops ashore, and helped to break up a counterattack. During the afternoon these big support craft teamed up with destroyers to silence other positions. They thrust close inshore, drew enemy fire to themselves and replied with tracers which gave the destroyers their cue.

[8] The "high degree of coverage and tenacity shown by these ships in beaching . . . and landing this vital equipment in the face of the heaviest mortar and artillery fire yet seen" was praised in the 4th Division Report. Bartley *Iwo Jima* pp. 60*n*, 62*n*.

The 1st Battalion of RCT 25, assigned to the inland thrust, had made only 600 yards by 1130. The 3rd Battalion, with the northerly assignment, was pinned down almost from the start and casualties ran high, especially among officers. Enemy fire aimed at supporting tanks also fell among the troops, adding to their misery. Not until 1400 was Colonel Lanigan ready to launch a concerted attack to the north, and by late afternoon his battalion had reached only the first ridge behind East Boat Basin.

In the meantime a chaotic condition was developing on the beaches, under fire throughout the day. At about 1100 the northerly wind veered to SE, which made the beaches a lee shore; but "hot cargo" — such as ammunition, rations, water and high priority equipment — had to be landed. Most of the movement to the beaches had been by amphtracs, which brought in supplies that were manhandled by shore and beach parties and stacked up on the beaches. Some LVTs, however, carried supplies to forward troops and others returned to their parent LSTs for more high priority cargo. At about noon regimental commanders began calling for their reserve battalions to land, and during the afternoon the division commanders committed their reserve regiments. These reserves were sent ashore from their transports by conventional landing craft, LCVP and LCM. The beaches were so steep that when these craft touched down they found it very difficult to hold on. Rising surf broke over their sterns, and the backwash of rollers flowed over the downed ramp into the bow and flooded a boat so that it could not retract. A current which set parallel to the beach also caused many to broach, and others were hit and damaged by enemy mortar fire. As a result of this cumulative damage, the beach was so littered with wrecked boats by nightfall that it was difficult to find a spot to land. Available salvage equipment was inadequate, and with heaped-up supplies also clogging the beach a very serious situation developed. It is a tribute to the shore and beach parties, who worked throughout the day under enemy fire without flinching, and the UDTs who also turned to, that the increasing number of troops ashore did not run out of ammunition and supplies.

Approximately 30,000 troops were landed on 19 February There were 2420 casualties, including 519 killed or missing in action; and 47 more died of their wounds. The beachhead established fell far behind the planned phase line. From East Boat Basin it extended inland, to and along the southeast edge of No. 1 airfield, across its southwestern end to the west beaches, returning to the east beaches along the northern base of Suribachi. The beachhead was only about 4000 yards long, 700 yards deep in the north and 1100 yards in the south, but it already contained six infantry regiments, as many artillery battalions and two tank battalions.

4. *Air Operations*

Admiral Durgin's escort carriers continued to supply observation and spotting planes, photographic flights, C.A.P. over the target, antisubmarine patrol, and strike missions for direct support of troops ashore. The observation squadrons (VOF) were especially useful in locating targets and spotting fall of shot for ships' gunners. Lieutenant Commander George Philip, skipper of destroyer *Twiggs*, recorded that this type had had a doubtful reception in the Pacific; but "his performance of a few minutes sold him. Work with the VOF was one of the highlights of the operation."

Of the fast carrier groups, TG 58.2 (Davison) and 58.3 (Sherman) operated about 65 miles northwest of Iwo Jima while TG 58.1 and TG 58.4 fueled and replenished off shore. After the prelanding strikes on the beaches, *Hancock* and *Lexington* sent fighter sweeps of twelve planes each against Chichi Jima and Haha Jima to destroy grounded planes and small craft. It proved to be an expensive mission. Five planes were lost operationally and a torpedo bomber was shot down by antiaircraft fire. During the afternoon Admiral Sherman sent some of his planes to report to Advance Commander Support Aircraft in *Estes*. This group made bombing, rocketing and strafing runs on designated targets on the hump of Iwo Jima that were not accessible to naval gunfire.

Since enemy planes could easily fly from Japan down the line of the Bonins to bomb ships at the beachhead, dawn and dusk air attacks were anticipated. The first of these came in at 1900 D-day; but, sighting two fast carrier groups en route, decided to make them the target. Over a period of two and a half hours an estimated 12 to 15 planes harassed TGs 58.2 and 58.3. Both task group commanders used radical maneuvers, cloud cover and smoke to conceal their ships' wakes and evade the attackers, and only two direct contacts were made. "Mighty Mo," the battleship *Missouri*, drew her first blood of the war by shooting down an enemy plane at a range of 9800 yards at 1953, and a second which approached nearer was splashed by the combined antiaircraft fire of several ships.

Task Group 58.5, the night carrier group, operated northwest of Iwo Jima and provided dusk C.A.P. over the island, night fighter cover, and night observers for naval gunfire.

The carrier planes inflicted very little direct damage. The performance of napalm or gasoline jelly bombs, which were expected to burn off camouflage and suck the oxygen out of dugouts, was disappointing, and a large percentage of them were duds.[9] Quarter-ton bombs were too small to smash Japanese installations. The principal contribution of carrier planes to the Iwo landings on D-day was to provide C.A.P. over the amphibious forces, which, in view of the fact that not one enemy air attack approached them, was hardly needed. But this was good practice for the Okinawa operation, where C.A.P. was desperately needed.

Darkness finally closed D-day, a day such as Iwo had never seen since it arose a hissing volcano from the ocean. The Marines dug themselves in where night overtook them. Gunfire support ships moved out to night withdrawal areas, leaving only *Santa Fe* and ten destroyers to supply star shell illumination and harassing fire on enemy positions. The Japanese tried a few infiltrations during the night, and on the west coast their feeble attempt at a counter-landing was wiped out by alert Marines. But the expected big counterattack never came off; banzai charges were no part of Gen-

[9] CTF 51 (Vice Adm. Turner) Report p. (V) (E) 6.

eral Kuribayashi's plan. He intended to conserve his man power, knowing that American sea and air power had closed all hope of reinforcement, and that it was hopeless to try to drive the Marines into the sea. But he intended to fight for every yard of ground, and did.

CHAPTER IV

The Conquest of Iwo Jima

19 February–16 March 1945

1. *The Struggle Ashore, 20–21 February* [1]

ROBERT SHERROD, the veteran correspondent who had come ashore on the afternoon of D-day and spent the night in a foxhole, picked his way forward early next morning among corpses. "Whether the dead were Japs or Americans," he recorded, "they had died with the greatest possible violence. Nowhere in the Pacific war had I seen such badly mangled bodies. Many were cut squarely in half. Legs and arms lay 50 feet away from any body. In one spot on the sand, far from the nearest cluster of dead, I saw a string of guts 15 feet long. Only legs were easy to identify; they were Japanese if wrapped in khaki puttees, American if covered by canvas leggings. The smell of burning flesh was heavy. . . ." [2]

The reduction and capture of Iwo Jima is a story of yard-by-yard advance against a tough, resourceful enemy who allowed no let-up, and who so used his terrain as to exact the maximum price in blood. The Marines, advancing in the open with little natural shelter, had to fight their way against an enemy burrowed underground and protected from everything but a direct hit. It was a costly and exhausting grind, calling for higher qualities of courage, initiative and persistence than a campaign full of charges, counter-charges and spectacular incidents that raise men's morale. It was

[1] All sources mentioned in Chap. III, Note 1, especially Vice Adm. Turner's Action Report; Sgt. Bill Miller USMC "Hot Rock, the Fight for Mt. Suribachi" and Capt. F. A. Scott USMC "Ten Days on Iwo Jima" *Leatherneck* XXVIII, No. 5 (May 1945) 15–19.

[2] *On to Westward* p. 180.

like being under the lash of a relentless desert storm, from which there was no shelter, day or night; but this storm lasted six weeks and rained steel, not sand. General Holland Smith said that "Iwo Jima was the most savage and the most costly battle in the history of the Marine Corps." And Admiral Nimitz observed that on Iwo "uncommon valor was a common virtue." [3]

Supporting the Marines, and a factor that may have tipped the balance, was the impact of naval gunfire support and naval aircraft whose shells, bombs and strafing wore the enemy down. No eight square miles in all World War II received such a sustained and heavy pounding by these means as did Iwo Jima. General Kuribayashi admitted the value of it. In a message to Tokyo at the height of the battle, he said: "I am not afraid of the fighting power of only three American Marine divisions if there is no bombardment from aircraft and warships. That is the only reason why we have to face such miserable situations." [4]

A pattern for the island campaign was promptly cut out. For daytime direct support, each Marine battalion had attached to it one or more destroyers with a liaison officer on board, and a Navy shore fire control party stayed with it ashore. At daybreak the heavy support ships closed the island to fire a preliminary bombardment on targets selected by divisional and regimental commanders the evening before. On the morning of 20 February (D-day plus 1) four battleships, three cruisers and an LCI mortar unit performed this service, each ship plastering her assigned targets for 50 minutes from 0740. After the Marines jumped off, the ships stood by for deep support on targets designated by the s.f.c.p.'s or by spotting planes. That afternoon *Washington* (Captain Roscoe F. Good) received a report from divisional headquarters of a strong point of enemy resistance near the southern end of airfield No. 2. And it was even stronger than we suspected. The Japanese had constructed more than 300 pillboxes, gun emplacements and traps in a space

[3] Isely & Crowl p. 501.

[4] Maj. Tokasuka Horie "Explanation of Japanese Defense Plan and Battle of Iwo Jima" 25 Jan. 1946. Horie, one of Kuribayashi's staff officers, was detached before the landings and sent to Chichi Jima, where he survived the war.

of 500 by 1000 yards. The air spotter, sent to investigate, reported many caves dug into a cliff and facing the Marines' front lines. He directed the battleship's main battery to one end of the cliff, then spotted three 16-inch salvos directly into its face at 50-yard intervals. These shells so ate into the cliff as to start landslides which sealed off most of the cave mouths. *Washington* was on the firing line with both main and secondary batteries for ten hours and twenty minutes on 20 February. Nobody could convince the Marines that battleships were obsolete!

Caves and excavated holes in the ground were the key to Iwo's defenses. On the extreme left, Colonel Liversedge's 28th RCT closed in on Mount Suribachi, supported by destroyer *Mannert L. Abele* and light minelayer *Thomas E. Fraser*. The latter, after illuminating the eastern slopes during the night, between 0715 and 1130 delivered preparatory and neutralization fire on the mountain's base from a point 1500 yards from the beach; then shifted fire to caves and other targets of opportunity on the slopes of the volcano. When relieved by her sister ship *Henry A. Wiley* at 1448 she had fired 775 rounds of 5-inch shell. Off the western slope of Suribachi, *Abele* supported the 3rd Battalion in a similar pattern, expending 971 rounds of 5-inch and 172 rounds of star shell. At 0830 RCT 28 jumped off to the assault. Only 50 to 70 yards were gained in the forenoon against well-placed, camouflaged pillboxes and caves, many of which were so close to the front lines that supporting weapons could not be used. When the tanks (delayed by lack of fuel) finally came forward at 1100, better progress was made; but RCT 28 gained only 200 yards that day towards the lower slopes of Suribachi.

The story was much the same on the right flank of the beachhead. Preceded by intense naval, air and artillery bombardment, the Marines jumped off at 0830 but found tough going from the start. On the extreme right the 4th Division was up against the first main line of Japanese defense and made slight progress. On the west coast the 5th Division did somewhat better; but the troops, mostly in the open, suffered heavy casualties from well-placed artillery and mortar barrages. By the end of D-day plus 1 the Marines occupied a line across the island that included No. 1 airfield. Now they were facing the main enemy line of defense in the higher, broken ground of the bulbous part of the island.

About noon 20 February occurred a change in the weather that hampered both air operations and unloading supplies. The wind veered from SSE to WSW and built up to 20 knots. At 1545 a sharp cold front passed over the island and the wind shifted to NNE, raising a heavy sea which added confusion to the already chaotic condition on the beaches. They became cluttered with wrecked boats and vehicles. The high surf, an insufficient supply of Marston mat to cover the soft ash, lost equipment, casualties, enemy artillery and mortar fire, all contributed to a horrible brew of congestion and confusion. As soon as the beach party pulled one wreck out of the way another landing craft came in and broached. Conditions would have been even worse but for the energy and skill of Admiral Hill's beach party commander, Captain Carl E. Anderson USNR. "Squeaky," as he was nicknamed from his high-pitched voice, commandeered men, bulldozers and weasels. Amphtracs and dukws justified themselves by rolling over the steep, soft beaches, carrying supplies to their destination without manhandling.[5]

In addition to morning and afternoon sweeps against Haha and Chichi Jima, aircraft from Task Force 58 and the escort carriers flew 545 sorties in 27 missions on 20 February, expending over 116 tons of bombs and 1331 rockets.

During the night of 20–21 February a destroyer was assigned to each battalion and a cruiser to each division ashore, for illumination and night harassing fire. The remaining ships withdrew to night operating areas and returned at dawn.

February 21 broke with showers and an 18- to 20-knot NE wind

[5] Bartley *Iwo Jima* p. 197. The Royal Navy liaison officer with the attack force remarked to this writer, about two months later, "On the beach was an extraordinary character, almost as wide as he was tall, wearing the insignia of a Navy captain, but delivering his commands in amazingly blasphemous language, with a strong Scandinavian accent. But he managed to get things done." That was "Squeaky" Anderson. Weasels were tracked vehicles, 15 ft. 9 in. long.

which continued to kick up choppy seas and heavy surf. At 0740 a heavy bombardment by naval gunfire and corps artillery opened in preparation for the Marines' jump-off at 0810. This was to be the daily pattern for the next three weeks. RCT 28 reached the base of Suribachi and some advance was made all along the line to the north of No. 1 airfield. Progress was painfully slow, as the Marines had to inch their way along, destroying pillboxes and sealing cave and tunnel entrances. Any position that was bypassed or missed was sure to come to life and start shooting again. Advance for the day was measured in yards and at the end of it No. 2 airfield was still in enemy hands.

Salvage work among the wrecked craft, vehicles and tanks on the beaches was hampered by the weather. Surf and sea conditions were such that unloading was limited to the big beaching craft and LSMs. During the day another RCT of the 3rd Marine Division, in floating reserve off the island, was landed and assigned to the hard-pressed 4th Division.

The Tokyo "Home and Empire" broadcast at the end of this day indicates that the enemy propaganda service was becoming really mad with Kelly Turner. The following is a partial translation: –

According to reports issued by the enemy, the man who commands the enemy American amphibious forces which effected landings on our Iwo Island is Vice Admiral Richmond Turner. He is the right-hand man to Commander in Chief Spruance of the enemy Fifth Fleet. He is the man who can be termed a devil man, being responsible for the killing of countless numbers of our own younger and elder brothers on the various islands throughout the central Pacific area. Turner's career in war against our own men began with the operations on the island of Guadalcanal.

This man Turner is called and known as the "Alligator" in the American Navy. He is associated with this name because his work is very similar to that of an alligator, which lives both on land and in the water. Also, the true nature of an alligator is that once he bites into something he will not let go. Turner's nature is also like this.

Spruance, with a powerful offensive spirit and Turner, with excellent determinative power, have led their men to a point where they are indeed close to the mainland, but they find themselves in a dilemma, as they are unable either to advance or retreat.

This man Turner, who has been responsible for the death of so many of our precious men, shall not return home alive – he must not, and will not. This is one of the many things we can do to rest at ease the many souls of those who have paid the supreme sacrifice.[6]

Nevertheless, "Alligator" Turner (the Japanese evidently got the name from the shoulder patch of the V 'Phib Corps) not only returned alive, but at the time we go to press (1960) is still very much alive.

2. *Carrier Strikes and Air Support, 21 February–1 March*[7]

On 21 February Task Groups 58.2 and 58.3 operated about 70 miles WNW of Iwo, providing C.A.P. and launching several bombing strikes. Admirals Sherman and Davison also sent a strafing sweep against Chichi Jima to interdict the airfield so it would not be used for staging. During the night of 20–21 February about 13 raids with a total of 18 to 20 planes came in on the task group. Several planes pressed in near enough to be fired upon; two were shot down. No damage was inflicted on the ships. The pattern of these attacks on Sherman's and Davison's groups reminded sailors of similar raids off the Gilbert Islands in November 1943, years and years ago as it seemed. But of very different design were the attacks on *Saratoga* that same evening by kamikazes from Hatori airbase near Yokosuka, which staged through Hachijo Jima in the Northern Bonins.

On the morning of 21 February *Saratoga* (Captain Lucian A. Moebus) and three destroyers were detached from TG 58.5 in order to provide C.A.P. the following night over the amphibious forces off Iwo Jima. Unfortunately the rest of the night carrier group, *Enterprise* with three cruisers and seven destroyers, was re-

[6] Foreign Broadcast Intelligence Service Bulletin 22 Feb. 1945.

[7] CTF 58 (Vice Adm. Mitscher) Action Report for 10 Feb.–4 Mar., 13 Mar. 1945, CTG 52.2 (Rear Adm. Durgin) Action Report for Iwo Jima, 21 Apr. 1945.

tained by Admiral Mitscher for night C.A.P. over TF 58; this gave old "Sara" too little protection. At 1628 that day, when she had just reached her operating area 35 miles NW of Iwo with most of her planes on board, bogeys were reported 75 miles out. These were evaluated by the air support commander as "friendly." Six fighters of *Saratoga's* C.A.P. were nevertheless vectored out to inspect the suspicious characters, and at 1650 came a "Tally-ho!" from a pilot, followed by the word "Splashed two Zekes." The sky was overcast and ceiling down to 3500 feet, favoring air attack. *Saratoga* went to general quarters, commenced catapulting night fighters at maximum speed, and sent them out in all directions. At 1659 her antiaircraft guns opened fire on six planes bursting out of the clouds. The first two, already blazing from hits, struck the water and bounced into the carrier's starboard side at the waterline, hurling their bombs inside the ship, where they exploded. "Sara" had just completed launching 15 planes when she received these hits, and had two standby fighters on the catapults when she received a bomb from a third aircraft which exploded on the anchor windlass. This knocked out a good section of the flight deck forward. The fourth attacker splashed; the fifth made a flat turning dive, crashed the port catapult and exploded. The sixth, also in flames, crashed an airplane crane on the starboard side; parts of it landed on No. 1 gun gallery and the rest went overboard. All this happened within three minutes, 1700–1703 February 21.

Saratoga's power plant was hardly touched, and she built up speed to 25 knots while fighting fires. The blaze on the hangar deck was brought under control by 1830; the fire in wing tank control twelve minutes later. But the flight deck was in no condition to recover airborne planes. Destroyer *McGowan,* which took over fighter control, instructed them to land on one of the escort carriers near Iwo, until "Sara" had jettisoned her burning aircraft.

At 1846, just as things were beginning to look up, there came a sinister glare of parachute flares, and five more kamikazes attacked. Four were shot down clear of the carrier; the fifth came in unobserved, dropping a bomb which exploded on or just over the flight deck, blowing a 25-foot hole in that deck as the plane bounced overboard. Even in this predicament there was something to laugh at. A confused pilot from a CVE landed his plane on *Saratoga's* deck, remarking as he alighted "Gee, I'm glad I'm not on that old Sara. All hell's broken out there!" A deckhand replied "Take a good look around, brother. This *is* hell!"

But old "Sara" was not yet dead. Although wounded in seven places, by 2015 she was able to recover planes on the after part of her flight deck. On Admiral Spruance's orders she steamed under her own power to Eniwetok, en route to a West Coast yard for repairs. She lost 36 planes by burning and jettisoning, and six by water landings, and sustained heavy casualties — 123 killed and missing, 192 wounded.[8]

The loss of *Saratoga's* services for over three months, and the discouraging results of this battle, coupled with the distaste of carrier-plane pilots for night work,[9] put a stopper on further development of special dusk-to-dawn carriers and planes. Admiral Mitscher was not favorably impressed by their performance. In the next operation, the one covering the Ryukyus, there was but one night-flying carrier, *Enterprise*. But, as we shall see, her performance in that operation caused the Admiral to change his mind about night fighters and bombers.

"Sara" was not the only flattop to catch it during the night of 21–22 February. At 1845, during twilight, escort carrier *Bismarck Sea*, operating with Admiral Durgin's group (to which *Saratoga*

[8] *Saratoga* Action Report 7 Mar. 1945.

[9] Discussed in letter from Cdr. William I. Martin (C.O. Air Group 90 in *Enterprise*) to Cominch 14 Apr. 1945. The reasons for this distaste were not so much the hazards of night flying as failure to receive target information from daytime fliers, dissatisfaction over not seeing targets, and irregular meals and hours. CTG 58.5 (Rear Adm. M. B. Gardner), in his Action Report of 12 March, stated that the effectiveness of a night carrier group was not properly tested during this operation. The losses of TG 58.5, 10–22 February, exclusive of *Saratoga's* in the 21 February attack, were eight planes (one over Yokosuka, one by "friendly" fire off Iwo, rest operational), five pilots and four other men, plus ten more planes jettisoned as a result of deck crashes. Admiral Spruance, in his endorsement to this report, observed that a special night carrier group was not a good solution because its requirements for daytime C.A.P. put too much load on the other groups. Night fighters were frequently called upon for emergency day missions; 71 per cent of their sorties in this operation were by day.

and *Enterprise* were temporarily attached) about 45 miles east of Iwo Jima, became a total loss to kamikaze attack. One Japanese plane attacking on her port bow was taken under fire but a second, coming in very low on the starboard side, was not seen until 1000 yards away. It was shot at until the guns could depress no more; already blazing, it crashed the ship abreast the after elevator, which dropped onto the hangar deck. About two minutes later a heavy explosion occurred. This started gasoline fires in planes on the hangar deck, the after end of which was blown out by a second explosion. The after part of the ship was a shambles and at 1905 Captain J. L. Pratt ordered Abandon Ship. *Bismarck Sea* burned and exploded for three hours, then rolled over and sank. Three destroyers and three destroyer escorts spent all night and until 1000 on the 22nd picking up survivors. Of her crew of 943 officers and men, 218 were lost.

Simultaneously with this fatal attack several Japanese torpedo bombers came in on the starboard side of escort carrier *Lunga Point*. The first, taken under fire at 1500 yards, launched a torpedo, then was caught by a shellburst and splashed only 200 yards away. The torpedo passed ahead. A second plane, closely following the first, dropped a torpedo which also crossed the carrier's bow safely; the plane then disappeared without being brought under fire. A third, close behind the second, after launching a torpedo which missed astern, hit the after part of the island with its wing, skidded across the flight deck with propeller chewing up the planking, then plunged into the sea over the port side. And a fourth plane was shot down. The fires in *Lunga Point* were soon quenched, the damage was slight, and nobody was killed.

Net cargo ship *Keokuk* [10] was cruising in formation with a group of LSTs and net tenders about 50 miles SE of Iwo Jima at 1720 February 21 when a Jill dived out of the clouds dead ahead, hit her on the starboard side just abaft the bridge, and slithered aft, wiping out all but one 20-mm gun of the starboard battery. All fires

[10] Designated AKN, an old train ferry converted to carry harbor nets and supplies for the net tenders.

were out by 1850, but *Keokuk* had 17 killed or missing and 44 wounded. *LST-477* was also hit by a kamikaze which apparently bounced overboard without doing much damage to this beaching craft or her embarked tanks.

Admiral Mitscher now ordered *Enterprise* to take *Saratoga's* place in close night support. Early 22 February she launched eight planes to search for "Sara's" missing pilots. Unfortunately two of these planes broke through a low, 500-foot cloud ceiling right over some of the fire support ships during an air alert, were mistaken for enemy and shot down. One crew of three was lost; the other, piloted by Ensign Henry G. Hinrichs USNR, was picked up by a PC which also mistook the men for Japanese and had the rail lined with armed bluejackets, in view of the enemy's propensity to toss hand grenades at would-be rescuers. Fortunately the "loud, continuous and explosive use of strong American invectives convinced them otherwise"; so much so that the patrol craft's skipper jumped over the side to aid the rescue.[11]

Enterprise had two main tasks off Iwo: to fly dawn and dusk C.A.P. over the escort carriers whose planes supported the troops by day, and to interdict the enemy airfield on Chichi Jima. On the evening of 23 February, her night fighter squadron, with the aid of five planes transferred from *Saratoga*, began hanging up a new record. Night and day for 174 consecutive hours, until midnight 2 March, this squadron kept planes airborne. Its pilots flew night, dawn, dusk and day air patrols, sweeps, and intruder missions on Chichi Jima. But the "jeep" carriers almost equaled this record of "Big E." Admiral Durgin's task group, during the 22 days that it furnished air support for Iwo (with only one day out for fueling), at one time kept planes airborne for 172 consecutive hours.[12] *Enterprise* remained off Iwo, under operational control of Rear Admiral Durgin, until 10 March. From her association with the escort carriers she acquired two new nicknames, "Enterprise Bay" and

[11] "History of Night Torpedo Squadron 90" p. 35, included in History Night Carrier Air Group 90.

[12] CTG 52.2 Action Report 21 Apr. 1945.

"Queen of the Jeeps." She entered Ulithi lagoon on 12 March for two days' upkeep before departing with TF 58 on the next operation to cover Okinawa.

Admiral Clark's TG 58.1 and Admiral Radford's TG 58.4 had been busy on D-day fueling and replenishing from the logistics group and filling up what would otherwise have been restful hours with antiaircraft practice. On 20 February "Jocko" Clark, who hated to see an idle plane on board, sliced off six whole deckloads to support the troops on Iwo Jima, and a few more next day.

During 23 February Task Force 58 fueled from Rear Admiral Beary's Servron 6 east of Iwo Jima and at 1850 shaped a northerly course for a high-speed run toward Tokyo. Next day the destroyers were topped off from the heavy ships, although hampered by high seas and strong winds. At about noon, destroyers were sent ahead to deal with Japanese pickets and give early warning of air attack. Weather forced a reduction of speed to 16 knots but the sea was so rough that *Moale*, hastening from TG 58.4 to take her picket station, smashed her bow and forecastle and flooded several forward compartments.

The first sweeps were sent off at 0715 February 25 when the task force was about 190 miles SE of Tokyo. The weather was so bad that most of the strikes hit secondary targets or those of opportunity. As the weather worsened rapidly during the forenoon, Admiral Mitscher at 1215 ordered all further operations canceled. This second strike on Tokyo was even less effective than the first.

Early in the afternoon, with unfavorable reports of weather over Tokyo for the next day, Admiral Mitscher decided to strike Nagoya on the 26th and shaped a course accordingly. En route, destroyers *Hazelwood* and *Murray* sank three Japanese small craft that were too tiny to be mentioned in postwar assessments. But a 100-foot-long Japanese picket boat, which refused to be disposed of easily, put up a spunky fight. She was picked up at 0030 February 26 by *Porterfield,* which opened fire with 5-inch and automatic weapons. The picket boat returned small-caliber shell fire, scoring hits which did considerable damage to instruments and radio sets around the destroyer's bridge structure, killed one man and wounded twelve. *Porterfield*, reporting that she had left the picket in a sinking condition, passed on; but the Japanesse vessel drifted into the inner screen of TG 58.3, where she almost collided with *Pasadena* and had the nerve to open fire on her at point-blank range, making 13 hits and wounding two men. The cruiser replied with 40-mm fire and passed on. Destroyer *Stockham* at about 0130 was ordered to destroy the enemy picket. She closed and opened fire with 5-inch and 40-mm guns. The boat still had considerable bite left, returned fire and hit *Stockham* several times with small bullets. By 0300 *Stockham* had silenced and dismasted the boat, leaving it awash in a sinking condition.

During that night both wind and sea made up and speed had to be reduced to 12 knots to avoid damage to the destroyers. Admiral Mitscher, realizing by 0514 February 26 that he could not reach a launching position off Nagoya in time, canceled the strikes and turned toward his fueling area, around lat. 23°30′ N, long. 141° E., where the task force fueled on the 27th. Admiral Radford's TG 58.4 was then detached to Ulithi, while the other three steamed westward to make their third call on Okinawa.

Early in the morning of 1 March they reached a position 60 to 70 miles SE of the "Great Loochoo." Even in that hornets' nest of enemy air activity tactical surprise was obtained and no airborne opposition developed. Naha, the flimsy capital of Okinawa, was well bombed. Carrier planes roamed at will over the future scene of battle, bombing and strafing every likely target. Very important for future operations were the photographic missions. It was a fair day for once, and the photo planes obtained almost perfect coverage of Okinawa, Kerama Retto, Minami Daito and Amami O Shima, obtaining data for charts which were made and distributed before the end of the month.

Retirement commenced as soon as planes were recovered that evening, except that Rear Admiral F. E. M. Whiting's cruisers (*Vincennes*, *Miami* and *San Diego*) with Desron 61 were detached to bombard Okino Daito (also known as Borodino Island), an islet

195 miles east of Okinawa where the enemy was reported to have a radar station. Three firing runs were made there in the early hours of 2 March. Task Force 58 continued southeasterly and entered Ulithi lagoon on 4 March 1945 to prepare for the next operation, the capture of Okinawa.

During this two weeks' cruise, 16 February to 1 March, TF 58 claimed to have shot down 393 enemy planes in the air, and believed that it destroyed over 250 on the ground. It is now impossible to check these claims from Japanese sources. Plane and pilot losses were heavy — 84 planes with 60 pilots and 21 crewmen in combat, 59 planes with eight pilots and six crewmen operationally.

Escort carrier planes were the winged workhorses of the Iwo Jima campaign. *Anzio's* planes destroyed two Japanese submarines;[18] and while Task Force 58 raided Tokyo and Okinawa, Admiral Durgin's "jeeps," almost within sight of Mount Suribachi, were feeding out call-bombing and rocketing missions, and providing C.A.P. and antisubmarine patrol, from D-day minus 3 to D-day plus 18. "The daily task of providing air support," observed Admiral Durgin, "is not broken even for replenishing and refueling. It is a continual grind from dawn to dark each day."

3. *The Land Battle, 22 February–16 March*

On 22 February, worst day yet for weather, with a cold, drizzling rain, General Schmidt decided to give his front lines a rest, and the weather was so foul that afternoon air strikes had to be canceled. On the 23rd, after preliminary bombardment, the Marines jumped off, with main effort directed towards No. 2 airfield. The 4th Division fought in misery in terrain honeycombed with mines, booby traps, buttressed pillboxes, caves and blockhouses, all mutually supporting. Gains of 200 to 300 yards were made on the right, but there was little change in the center or on the left.

[18] See end of Chap. I.

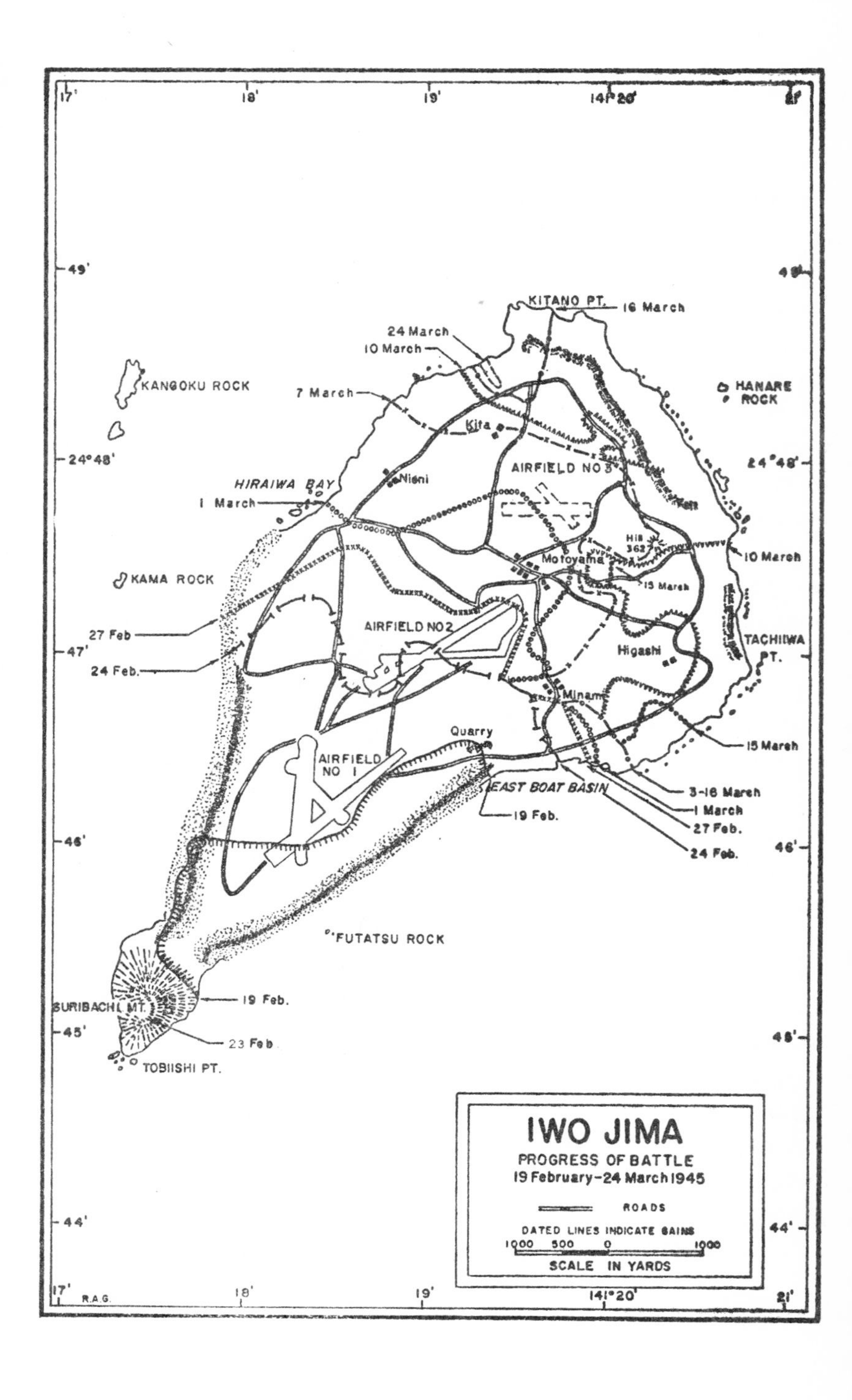
IWO JIMA
PROGRESS OF BATTLE
19 February–24 March 1945
ROADS
DATED LINES INDICATE GAINS
1000 500 0 1000
SCALE IN YARDS
KITANO PT.
16 March
24 March
10 March
7 March
KANGOKU ROCK
HANARE ROCK
Kita
AIRFIELD NO 3
Nishi
HIRAIWA BAY
1 March
Hill 362
Motoyama
10 March
15 March
KAMA ROCK
27 Feb
24 Feb.
AIRFIELD NO 2
TACHIIWA PT.
Higashi
Minami
15 March
Quarry
AIRFIELD NO 1
EAST BOAT BASIN
3-16 March
1 March
27 Feb.
24 Feb.
19 Feb.
FUTATSU ROCK
SURIBACHI MT.
19 Feb.
23 Feb
TOBIISHI PT.
17'
18'
19'
141°20'
21'
49'
24°48'
47'
46'
45'
44'
R.A.G.

The great event of 23 February was the successful scaling of HOTROCKS, the code name for Mount Suribachi. General Kuribayashi ordered his troops there to hold out to the last. But things got so hot on HOTROCKS – whose every slope could be reached by naval gunfire, air bombing and rocketing – that the local commander became desperate, and sent a message to headquarters requesting permission to make a banzai charge, rather than sit tight and be smothered. Whether or not the General deigned to reply is not known; but in any event, Colonel Harry ("the Horse") Liversedge USMC gave neither commander any time to make up his mind. Early on the 23rd a 40-man detachment from Liversedge's 28th Marines, commanded by 1st Lieutenant H. G. Schreier USMC, scaled the volcano. As they scrambled over the rim of the crater they were challenged by a small defense force on the opposite edge and a hot little fight developed. Before it ended, one of the Marines picked up a length of iron pipe, lashed to it a small American flag that he had brought up in his pocket, and raised it at 1020. This is the scene which we have used as a frontispiece to this volume. The flag was too small to be seen through the fog of battle, but fortunately a bigger one was coming up. A Marine had thoughtfully borrowed a big battle ensign eight feet long from *LST-779*, which had beached near the base. He carried it up the mountain, and Joe Rosenthal, Associated Press photographer, arrived in time to take the picture of the second flag-raising, at 1037, which became the most famous photograph of the Pacific War. It inspired the bronze monument to the Marine Corps by Felix de Welden that has been erected near Arlington National Cemetery, overlooking the Potomac.[14]

Secretary of the Navy James V. Forrestal was coming ashore with General Smith from *Eldorado* during the preliminaries. Symbolically, they touched Beach Green just as the second Stars and Stripes was flung to the strong north wind. "It was one of the proudest moments of my life," said General Smith; and the Secretary, turning to him, said gravely, "Holland, the raising of that flag

[14] Bartley pp. 73–78; *Coral and Brass* pp. 259–262.

on Suribachi means a Marine Corps for the next 500 years." [15] Old Glory, visible all over the island and far off shore, lifted the spirits of all hands.

But the end was not yet near. Even the 28th Regiment could not leave Suribachi and join the rest of the 5th Division on its way north, because the volcano slopes were a rabbit warren of caves and tunnels. Although some 600 Japanese had been killed in the assault, at least 1000 more were still there, holed up like mites in an over-ripe cheese.

Unloading conditions continued bad, even after a shift was made to the western beaches to avoid the cluttered wrecks of landing craft on the eastern side. Wind seemed to go around in circles at Iwo Jima, making first one side of the island and then the other a lee shore. Beach gradients everywhere were so steep that pontoon causeways broached, so the rest of the LSTs equipped with pontoons used them as lighters. Ordinary landing craft could not be used, as the backwash of each wave flooded them through the ramps, and all beaching craft had to keep motors running and use breastfasts in addition to two stern anchors.[16]

February 24 was a day of very heavy fighting in which significant gains were made. *Idaho* and *Pensacola* delivered an hour's naval bombardment of the heavily fortified area just north of No. 2 airfield; planes from the escort carriers then bombed it for a quarter of an hour and the Marines jumped off at 0915. During the day some of their tanks managed to reach the airfield by a rough road which first had to be cleared of mines. A foothold was secured near the middle of No. 2 airfield and gains of up to 800 yards were made on the left flank.

A feature of gunfire support rendered during the first week on Iwo Jima was the work of the LCI mortar unit under Lieutenant

[15] Walter Millis ed. *The Forrestal Diaries* (1951) pp. 29–30.

[16] Notes from Commo. Robert C. Johnson USNR of the Seabees at Iwo Jima 21 Apr. 1945. From same source, 160 landing craft were damaged beyond repair the first two days.

Commander Stanley J. Kelley USNR. Thirty LCI(M)s were assigned, but owing to breakdowns not all were available at the same time. They provided direct support on call, and harassing fire to break up enemy counterattacks. With their shallow draft they could work close inshore on the flanks and often were in a position to shoot up gullies against enemy targets that were not visible to the Marines. Much of their fire was delivered at night. So impressed were the Marines with the performance of Kelley's craft that on 22 February the landing force commander sent them a special message: "Ships of mortar support group have been doing a splendid job. Believe your fire has had great effect in preventing large scale counterattacks." [17] Ammunition shortages curtailed their support at times, but when they retired to Saipan on 26 February they had expended over 32,000 mortar projectiles. Although frequently taken under fire by enemy batteries the only one damaged was *LCI(M)–760*, by a near miss.

Beginning 25 February the Marines ashore made slow but steady progress, gradually pushing Japanese defenders into the northern part of the island. The 3rd Division having completed landing on 24 February, the final drive was made by three divisions abreast, 4th on the right, 3rd in the center, and 5th, proud of having taken Suribachi, on the left flank.[18] By 1 March, No. 2 airfield and the village of Motoyama were in their hands. The naval gunfire support plan continued as on D-day, with destroyers assigned to battalions and heavier ships to divisions, or engaged in area bombardment. This continued until 9 March, when the enemy was contained in a narrow strip along the north and northeast coasts of the island. With fewer targets to take under fire, fewer ships were assigned.

Routine fire support duties were varied by many alarums and excursions. Few ships, however, had such a lively experience as destroyer *Terry* (Lieutenant Commander William B. Moore) on

[17] CTG 52.6 (Com. Mortar Support Group) Action Report 2 Mar. 1945.

[18] This advance is well described in Robert Sherrod *On to Westward* pp. 207–215.

1 March. In a screening station northwest of the island, she was ordered at 0215 to search for a submarine contact which had been lost by another destroyer. At 0245 a low-flying Japanese plane coming from the direction of Kita Jima closed and dropped a torpedo at about 1000 yards' range. The plane had been picked up by radar and tracked; the recognition officer saw it drop the torpedo and sang out "Torpedo Away–" The skipper put rudder hard over and rang up flank speed, which enabled *Terry* to escape, the torpedo passing about 50 yards astern.

At 0720, en route to her next assignment, a screening station north of Iwo Jima, *Terry* was passing Kitano Point at the north end of the island and about 5200 yards off shore, when salvos from a Japanese coastal battery began straddling her. Lieutenant Commander Moore rang up flank speed and began counterbattery fire with his after guns. The destroyer received a 6-inch hit on the starboard side of her main deck over the forward engine room, losing eleven men killed and 19 wounded and suffering extensive damage. The Japanese battery fired continuously until about 0730, when *Nevada* and *Pensacola* silenced it.

On the same day, *Colhoun*, anchored off the northeastern coast of the island to repair damage received in a collision, absorbed a three-gun salvo from an 80-mm dual-purpose battery. It wrecked No. 2 torpedo tube, exploded the air flask of a torpedo, caused extensive damage, killed one man and wounded 16.

The same shore battery that bopped *Terry* almost got the number of ammunition ship *Columbia Victory*, anchored off the beach close to V Amphibious Corps headquarters. A salvo fell near enough to her fantail to wound a man. The skipper promptly slipped his cable and got under way, pursued by enemy salvos. Generals Smith and Schmidt watched this performance with hearts in their mouths, as one hit on the ammunition ship would have sent them as well as her to kingdom come.[19]

[19] Rear Adm. Hill Action Report p. III 9; *Coral and Brass* pp. 217–218.

Beach and unloading conditions improved after 25 February. New beach exits were constructed, a lateral road leading inland was covered with Marston matting, good progress was made cleaning up wrecked landing craft and vehicles. But weather and surf conditions still prevented anything smaller than LST, LSM and LCT from unloading. Late on 2 March landing operations were shifted to the western group of beaches, and thereafter both sets of beaches were used whenever wind and surf permitted.

Escort carrier planes and B–24s from the Marianas continued to provide air support. Base development work on No. 1 airfield was pressed by Seabees. On the 27th (D-day plus 8) the first light Piper Cub observation plane, designated OY–1, was launched successfully from *LST–776*, which had been equipped with a special gear of booms and cables (the so-called "Brodie") for launching and recovering these small aircraft.

PBMs began to arrive that day to operate searches from their floating bases, tenders *Hamlin*, *Williamson* and *Chincoteague*, and the first searches went out on the 28th. But the sea off Iwo proved to be too rough and too full of flotsam to operate PBMs profitably, and they began to withdraw to Saipan 6 March when A.A.F. fighters arrived to take over covering duties. Thereafter searches were flown by PB4Ys, using the Iwo No. 1 airfield, which had received its first twin-engine plane, a C–47, on 3 March. Next day the island received its first call from a B–29, returning low on gas from Japan. The CVEs began to pull out on 9 March. Last of the heavy bombardment ships departed 12 March, leaving only destroyers and LCI(G)s for fire support.

Vice Admiral Kelly Turner, the "devil man" who the Japanese vowed would never return home alive, departed in *Eldorado* 4 March, after appointing Rear Admiral Harry Hill S.O.P.A., Iwo Jima. Transdiv 33 left the same day, taking to Guam one regiment of the 3rd Marine Division, which had suffered severely in the fighting. The other two regiments were ordered to remain until relieved by the 147th Infantry U. S. Army. Major General James E. Chaney

USA, commander of the future Army garrison, arrived with his headquarters on 27 February and the bulk of his troops began disembarking 21 March.[20] This overlapping of Marines and Army was a good thing, as it gave the GIs an opportunity to learn the peculiar methods that had been developed to meet the enemy tactics before becoming responsible for the final dig-out and mopping-up.

[20] Rear Adm. Hill Action Report pp. III 9, 14, XII 6. They arrived in cargo ships *Zaurak*, *Alkaid*, *Alderamin* and *Celeno*, escorted by DEs *John L. Williamson* and *French*.

CHAPTER V

Securing the Island[1]

17 March–1 June 1945

1. *The Mopping-up Process*

ALTHOUGH Iwo Jima was declared "secured" at 1800 March 16, and "operation completed" at 0800 on the 26th, there was a good deal of ground fighting between these two dates, and even later. The Marines suffered 3885 casualties between 11 and 26 March.

It took a week's work – 16 to 24 March – to overcome an exceptionally tough pocket of resistance, a rocky gorge that led down to the sea not far west of Kitano Point. By the 24th it was reduced to an area of about 2500 square yards. General Kuribayashi's radio informed Major Horie at Chichi Jima on the 21st: "We have not eaten or drunk for five days. But our fighting spirit is still high. We are going to fight bravely till the last." On the 24th Horie received the last word from his commanding general: "All officers and men of Chichi Jima, goodbye."[2]

These Japanese defenders did not simply hole up and die; they continued to do all the mischief they could. On 26 March, shortly before dawn, a body of about 350, including a large number of officers wearing swords, crawled out of the gorge. They were heavily armed with knee mortars, rifles and hand grenades (some of them

[1] Bartley *Iwo Jima* and Action reports cited earlier, especially those of Generals H. M. Smith and Harry Schmidt USMC.

[2] The Horie document (see Chap. IV Note 4).

American); a few were even wearing U. S. Marine uniforms. They took by surprise an insufficiently guarded VII A.A.F. and Seabee camp just south of Hirawa Bay. The Marine 5th Pioneer Battalion, which fortunately had bivouacked in this area, hastily formed battle line, and after a bitter struggle, lasting three hours, killed or drove off all attackers. The Japanese left some 250 of their number dead, but succeeded in killing 53 and wounding 119 American officers and men. General Kuribayashi may have been killed in this foray; but his body was not identified, and it seems more likely that this brave and resourceful officer committed hara-kiri in his subterranean command post.[3] The Japanese naval commander, Rear Admiral T. Ichimaru, also disappeared.

The smoke of this battle of 26 March had hardly cleared when General Harry Schmidt USMC announced that the Iwo Jima operation was completed. To all intents and purposes it was, with airfield No. 1 already doing business for the B–29s. Admiral Nimitz, upon his first visit to the island on the 24th, ascertained that so far 65 Superforts had been saved from destruction by being able to make emergency landings on Iwo, and between 24 March and 21 April about 230 more used the island facilities.

On 25 March, when the Japanese air forces attempted their last raid on Iwo, they were picked up by radar and intercepted by island-based P–61s which shot down several and drove off the rest.

General Schmidt closed his command post and departed on the afternoon of 26 March. The 3rd Marine Division began loading for Guam next day. The 147th Infantry Regiment U. S. Army, which had begun landing on 21 March, now took over responsibility for mopping-up and garrison duty. Major General James E. Chaney USA became island commander.

Down to 1800 March 27 the Marine Corps and Navy casualties incurred in capturing Iwo Jima were as follows: —[4]

[3] HQ Army Garrison Force G–2 Weekly Report No. 1, 2 Apr.; data obtained by the writer at Iwo 21 Apr. 1945. Different figures in Bartley p. 192.

[4] Bartley pp. 220–221.

	MARINE CORPS		NAVY [5]
	Officers	*Men*	*Officers and Men*
Killed in action	215	4,339	363
Died of wounds	60	1,271	70
Missing, presumed dead	3	43	448
Wounded in action	826	16,446	1,917
Combat fatigue casualties	46	2,602	?

Up to and including 26 March the count of Japanese killed and sealed up in caves was 20,703,[6] and only 216 had been taken prisoner. General Harry Schmidt then estimated that only 100 to 300 of the enemy were left alive on the island, which proved to be too optimistic.[7]

The Army now organized a systematic mop-up. An officer and ten men, Nisei who spoke Japanese, accompanied by prisoners who lent themselves to this work, broadcast invitations to surrender through loud-speakers, promising the Japanese good usage and plenty to eat and drink.[8] Caves on the northwest coast of the island and northeast of the East Boat Basin, whose occupants proved deaf to these appeals, were blasted by flame-throwers and explosives and sealed. These methods netted 867 more prisoners in April and May, during which time 1602 more Japanese were killed. Isolated pockets long held out in various parts of the island. During the week of 2 April about 200 Japanese attempted to rush an infantry command post just above East Boat Basin; this fight lasted all night and all Japanese participating were killed. They also managed to blow

[5] Including Navy Medical and Dental Corps officers and hospital corpsmen serving with Marines, Seabees, crews of gunfire support ships, aircraft carriers, transports and air units; but not including losses of TF 58 in strikes on Tokyo. There were also 37 casualties in Army units attached to V 'Phib Corps.

[6] Writer's notes from Col. John K. Gowen, Head of Intelligence Section A.A.F. Command at Iwo, 26 Apr. 1945.

[7] Writer's notes at Iwo Jima 21 Apr. 1945.

[8] A merry peasant-type Japanese soldier, nicknamed "Tojo," was particularly effective on these propaganda forays. He became a great pet of the soldiers, who, in answer to his request for a few English words of politeness, taught him the most horrible blasphemies. It became routine for any work party passing "Tojo's" group to call out "Hey, Tojo! How are you today, Tojo?" upon which the little fellow would come to attention, spread a broad grin, bow politely and call out an obscenity which he had been led to believe meant "Thank you very much!"

up a dump of 6000 cases of dynamite, which rocked the island and caused a number of casualties.[9]

2. *Air Base and Conclusion*

On 1 April a submarine gasoline pipeline, buoyed at its seaward end, was brought ashore to reduce dependence on drummed gas, and four 1000-gallon gas tanks were set up ashore. Aviation gas could now be delivered directly from tankers. A second pipeline was later established on the west side. Seabees began to construct No. 3 airfield in the north part of the island on 3 April. The 7th was a red-letter day, marking the first B–29 raid on Japan escorted by P–51 fighter planes based on Iwo. About 100 participated and they were aloft seven hours; 54 B–29s used Iwo fields during the day. Possession of Iwo more than doubled the efficiency of the Superfortress bombing missions against Japan.

The writer, landing at Iwo 20 April 1945, counted 5330 crosses and stars in the Marine Corps cemetery. But there were about 31,000 soldiers, Air Force ground crews and Seabees on the island very much alive, healthy and in high spirits. Army officers said they wouldn't trade Iwo for any South Pacific island. The weather was cool and pleasant, and there was complete absence of mosquitoes and other wild life. The fact that everyone was active and helping the war effort kept morale high. The Seabees,[10] three of whose battalions landed on D-day, and who started to activate No. 1 airfield on D-day plus 5, did outstanding work; General Holland M. Smith on his departure sent a message: "Let us remember the skillful work of the Seabees who, laboring under fire, immediately began to transform this barren wasteland into a powerful advance base." Over 7600 of them were on the island 20 April; their sick list, an average of only 40 per day, was less than it had been in the United States.

[9] HQ Army Garrison Force G–2 Weekly Report No. 2, 8 Apr.

[10] These were the 8th Naval Construction Regiment, comprising the 8th, 90th, 95th, 106th and 23rd Naval Construction Battalions, and the 41st Naval Construction Regiment, composed of the 31st, 62nd and 133rd NCBs. (Notes from their War Diary, seen at Iwo 20–22 Apr. 1945.)

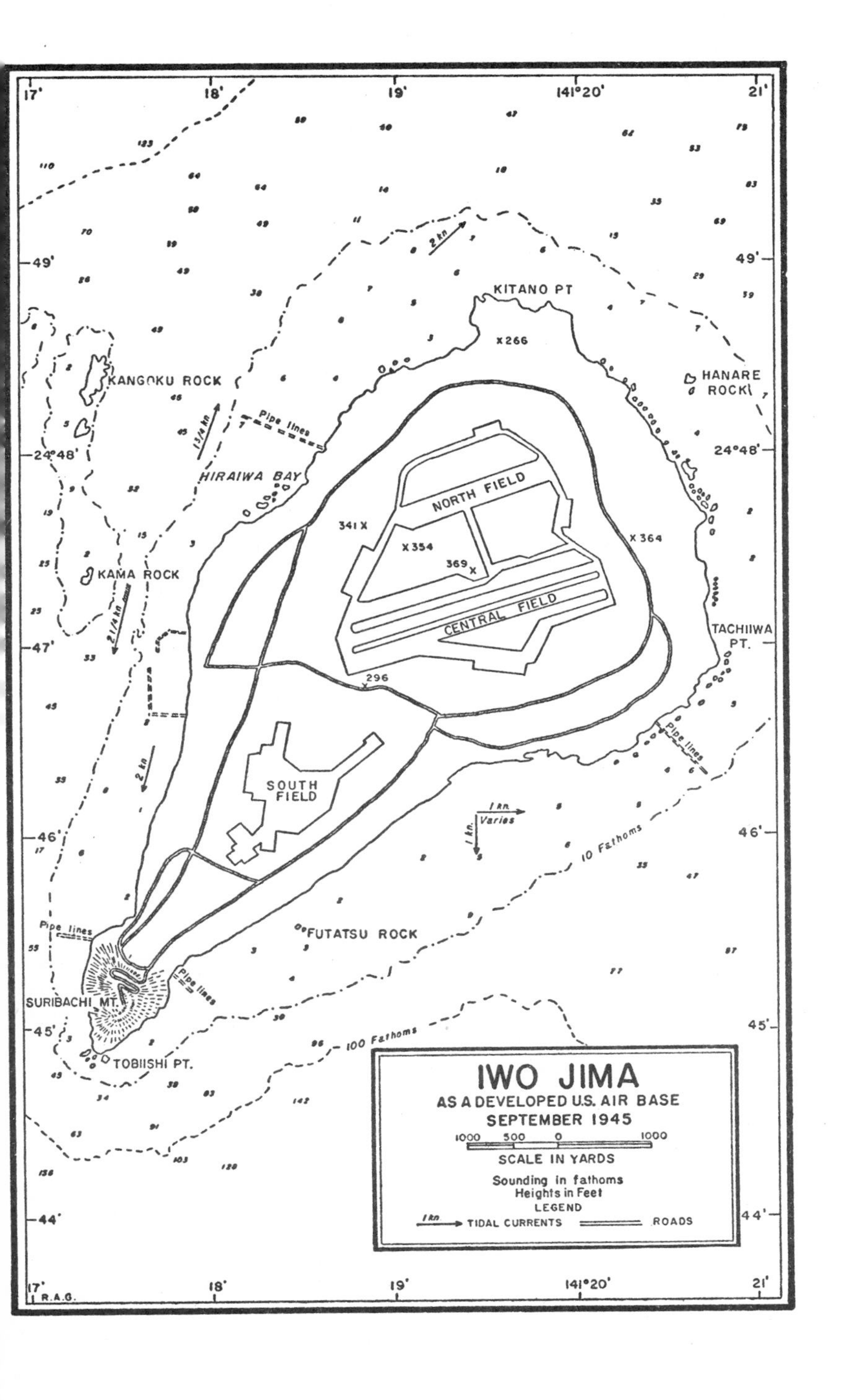
IWO JIMA
AS A DEVELOPED U.S. AIR BASE
SEPTEMBER 1945
SCALE IN YARDS
Sounding in fathoms
Heights in Feet
LEGEND
TIDAL CURRENTS
ROADS
KITANO PT
HANARE ROCK
KANGOKU ROCK
HIRAIWA BAY
NORTH FIELD
CENTRAL FIELD
SOUTH FIELD
KAMA ROCK
TACHIIWA PT.
FUTATSU ROCK
SURIBACHI MT.
TOBIISHI PT.
Pipe lines
10 Fathoms
100 Fathoms
R.A.G.

Survey ship *Sumner* (Commander Irving M. Johnson USNR) was busy making soundings and erecting beacons off shore; she had already published a preliminary chart of the island and surrounding waters.[11]

Above all, let us not forget the United States Marines, who conducted this, one of the toughest battles in their entire history, with exemplary endurance, skill and valor. Never before had that great fighting arm of the United States Navy covered itself with so much glory; the more so because it was not a spectacular battle, but one of steady slugging against a relentless, dug-in enemy. Battle casualties amount to 30 per cent of the entire landing force, 60 per cent in the infantry regiments of the 3rd Division and 75 per cent in the infantry regiments of the 4th and 5th Divisions. During the five weeks of the campaign, 7500 battle replacements were provided most of them coming under fire for the first time.[12]

The chief beneficiary of the seizure of Iwo Jima was the Army Air Force. Before the end of the war about 2400 B–29s landed on the island, carrying crews of some 27,000 men. One, nicknamed by her crew the "Oily Boid," crash-landed after being shot up over Tokyo so many times that the ground crew would bet every time a B–29 landed that it was she. Once a B–29 came down when the weather was so thick that the pilot had to land by guess, and when the plane stopped one wing was hanging over the cliff.[13] Air-sea rescue planes based on Iwo Jima also rescued many crews of planes that splashed. Not all would have been lost without the island's facilities; but the fact that these facilities were there gave a tremendous boost to aviators' morale. There is no doubt that the capture of Iwo Jima, expensive as it was, became a major contribution to victory over Japan.

Unfortunately, and, in my opinion, unjustifiably, there developed two controversies over this operation, one within the Marine Corps

[11] *Sumner* Monthly Report of Survey Activities for Mar. 1945; conversations with Cdr. Johnson at Iwo.
[12] Maj. Gen. Harry Schmidt Action Report 20 May 1945.
[13] Honolulu *Advertiser* 2 June 1945.

and the other in criticism of the Marine Corps. Marine historians have made much over the fact that General Schmidt originally asked for ten days' preliminary naval bombardment but Admirals Spruance and Turner would provide only three. Lieutenant General Holland M. Smith, in his pungent postwar narrative, denounced this decision, brushed off the reasons for it,[14] and implied that the adamant attitude of the Navy caused unnecessary casualties.

This serious charge deserves examination. All accounts agree that the nature of the defenses on Iwo was such that only direct hits on specific targets paid off. Aside from a lucky hit, about all that area bombardment could do was to blast off camouflage and reveal hidden targets. General Kuribayashi had purposely designed his defenses to minimize the effect of bombardment, so that rules about dropping so many rounds of shell per hundred square yards meant nothing. There is no reason to believe that ten or even thirty days of naval and air pounding would have had much more effect on the defenses than the bombardment that was delivered. The defenses were such, by and large, that the only way they could be taken out was the way they were taken out, by Marine Corps infantry and demolitions. Combat engineers of the 5th Marine Division destroyed 5000 cave entrances and pillboxes in their divisional zone of operations alone. As many as 1000 caves and underground entrances were blasted on Mount Suribachi.[15] Aërial bombardment and naval gunfire simply could not reach underground into the maze of caves and tunnels; yet these had to be cleared or sealed shut before the island could be secured as an air base on the Bonins' road to Tokyo. Robert Sherrod well said (in a dispatch that appeared in *Time* magazine on 12 March): "On Iwo the Japs dug themselves in so deeply that all the explosives in the world could hardly have reached them."

Commodore W. R. Carter has estimated that Iwo Jima, one-

[14] The reasons were (1) that the carrier strikes on Tokyo, necessary to keep the kamikazes away, could not be extended beyond three days; (2) difficulty in replenishing ships' ammunition so far from base; (3) by the law of diminishing returns, three days' bombardment should accomplish about 90 per cent of the maximum.

[15] 1st Lt. Walker Y. Brooks USMC "Engineers on Iwo" Marine Corps *Gazette* (Oct. 1945).

fifteenth the area of Saipan, had one-third more bombardment ammunition expended on it than was expended on the big Marianas island. The total amounted to 14,650 tons.[16]

The other and more serious controversy began with an attack on Navy strategy and Marine Corps tactics by the Hearst and McCormick press. This was largely a rehash of the arguments used against taking Tarawa in 1943. Why sacrifice men for a useless piece of real estate? Why do the Marines squander lives, in contrast to General MacArthur who saves them? To these criticisms Hanson W. Baldwin patiently and convincingly replied in the *New York Times*.[17] He pointed out that Iwo was necessary to protect and enhance the B–29 strikes on Japan and that there was no easy alternative. He defended Navy strategy and Marine Corps tactics as the best suited to the situation. He replied to armchair critics who demanded "Why wasn't poison gas used?" by pointing out that poison gas is a defensive weapon, the use of which on Iwo would have done the invaders more harm than good. He observed that many false notions about what can be accomplished by air and naval bombardment of islands stemmed from the fall of Pantelleria in the Mediterranean in 1943, where the Italian defenders had no heart to fight it out on the ground.[18] He reminded the public that it cannot have an omelet without breaking eggs, and that the infantryman, in the last resort, is the one who has to push a campaign through to victory. All this is as true today as it was in 1945.

Peleliu, Iwo Jima and Okinawa were three operations conducted in whole or in part by the Marines after the Japanese had adopted their new tactics of defense in depth against an amphibious invasion; and Iwo Jima was the hardest nut to crack because there the coastal shell, too, was tough. But in all three the Japanese made a highly intelligent use of natural features to exact the utmost in casualties. A comparison of casualties in the three regimental combat teams

[16] *Beans, Bullets and Black Oil* pp. 289–290.
[17] Five installments, 5–9 March 1945.
[18] See Vol. II Chap. XII.

that suffered most in each of these three operations is instructive.[19]

On Peleliu the 1st Marine RCT had 1749 casualties, highest of the three involved. On Iwo Jima the 26th RCT of the 5th Marine Division suffered 2675 casualties. On Okinawa the 29th RCT of the 6th Marine Division had 2821. These comparisons indicate that losses at Iwo were not disproportionate to those in similar operations at that stage of the war.

Robert Sherrod wrote a succinct conclusion to this operation. "To the Marines, Iwo looked like the ugliest place on earth, but B–29 pilots who made emergency landings months later called it the most beautiful. One pilot flew eleven missions in the three months following the island's capture, and landed on it five times. Another said, 'Whenever I land on this island, I thank God and the men who fought for it.' "[20]

[19] This yardstick is best, as the total number of Marines in the three operations differed widely. The average combat strength of a Marine Corps RCT in World War II was 7500 officers and men.

[20] Sherrod *On to Westward* p. 153.

PART II

Okinawa

CHAPTER VI

Preparing for the Ryukyus

October 1944–March 1945

1. *Okinawa and the Okinawans*[1]

PLACE one leg of a pair of dividers on Shanghai, step off a radius of 450 miles, place the other leg on the tip end of Kyushu (the southernmost island of Japan proper), and swing it south and west, to the point where it hits Formosa. This outer leg will describe a 90-degree arc, about 700 miles long, through the Nansei Shoto. It will pass through Amami O Shima, and miss Okinawa and the Sakishima Gunto by a hair. And the quadrant that this arc subtends is the Tung Hai, the East China Sea. The Nansei Shoto (which means Southwestern Islands) are a series of drowned volcanic summits, about 140 in number, with a total land area of 1850 square miles, less than that of the State of Delaware. Over one quarter of this area, 485 square miles, is comprised in the central island of the chain that especially interests us: Okinawa.

The Nansei Shoto, commonly known as the Ryukyus,[2] are divided into three main groups (*Guntos*). Nearest Japan and longest under Japanese domination is the Amami Gunto. In the center is the Okinawa Gunto, which includes Okinawa, the Kerama Retto,

[1] Okinawa Studies, Nos. 1 and 2, issued by Office of Strategic Services in Honolulu (Alfred M. Tozzer, director) March 1944. Other useful documents are "Joint Staff Study – Okinawa Operation" 6 Dec. 1944; Cincpac-Cincpoa Info. Bull. No. 161–44 *Okinawa Gunto* 15 Nov. 1944; Second Supplement to same, 28 Feb. 1945; G. H. Kerr *Okinawa, the History of an Island People* (1958), an excellent scholarly history of the island.

[2] "Loochoo" or "Lew Chew" and "Ryukyu" are the Chinese and Japanese pronunciations of the same name, said to have been given by a Chinese poet in the seventh century, meaning "bubbles on the water" or something similar.

Ie Shima and several smaller islands. The south part of the arc, nearest Formosa, is the Sakishima Gunto. With Formosa, these islands form an eastern wall protecting the Japanese lifeline through the East China Sea. Whether the Allied Nations wished to invade Japan directly, or by way of China, airfields and an advanced naval base had to be set up somewhere in the archipelago. Formosa was the only alternative to the Ryukyus; and Formosa had been ruled out in September 1944. Once the Joint Chiefs of Staff had decided to seize and exploit "one or more positions in the Nansei Shoto" (as stated in their directive of 30 October), there could be no doubt that Okinawa would be position number one.

Okinawa or "The Great Loochoo" has plenty of room for airfields, and two partially protected bays on the east coast suitable for a naval base. Its position is extraordinarily central. The nearest points in China, Formosa and Japan proper lie respectively 360 miles WNW, 340 miles WSW and 340 miles NNE. The 500-mile radius from Naha, the principal town of Okinawa, includes most of Kyushu, all Formosa and passes behind Shanghai and Foochow. The 600-mile arc includes Cape Engaño on Luzon and the Inland Sea of Japan. Iwo Jima is 760 miles distant. The 830-mile radius clips Hong Kong, Manila and the entrance to Tokyo Bay. But Okinawa was a long way from home for the United States Navy. Leyte, the nearest point where ground troops could be staged early in 1945, lies 900 miles to the southward. Ulithi and Guam are over 1200 miles away, and Pearl Harbor lies 4040 miles to the eastward on a great circle course – about the same as the air line from Berlin to Juneau, Alaska.

The Ryukyus are inhabited by a race apart. Their blood seems to be a mixture of Chinese, Malayan and Ainu. From early times there were one or more kings of the Ryukyus, and a single dynasty ruled from 1187 to 1879, when the islands were annexed by Japan. During the Middle Ages the king paid tribute to China, principal source of such culture as his people acquired; and, to be on the safe side, he gave a "cut" to the Japanese shogun or Prince of Satsuma, whose seat was in Kyushu. During the two centuries of Japanese isolation (1636–1853), when no foreign ships except a few Dutchmen were allowed to trade with Japan, and the Japanese were forbidden to go abroad, the Ryukyu kingdom acted as go-between in a smuggling trade between China and Japan; and as this trade brought rich profits to the Satsuma shoguns they permitted the Ryukyus to remain independent. The kings were real rulers, but paid tribute to the Emperor of China as their sovereign overlord; it was observed that their ancient castles at Shuri, Zachini and Nakagusuku faced the west, as a sign of fealty to China.

Except for an occasional Portuguese ship, the first European vessels to visit the Ryukyus arrived in the last decade of the eighteenth century. These visitors found the Okinawans polite but suspicious and evasive, anxious to protect themselves from prying foreigners, but with no armed forces to defend themselves.[3] In the 1840s France endeavored to establish a protectorate over the Ryukyus, but did not press the matter when the king politely declined. She did leave a Catholic mission at Naha, but neither Christianity nor Buddhism nor Islam made much inroad against the primitive animism and ancestor worship of the Okinawans. Commodore Matthew C. Perry USN in 1853 raised the American flag near Shuri on one of the hills that cost us dear to capture in 1945; he forced the regent (the king being a minor) to sign a treaty guaranteeing friendly treatment to American ships, and even established a temporary coaling station at Naha harbor.[4] Other nations then made treaties with the kingdom of the Ryukyus, but these were no protection when Emperor

[3] Captain Basil Hall, on his way home in 1816 after a visit to Okinawa, had an interview with Napoleon at St. Helena. In describing the Okinawans to the Emperor, "Nothing struck him so much as their having no arms. '*Point d'armes!*' he exclaimed. '*C'est à dire point de canons – ils ont des fusils?*' 'Not even muskets,' I replied. '*Eh bien donc – des lances, ou au moins, des arcs et des flêches?*' I told him they had neither one nor the other. '*Ni poignards?*' cried he, with increasing vehemence. No, none. '*Mais!*' said Buonaparte, clenching his fist and raising his voice to a loud pitch, '*Mais! sans armes, comment se bat-on?*' I could only reply that as far as we had been able to discover, they had never had any wars, but remained in a state of internal and external peace. 'No wars!' cried he, with a scornful and incredulous expression, as if the existence of any people under the sun without wars was a monstrous anomaly." Hall *Voyage to Loo-Choo* (Edinburgh 1826) p. 315.

[4] One of Commo. Perry's trophies, a great bronze gong dated 1458, hangs in the yard of the Naval Academy at Annapolis.

Meiji embarked on the policy of expansion which was doomed to be liquidated in 1945. The Emperor invaded the islands in 1875 and the Okinawans countered with passive resistance. Three years later, when General Ulysses S. Grant was about to visit China, a rumor reached Tokyo that the Okinawans intended to appeal to him for protection. Meiji then moved fast, reinforced his garrison in the islands, deposed the king, abolished the tribute to China and formally annexed the Ryukyus to Japan in 1879.

A semicolonial régime was maintained there until 1920. The Okinawans, despised by the Japanese for their poverty, lack of culture and failure to appreciate *bushido*, had the benefit of Japanese schools, but otherwise were treated as an inferior race. They seldom intermarried with the Japanese, continued to speak their own language and to observe their ancient rites and customs. Thousands of Okinawans emigrated to Hawaii, where they received news of every Japanese defeat with delight. This pacifist tradition and resentment against the "superior race" made it easy for United States forces to deal with the Okinawans as soon as they discovered that the stories of American brutality told them by the Japanese were untrue.

Compared with Japan or even with China, these islands were undeveloped and overpopulated. The southern part of Okinawa, in which we were chiefly interested, had a population density of 2700 per square mile as against 243 for Saipan, and 647 for Rhode Island. A population of over 800,000 [5] in 1940 owned only 331 motor cars, of which 88 were buses; two of the three narrow-gauge railroads were horse-drawn; there were only five movie houses in the entire archipelago. Most Okinawans lived in thatched huts or small frame houses, each surrounded by a stone wall and garden and clustered in villages of a few hundred or more inhabitants. They were predominantly farmers, each family owning several tiny fields in which were raised barley, sugar cane, beets, cabbages and sweet potatoes. There were only three towns of any size —

[5] For the entire Ryukyus 818,624; 463,000 for Okinawa.

Naha the capital, Shuri the ancient capital, and Toguchi on the Motobu peninsula.

Okinawa itself is shaped like a comic-strip dog, with an elongated neck and an overgrown jowl. The northern part is barren and mountainous, except for a portion of the Motobu Peninsula, the dog's uplifted ear. Three quarters of the population live in the southern portion, south of the Ishija Isthmus, the dog's neck. Naha, the one small harbor, is just forward of his stubby tail, on which the Naha airfield was situated. On the southeast coast there are two extensive bays protected by the Eastern Islands: the Nakagusuku Wan (Buckner Bay) between the dog's hind feet and forelegs, and the Kimmu Wan between forelegs and neck. Besides the Naha airfield three other important airdromes had been constructed by the Japanese by 1944: – the Yontan and Kadena fields close to the west coast, and the Yonabaru on the east coast. In addition there was a small airfield on the island of Ie Shima, which on the map looks like a bumblebee making for the dog's ear.

From the sea, the island had the appearance of a peaceful rural community, intensively cultivated. The countryside, with steep limestone hills, umbrella-topped pines, small cultivated fields and patches of woodland, recalled those Italian landscapes seen through the windows of Tuscan and Sienese paintings. But no church towers or domes break the skyline. Corresponding to the temples of other Oriental countries are the family tombs of the Okinawans. These large circular structures – built flush to a hillside and roofed with stone – dot the landscape, facing in the direction of Mother China. In front of each tomb is a porch, where the bodies of the dead are left exposed for a period of three years, after which their bones are cleaned and deposited in a handsome urn which is placed within the tomb. The suitability of these structures for machine gun installations was not overlooked by the Japanese Army, and American aviators occasionally bombed those suspected of interesting others than native morticians.

Such, in brief, is the nature of the island which was wanted as a

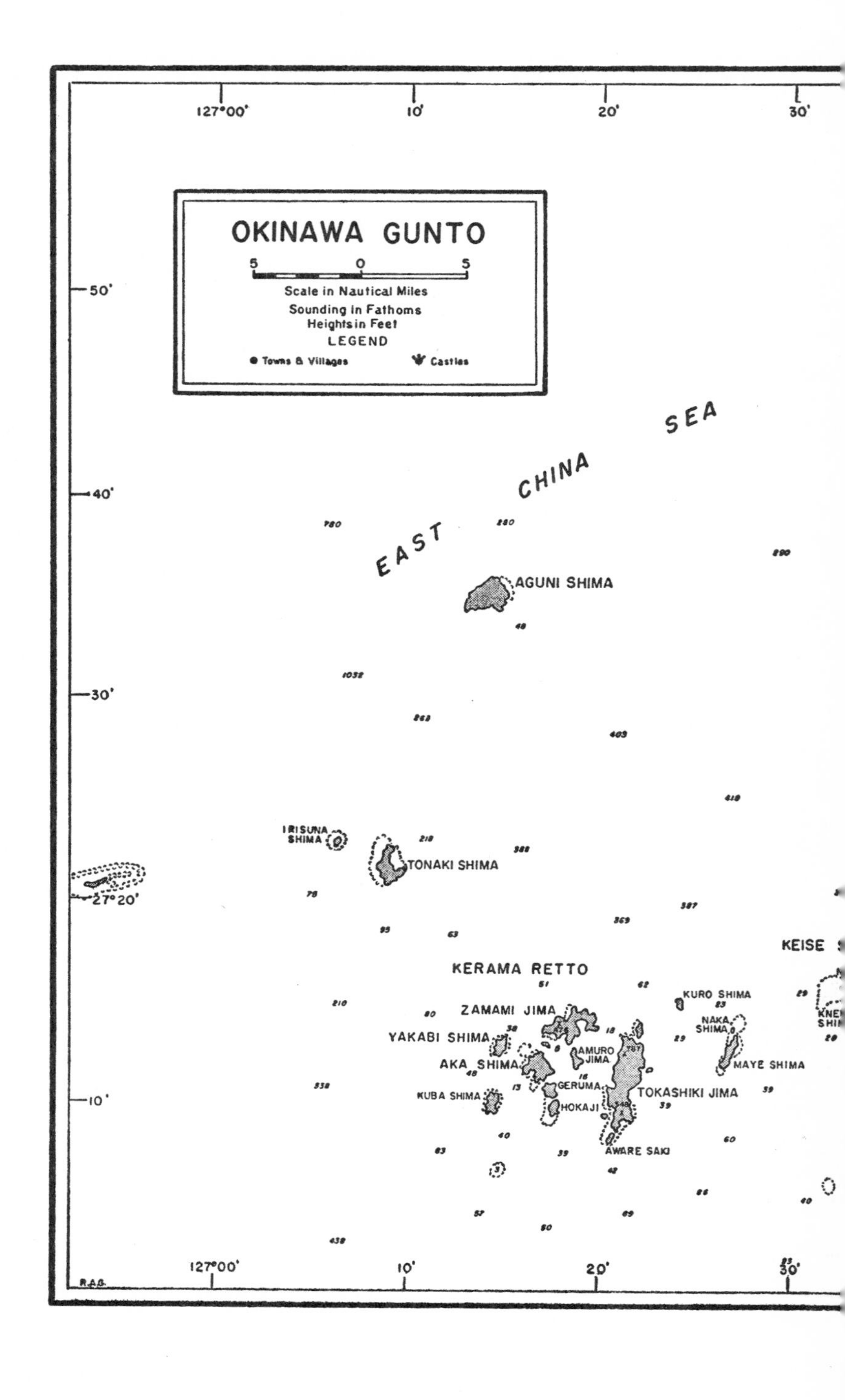

OKINAWA GUNTO
Scale in Nautical Miles
Sounding in Fathoms
Heights in Feet
LEGEND
Towns & Villages
Castles
127°00'
10'
20'
30'
50'
40'
30'
27°20'
10'
EAST CHINA SEA
AGUNI SHIMA
IRISUNA SHIMA
TONAKI SHIMA
KERAMA RETTO
ZAMAMI JIMA
YAKABI SHIMA
AKA SHIMA
KUBA SHIMA
AMURO JIMA
GERUMA
HOKAJI
TOKASHIKI JIMA
AWARE SAKI
KURO SHIMA
NAKA SHIMA
MAYE SHIMA
KEISE
R.A.B.

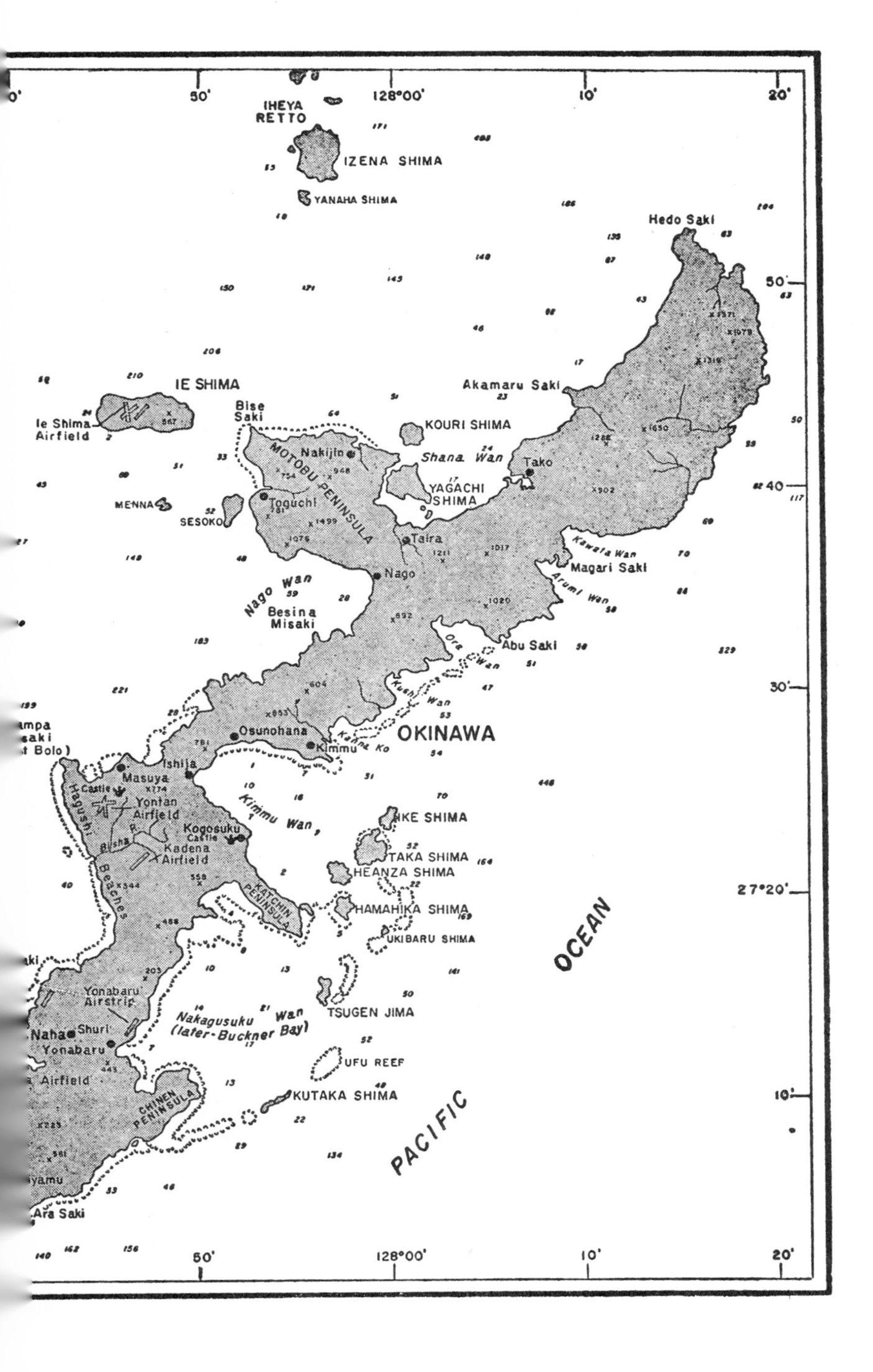

IHEYA RETTO
IZENA SHIMA
YANAHA SHIMA
Hedo Saki
IE SHIMA
Ie Shima Airfield
Bise Saki
Akamaru Saki
KOURI SHIMA
Nakijin
MOTOBU PENINSULA
Shana Wan
Tako
YAGACHI SHIMA
Toguchi
MENNA
SESOKO
Taira
Kawata Wan
Magari Saki
Nago
Nago Wan
Arumi Wan
Besina Misaki
Abu Saki
Ora Wan
Kushi Wan
OKINAWA
Osunohana
Kimmu
Kanna Ko
Ishija
Masuya
Castle
Yontan Airfield
Hagushi Beaches
Kimmu Wan
IKE SHIMA
Kogosuku Castle
TAKA SHIMA
Bisha R.
Kadena Airfield
HEANZA SHIMA
KATCHIN PENINSULA
HAMAHIKA SHIMA
UKIBARU SHIMA
OCEAN
Yonabaru Airstrip
Nakagusuku Wan (later-Buckner Bay)
TSUGEN JIMA
Naha
Shuri
Yonabaru
UFU REEF
Airfield
CHINEN PENINSULA
KUTAKA SHIMA
PACIFIC
Ara Saki
128°00'
50'
10'
20'
27°20'
30'
40

springboard for Japan, and whose securing would cost the United States more casualties than had been incurred in taking any other island in the Pacific.

2. *Planning Operation* ICEBERG

Planning for this massive operation, described by British observers as "the most audacious and complex enterprise yet undertaken by the American amphibious forces,"[6] started with a Cincpac-Cincpoa staff study, dated 25 October 1944, beginning "The Joint Chiefs of Staff have directed the Commander in Chief Pacific Ocean Areas to occupy one or more positions in the Nansei Shoto, with a target date of 1 March 1945." This staff study defined objectives, allotted forces and gave a rough outline of procedure. Rear Admiral Reifsnider,[7] designated to command the amphibious group to land on the northern half of the Okinawa beaches, arrived at Pearl Harbor 24 November 1944 for planning. He worked with the staffs of Commander Amphibious Forces Pacific (Admiral Turner), Commander Tenth Army (General Buckner), Commander III 'Phib Corps (General Geiger USMC). Rear Admiral John L. Hall,[8] to command the amphibious group that effected the southern landings, and Rear Admiral Blandy, in charge of amphibious support force and of all preliminary operations, were already there. They also

[6] British Combined Operations Observers Pacific Ocean Areas (Cdr. R. K. Silcock RN, Col. G. I. Malcolm, Grp. Capt. W. G. Tailyour RAF), Report to British Joint Staff Mission, Washington, 18 Apr. 1945.

[7] Lawrence F. Reifsnider, b. Maryland 1887, Naval Academy '10. Served in *Delaware, Maine, Rhode Island* and *Ozark;* qualified for submarine duty; C.O. of *C-1* in 1916 and fitted out several submarines to late 1917; C.O. of *E-2* and *O-5* during World War I. Shore duty 1919–1921; exec. *Chicago* to 1923; Comsubdiv 14 to 1925; duty at Naval Academy to 1928. C.O. *Corry, Broome* and *Evans* to 1930, duty in Bunav, 1st Lieut. *New Mexico* 1933–1935; senior course Naval War College, public relations officer Navy Dept. 1936–1937. C.O. *Memphis,* chief of U.S. Naval mission to Colombia, Comtransdivs 5 and 10, 1941–1943, and of Sopac Amphibious Group, July 1942 (see Vol. VI). Com 'Phib Group 4 in June 1944 (see Vol. VIII). After V-J Day commanded occupation Sasebo and Nagasaki; 4 Oct. 1945 Com V 'Phib Forces Western Japan; Com Administrative Command 'Phib Forces Pacific 1946; Com Eight and Gulf Sea Frontier 1947; retired 1949 as Vice Admiral.

[8] Brief biog. in Vol. IX, and see Vols. X and XII indexes.

took an active part in the planning of Operation ICEBERG, code name for the invasion of the Ryukyus. The operation plan of Admiral Spruance, Commander Fifth Fleet, was issued on 3 January 1945. Next came the detailed operation plan of Vice Admiral Turner, dated 9 February.

Here let us consider the plan as a whole, keeping in mind that the four principal commanders were Admiral Spruance, Vice Admiral Mitscher (CTF 58), Vice Admiral Turner, who had charge until the beachhead was established, and Lieutenant General Simon Bolivar Buckner USA, commanding Tenth Army. Like the Gilberts and Marshalls and Marianas and Iwo Jima, this was a Central Pacific show. General MacArthur and Seventh Fleet were still engaged in liberating the Philippines.[9]

D-day for Okinawa (L-day in the plan) was finally set for 1 April 1945. In order to obtain control of both air and ocean before invading an island so close to Japan, enemy air power, especially in view of the kamikaze technique, had to be pared down as far as possible before the expeditionary force hit the Ryukyus. Not much opposition was anticipated from the now decrepit Japanese Navy.

The Okinawa plan contemplated a week of preliminary strikes from the fast carriers and by B–29s based on the Marianas. Until the Iwo Jima airfields were activated, the distance of Okinawa from the nearest Army Air Force bases was too great (800 miles) for anything smaller than a Superfort to splice out the work of carrier-based bombers. Generals Arnold and LeMay of the Strategic Air Force were reluctant to have their costly B–29s directed to what they regarded as a mere tactical mission, but agreed to coöperate. The question of how they should coöperate, and for how long, was acrimoniously debated between General LeMay and Admiral Nimitz in early March. According to the so-called "Strategic Air Force Charter" (a directive of 1 April 1944 from the Joint Chiefs

[9] See Vol. XIII. About 24 Jan. 1945 Admiral Halsey, Vice Adm. McCain and Vice Adm. Wilkinson (Com III 'Phib) left the Philippines for Pearl Harbor in order to plan Operation OLYMPIC, the invasion of Kyushu that never took place.

of Staff), the B-29s constituted an independent kingdom under "Hap" Arnold within the Cincpac-Cincpoa empire; but Nimitz retained the right to direct the employment of the big bombers in a tactical or strategic emergency, which he considered this to be. Accordingly, on 27 March, when the advance expeditionary force for Okinawa put in at Kerama Retto, the B-29s flew the first of two missions against Japanese airfields and an aircraft factory on Kyushu.[10]

Two naval bombardment forces were brought up to the Ryukyus eight days before the landings, in order to give Okinawa and the vicinity a complete working-over. Admiral Blandy's amphibious support force of escort carriers, minecraft, light gunboats and the like, and Admiral Deyo's [11] bombardment group of battleships and cruisers, were given this job. Also under Admiral Blandy's command was placed a complete attack group, lifting an infantry division to take the Kerama Retto, a cluster of smalls islands off Okinawa. Here, six days before the main landings, he would set up an advanced fueling and repair base. No previous amphibious operation had included such important and vital preliminaries. Admiral Spruance, recognizing this, decided to be on the spot in *Indianapolis* from L-day minus 8.[12]

[10] Craven & Cate V 38, 629-631. In *The New Yorker* for 14 June 1958 is a souped-up account by Lt. Col. St. Clair McKelway, public relations officer on General LeMay's staff, of how he "blew his top" over this situation and tried to send a message to General Arnold demanding that Admiral Nimitz be court-martialed for obstructing the war effort!

[11] Morton L. Deyo, b. Poughkeepsie 1887, Naval Academy '11. Served in *Virginia, Duncan, Washington* and *Jenkins* to 1917; in *Allen* on the Queenstown station and in destroyer training at Boston in World War I. C.O. *Morris* 1919; aide to Com One 1920-1921; aide to Admiral S. S. Robinson, Com Battle Fleet and Cincus, 1921-1925. Instructor Naval Academy 1926-1929; C.O. *Sloat* and *Upshur* to 1932. Senior Course Naval War College and on staff thereof to Dec. 1934, when became exec. of *Milwaukee*. Operations officer staff of C in C Asiatic Fleet 1936-1939; aide to SecNav 1940 to Apr. 1941. Comdesron 11, 1941 (see Vol. I). C.O. *Monticello* Feb.-June 1942; C.O. *Indianapolis* July-Dec. 1942 (see Vol. VIII). Rear Adm. and Comdeslant in *Denebola* to 1943; commanded bombardment group in *Tuscaloosa* (flag) in operations OVERLORD and DRAGOON, 1944 (see Vol. XI). Comcrudiv 13 in *Santa Fe* with TF 38, Nov. 1944; and had this Okinawa command, relieving Vice Adm. Oldendorf after the latter's injury, to May 1945. Following V-J day, directed occupation landings in Kyushu and western Honshu and commanded Northern Japan Force. Com One 1946; retired as Vice Adm. 1949.

[12] He chose this 14-year-old heavy cruiser as his flagship because she was fast

Both planners and commanders were highly apprehensive of what enemy air might do to our forces before they had secured airfields on Okinawa. For the Japanese had several airfields in Okinawa and nearby islands, airdromes 150 miles away in the Amami Gunto, about 230 miles away in the Sakishima Gunto, and 65 airfields on Formosa, as well as 55 on Kyushu. Since no other operation would be going on at the time except the liberation of the Southern Philippines, there was no reason why the enemy should not concentrate his available aircraft, estimated at 2000 to 3000 planes, on the Allied expeditionary force and shipping off Okinawa – which is just about what he did. Nor was there any reason to suppose that he would not continue and even develop the effective kamikaze technique.

The Joint Expeditionary Force commanded by Vice Admiral Turner – gathered together from the West Coast, Oahu, New Caledonia, Espiritu Santo, the Solomons, the Philippines and the Marianas, and staged through Ulithi, Leyte and Saipan – would all be present off Okinawa on L-day, 1 April. Richmond Kelly Turner, having fairly earned the sobriquet that Napoleon bestowed on General Kléber (*l'enfant gâté de la victoire*), might have indulged in a little careless swagger. Having wrested one position after another from the enemy he was in fine fettle. He had been attacked in the American press for wasting lives, and compared unfavorably with General MacArthur, whose maxim "Hit 'em where they ain't" was hardly applicable to islands where enemy positions covered every beach and Japanese soldiers occupied every square rod of ground. Little he cared for that. He was still the same driving, swearing, sweating "Kelly" whose head could conceive more new ideas and retain more details than could any other flag officer in the Navy. He undertook the planning of the Ryukyus operation with more than ordinary meticulousness, and his voluminous plan was ready in time for subordinate commanders to study; it was so detailed that little was left for them to do.

The entire III Amphibious Corps (Major General Roy S. Geiger

---

enough to keep up with the carriers, yet old enough to be risked at the objective in an amphibious operation.

USMC), comprising three Marine divisions (the 1st, veterans of Guadalcanal and Peleliu; the 2nd, veterans of Tarawa and Saipan; the 6th, going into battle for the first time) and four infantry divisions of the XXIV Army Corps (the 7th, veterans of Attu, Kwajalein and Leyte; the 96th, veterans of Leyte; the 77th, veterans of Guam; and the 27th, veterans of Makin and Saipan), were to be employed in the invasion of Okinawa. A fifth infantry division, the 81st, was held in reserve at New Caledonia. The entire expeditionary force constituted the Tenth Army, under command of Lieutenant General Simon Bolivar Buckner, son of the like-named hero of the Southern Confederacy. If these plans worked out, some 172,000 combatant and 115,000 service troops would be landed on Okinawa before the operation was over.[13] About 77,000 Japanese troops were expected to be there to receive them.[14]

Troop-lift for this large force was a problem that vexed the planners, since war was still going on in Europe. Eight transport squadrons, each comprising about 15 assault transports, six assault cargo ships, 25 LST, 10 LSM and one LSD, were required. Four transrons could be culled from those used at Lingayen, but all eight would first have to do a job at Iwo. Two new transrons used at Iwo would be pulled out as soon as they had set the troops ashore, and proceed to Saipan or Espiritu Santo to load one assault and one reserve division for the Ryukyus. Two other new transrons were counted on to leave Pearl Harbor in early February for training, rehearsals, and loading of assault divisions at Guadalcanal and Nouméa.

The actual landings were planned for a four-division front, over five miles of beaches on the west coast of southern Okinawa. They were selected between two points known as Zampa-misaki and Kezu-saki. For want of a better name these were called "the Hagushi beaches," after a village at the mouth of the Bisha River that bisects the coastline and makes a convenient boundary between

[13] Joint Staff Study of 25 Oct. 1944.
[14] Estimate immediately before L-day. The 25 Oct. estimate was less than 50,000.

the Marines' sector on the north and the Army's on the south. Photographic reconnaissance showed that these beaches lay behind the usual shelflike coral reef, which meant that the first assault waves must be boated in amphtracs at or near high water, 0900. The mean range of tides there is 4.1 feet; but on L-day, which was Easter Sunday, there would be a spring tide of 5.2 feet.

The reason for choosing these particular beaches was the fact that they lay close to two important enemy airfields – Yontan behind the Marines' sector, and Kadena behind the Army's. In earlier operations it was deemed best if possible to land at some distance from airfields, which the Japanese usually defended fanatically. But at Okinawa it was the essence of victory that airfields be secured promptly, so that land-based planes could help the carrier planes to ward off enemy air attacks and eventually relieve them.[15]

From the landing beaches, the Marines would fan out to the east and north, and XXIV Corps to the east and south, capturing the two airfields within three days, the "waist" of the dog in fifteen, and the southern half of the island in thirty to sixty days. It was not expected that troops would advance beyond the Ishija Isthmus – the dog's neck. Mountainous northern Okinawa could be left to the enemy for the time being.

Phase II of the operation, the seizure of Motobu Peninsula (the dog's ear) and of Ie Shima, the little island with a big airfield, was planned to start about one month after the landings; and during that phase the conquest of Okinawa was expected to be completed.

A careful plan was worked out for the support of this operation by submarines of the Pacific Fleet. Besides wolf-packs hunting Japanese shipping in the unmined areas of the East China Sea, off Indochina and the coast of Honshu, "lifeguard" service was provided in the waters where TF 58 planned to strike.

Admiral Mitscher's fast carrier groups, TF 58, were depended upon to make preliminary neutralization strikes on Tokyo, the

[15] There was an alternate plan for landing on the eastern coast of Okinawa, between the dog's fore and hind legs, in case the wind backed to the westward and raised a dangerous surf on the Hagushi side.

Ryukyus, Formosa and airfields on the Japanese home islands, then to support the actual operation. In the latter mission they were to have the help of 18 escort carriers. Luzon-based planes of the Allied Air Forces Southwest Pacific were expected to keep Luzon Strait clear, and on 21 March Admiral Nimitz asked them to support the Ryukyus operation by strikes on Formosa. The Superfortresses based on the Marianas, now augmented to several hundred, were prepared to hammer at Tokyo, and industrial targets in Japan, right through the campaign.

3. *Japanese Preparations* [16]

The Japanese high command expected the Okinawa operation at about the correct date, and did everything in its power to put up a stiff ground defense supported by air and surface attack. This was in accordance with the "Outline of Army and Navy Operations" approved by the Emperor and promulgated 20 January 1945. Okinawa was designated one of the key strongpoints to be developed, the others being Iwo Jima, Formosa, Shanghai and the south coast of Korea. The defense of any or all these places was frankly stated to be a delaying action: –

> When the enemy penetrates the defense zone, a campaign of attrition will be initiated to reduce his preponderance in ships, aircraft and men, to obstruct the establishment of advance bases, to undermine enemy morale, and thereby to seriously delay the final assault on Japan. . . . Preparations for the decisive battle will be completed in Japan proper in the early fall of 1945.
>
> In general, Japanese air strength will be conserved until an enemy landing is actually under way on or within the defense sphere.

On 6 February the Japanese Army and Navy agreed to concentrate all air forces in the homeland around the perimeter of the East China Sea, and to emphasize training in kamikaze tactics. It was

[16] Rear Adm. Toshiyuki Yokoi "Kamikazes and the Okinawa Campaign" U.S. Naval Institute *Proceedings* LXXX (1954) 505–513; General of the Army Douglas MacArthur *Historical Report* II 543–555.

hoped that around 2000 aircraft could be assembled by 1 April, which happened to be Okinawa L-day, and that airplane production, which had declined to 1900 in January (and, as it turned out, to 1260 in February), owing to plant dispersal in anticipation of air raids, could soon be increased.

Less than two weeks after this agreement, on 19 February, American forces invaded Iwo Jima. As we have seen, the Japanese were unable to exert any great air effort on behalf of that hot little island, and the Japanese high command wrote it off on 22 March.

In the meantime the B–29s had begun their series of air raids, using incendiary bombs, on large urban areas of Japan. These, in the words of the Japanese collaborators to General MacArthur's *Historical Report,* "rocked the nation to its very foundations." The attack the night of 9–10 March, in particular, was "indescribably horrifying. Well over 250,000 houses were destroyed, rendering more than a million persons homeless, and 83,793 were burned to death." [17]

Air force training, with special emphasis on the kamikaze technique, was now accelerated in expectation of an attack on the Ryukyus. In a new Imperial General Headquarters directive of 20 March, these islands were designated "the focal point of the decisive battle for the defense of the Homeland." A massed air attack on our amphibious forces, both by kamikazes and conventional bombers, was planned and designated Operation TEN-GO. Already the high command had learned through Intelligence channels that the invasion force was beginning to leave Ulithi. C. in C. Combined Fleet (Admiral Toyoda) ordered Commander Fifth Air Fleet (Vice Admiral Matome Ugaki) in Kyushu to concentrate on enemy transports. Ugaki protested that if he did not send his aircraft out at once to attack anything encountered, they might all be destroyed on the ground.[18] The prohibition was then removed, but too late; Fast Carrier Force Pacific Fleet were about to swing into action again.

[17] MacArthur *Historical Report* II 551. Note that this was more destructive than the explosion of the first atomic bomb over Hiroshima.
[18] That is just what Admiral Nimitz wanted done, by the B–29s.

4. *The Fast Carriers' Contribution, 18–31 March*[19]

Vice Admiral Marc Mitscher's Task Force 58 sortied from Ulithi 14 March for an initial attack on Kyushu airfields. After replenishing on the 16th, the force began its run-in and reached launching position, about 90 miles southeast of the island, at dawn 18 March. Air opposition over Kyushu was light during the morning strikes, and the pilots were puzzled to find few planes grounded — for the good reason that, well alerted, they had taken off to attack the carriers. Consequently the TF 58 pilots expended their bombs on hangars and barracks. Afternoon strikes were directed against fields farther inland. Search planes located a concentration of warships, including battleship *Yamato*, around Kobe and Kure.

In the enemy counterattacks — for which Admiral Ugaki expended 50 of his carefully hoarded planes — Rear Admiral Radford's TG 58.4, operating about 75 miles south of Shikoku, received all the damage on 18 March. *Enterprise* was hit by a dud bomb at 0725, and a Betty trying to crash *Intrepid* was shot down so close aboard that two men were killed and 43 wounded; burning fragments started a fire in the hangar deck. Three Judys went for *Yorktown* shortly after 1300. Two missed; a third dropped a bomb which hit the signal bridge, passed through one deck, and exploded near the ship's side — blowing two big holes, killing or mortally wounding five men, and wounding another 26.

On 19 March Task Force 58's strikes were directed against Japanese ships in the Inland Sea and at Kure and Kobe. Seventeen ships, including such monsters as *Yamato* and carrier *Amagi*, were hit and damaged, but none seriously.

Shortly after sunrise Admiral Davison's TG 58.2 caught it. *Wasp* (Captain O. A. Weller) had just secured from general quarters and

[19] Com Fifth Fleet (Admiral Spruance) Action Report 21 June 1945; CTF 58 (Vice Adm. Mitscher) Action Report 17 July, and those of CTG 58.1 (Rear Adm. Clark), 58.2 (Rear Adm. Davison), 58.3 (Rear Adm. F. C. Sherman), and TG 58.4 (Rear Adm. Radford).

two thirds of her planes were away on strikes. An enemy plane arrived directly over the ship undetected, dived, and at 0710 dropped a bomb which penetrated to the hangar deck, exploded a plane, passed through crew quarters on No. 2 deck and burst in the galley on No. 3 deck, causing great slaughter among cooks and mess attendants who were about to serve breakfast. Fires broke out on five decks simultaneously, six water mains were ruptured, and avgas poured down onto the lower decks, adding to the blaze. Yet, so efficient was damage control that the fires were out in fifteen minutes and *Wasp* was recovering planes by 0800. A few minutes later a second kamikaze missed the carrier by a few feet, nicking the exterior plane elevator, and exploding alongside. Casualties resulting from the bomb explosion were very heavy — 101 killed or died of wounds, 269 wounded; but *Wasp* continued to operate for several days before retiring for repairs.[20]

Admiral Davison's flag carrier *Franklin*, "Big Ben" as her crew called her, was launching her second strike of the morning at 0708 when hit by two bombs from a plane which approached undetected. The first bomb exploded on the hangar deck at about frame 82, wrecking the forward elevator, spreading destruction throughout the hangar and No. 3 deck and lighting huge fires among parked and armed planes. Everyone on that part of the hangar deck was killed, and the fire spread quickly. The second bomb struck the flight deck at about frame 133, exploded above the hangar deck and spread fires through planes which were tuning up to launch. This explosion blew the after elevator up and to one side. Almost immediately the entire ship was enveloped in flames and a pall of heavy black smoke.

Captain Leslie H. Gehres, on the bridge, was knocked down by the first explosion. On picking himself up he noted the fires on the starboard side forward and ordered full right rudder in order to bring the wind on the port side, with the thought of keeping the flames away from planes on the after flight deck. When he managed to make his way inboard he saw that the after part of his ship

[20] *Wasp* Action Report; Carlyle Holt in Boston *Globe* 23 and 24 Oct. 1945.

was also on fire; he swung her to port to bring the wind on her starboard beam, and slowed to two-thirds speed. The bombs in the planes began a long series of explosions, some very violent. Admiral Mitscher, who was on board *Bunker Hill*, heard six enormous explosions in *Franklin* when she was still below the horizon.

One of the more spectacular displays was put on by twelve 11¾-inch "Tiny Tim" rockets with which a dozen fighter-bombers on the flight deck were armed. As described by Commander Joe Taylor, the executive officer, "Some screamed by to starboard, some to port, and some straight up the flight deck. The weird aspect of this weapon whooshing by so close is one of the most awful spectacles a human has ever been privileged to see. Some went straight up and some tumbled end over end. Each time one went off the fire-fighting crews forward would instinctively hit the deck." [21] Before the fires were brought under control all ready ammunition in lockers and gun mounts abaft the island structure had exploded.

Admiral Davison ordered *Santa Fe* to stand by and assist *Franklin*, and with members of his staff and Admiral Bogan (on board as observer) transferred to a destroyer in order to shift his flag to *Hancock*. As he was leaving, the Admiral advised Captain Gehres to issue the order "Prepare to Abandon Ship," but the skipper replied that he thought he could save her. While waiting to go alongside, *Santa Fe* began picking up survivors who had been forced overboard by the heat and flames. As soon as some measure of communication was regained within the ship, Captain Gehres passed the word to direct all but key officers and men to abandon ship. These men took to the water as best they could. Many were rescued by destroyers which were following the carrier for that purpose.

Shortly after 0930 *Santa Fe* closed, Captain Hal C. Fitz slamming her alongside the exploding carrier and holding her with his engines. By that time the fire on the forward part of *Franklin's* flight deck was under control, and wounded men were transferred to her deck. Fire and engine rooms now reported to Captain Gehres that, owing to intense smoke and heat, they had to be evacuated.

[21] Exec's Report enclosed with *Franklin* Action Report 11 Apr. 1945.

By about 1000 all way was lost and the ship lay dead in the water. By noon *Franklin* reported that her skeleton crew had brought the fires practically under control and stabilized the ship's list at 13 degrees, and all wounded had been evacuated. *Santa Fe* took on board 826 men in 30 minutes, and stayed alongside for three hours.

Pittsburgh (Captain John E. Gingrich) now reported that she was ready to pass the towline to *Franklin*, as Captain Gehres had requested. *Santa Fe* pulled clear and *Pittsburgh* brought the heavily listing carrier around to a southerly course – a difficult task in the easterly wind that was blowing. The cruiser gradually worked up to six knots as she and her tow, screened by *Santa Fe* and destroyers, made headway southward. Rear Admiral M. B. Gardner of TG 58.5 took over command of TG 58.2.

By 0300 March 20 *Franklin* had begun to regain power and reported that she could make two knots. By 0932, she had regained steering control in the pilothouse, although still without a compass; and at 1100 she was ready to make 15 knots. The appearance of her flight deck was graphically compared to that of a half-eaten Shredded Wheat biscuit. The tow gradually built up speed and at 1235 *Franklin* was clear of *Pittsburgh* and under her own power. "Down by the tail but reins up!" reported Captain Gehres. Admiral Spruance signaled on the 24th that the ability, fortitude and sheer guts of skipper and crew in saving their ship were in the highest degree praiseworthy.[22] She was by far the most heavily damaged carrier in the war – in much worse shape than *Lexington* at Coral Sea or *Yorktown* at Midway – to be saved. Under her own power and with only one stop, at Pearl Harbor, she made the 12,000-mile voyage to New York. Vice Admiral A. W. Fitch, the former carrier commander at the Battle of the Coral Sea, declared without exaggeration, "Only by the outstanding skill, stamina and heroism of the officers and crew" could this have been done; that there was no precedent in the annals of sea warfare for a capital ship returning to port after such severe damage.[23]

[22] Com Fifth Fleet to C.O. *Franklin* 0100 Mar. 25.
[23] *New York Times* 22 May 1945, with list of those decorated.

Actual casualties in *Franklin* were 724 killed or missing and 265 wounded; and there would have been 300 more killed but for the heroic work of Lieutenant Commander Joseph T. O'Callahan USNR Catholic chaplain, who not only administered last rites but organized and directed fire-fighting parties, and led two sailors below to wet down a 5-inch magazine that threatened to explode. Lieutenant (jg) Donald A. Gary, who discovered 300 men trapped in a pitch-black mess compartment, found an exit, and returned thrice through smothering smoke to lead them to safety.[24] No fewer than 1700 men were rescued from the water by cruisers and destroyers.[25] Among those killed was Captain Arnold J. Isbell, the distinguished commander of Atlantic hunter-killer groups.[26] He was on board *Franklin* waiting for transfer to *Yorktown,* to which he had been ordered as commanding officer.

Something more than courage – know-how – was required to conquer fires such as those that raged in *Franklin.* Neither she nor many of the other ships crashed by kamikazes off Okinawa could have been saved but for the fire-fighting schools and improved technique instituted by the Navy in 1942–1943. The initial impulse came from Lieutenant Harold J. Burke USNR, deputy chief of the New York City fire department. He interested Rear Admiral Edward L. Cochrane, Chief of the Bureau of Ships, in the new fog nozzle, which atomized water to a fine spray and quenched a blaze much more quickly than a solid stream. Burke and Lieutenant Thomas A. Kilduff USNR, formerly of the Boston Fire Department trained over 260 officer instructors and established schools with mock-up ships at every continental naval base, and on several Pacific islands. At one of these, the damage control party of every new warship was trained before going to sea. The major object of this instruction was to "get the fear of fire out of the sailor"; to teach

[24] Story by Richard W. Johnston, who was on board, in Honolulu *Advertiser* 1 May 1945.

[25] Bupers breakdown and *Santa Fe* Action Report. The casualties are a record for any United States ship which survived an enemy attack, and are exceeded only by those of *Indianapolis* for a ship sunk.

[26] See Vol. X 109.

him that, if properly equipped with fire mask and helmet, handling an all-purpose nozzle and applicator, he could boldly advance to the source of a blaze and not get hurt.

The big carriers, which already had fourteen fire mains dependent on ship's power, were now given two more, operated by individual gasoline engines. One of these in *Franklin* threw fog for eight hours continuously when all other mains were knocked out by power failure. All ships were equipped with 160-pound handy billies, and the destroyers and larger types with 500-pound mobile pumps, each operated by its own gas engine. Hoses and couplings were made standard throughout the Navy. Portable oxyacetylene steel-cutting outfits and rescue breathing-apparatus were provided. A foamite system was placed at every hundred feet of a carrier's deck. The foam generators in destroyers, originally located in the engine spaces, were moved topside. Salvage vessels (ARS) were especially fitted out to help fight fires in other ships; and occasionally – though seldom in the Pacific – fire-fighting teams were flown out from a shore base to burning ships at sea.[27]

Following the Inland Sea strikes on 19 March, TF 58 retired slowly, sending fighter sweeps over southern Kyushu to keep enemy aircraft grounded. A quiet morning on the 20th was followed by a very lively afternoon. Admiral Davison's TG 58.2, still covering *Franklin*, came under attack by enemy aircraft. At 1454 *Hancock* opened fire on a Zeke coming in on her port beam at about 500 feet. *Halsey Powell*, which had just topped off fuel alongside, cast off and was in the process of getting clear when the burning Zeke, having missed the flight deck of *Hancock*, crashed the destroyer's main deck near the after 5-inch mount. Her steering gear was jammed, a collision with *Hancock* narrowly averted, speed was reduced to about ten knots, and 12 men were killed and 29 wounded.[28] The

[27] See Vol. I 329 for an early instance of this, to salvage *Wakefield*. Navy Dept. Press Release 8 Sept. 1945; information from Lt. Cdr. T. A. Kilduff USNR, 1946 and 1960.

[28] *Halsey Powell* Action Report 4 Apr. 1945.

kamikaze's bomb went right through *Halsey Powell's* hull without exploding. Between 1600 and 2000 some 15 to 20 aircraft attacked TG 58.2 and at 1626 one plane bombed and strafed *Enterprise*. The bomb missed but fires were started on "Big E's" flight deck as a result of "friendly" antiaircraft fire, impairing her ability to operate night fighters.

Task Force 58 was shadowed during the night, but no serious attack developed until about 1400 March 21 when a large bogey was picked up by radar to the northwest of the task force. Extra fighters were launched, to a total of 150, of which 24 from Task Group 58.1 intercepted the enemy about sixty miles out. The raid numbered 48 aircraft, 18 of them Bettys carrying the new one-man piloted bomb slung under their bellies. This gimmick, called *oka* (cherry-blossom) by the Japanese and *baka* (screwball) by us, was a 4700-pound bomb provided with rocket propulsion and a human pilot. Fortunately for us the Japanesse did not have many of them, as they were so small and fast (up to 600 m.p.h.) as to be almost impossible to shoot down once cast off from the parent plane. In this instance the weight of the *baka* deprived the Bettys of all power to maneuver, and so made them and their fighter escort an easy prey to the carrier-based Hellcats.

On 22 March TF 58 replenished from Admiral Beary's Logistic Support Group. The same day Admiral Mitscher reorganized his force into three task groups, leaving TG 58.2 to support the crippled carriers *Franklin*, *Enterprise* and *Yorktown*.

The carrier airmen claimed to have destroyed 528 aircraft in the air and on the ground in this two-day strike, operating within range of Japanese air bases. Japanese authorities admit that "losses were staggering": 161 lost out of 193 aircraft committed, in addition to an indeterminate number destroyed on the ground. These losses prevented heavy participation by Japanese air forces in the defense of Okinawa until 6 April. Admiral Ugaki, however, claimed that his "eagles" had sunk five carriers, two battleships and three cruisers, and that the Americans would have to postpone their attack on the Ryukyus. Imperial General Headquarters doubted the accuracy of his figures but hoped for the best.

Once again, as in the Formosa air battle of October 1944,[29] the Japanese were victims of their own propaganda. On 23 March, when TF 58 began its last pre-landing bombings of Okinawa and Admiral Blandy's Advance Expeditionary Force appeared in the Kerama Retto, the Japanese high command assumed that the one was a Parthian shot of fast carriers returning crippled to Ulithi, and that the other was a diversion.[30] Within two days they learned better, and on 25 March issued an alert for the concentrated air attack on the amphibious forces, Operation TEN-GO.

By that time it was too late for the kamikazes to interfere with the landings; TEN-GO was no go until 6 April, when, as we shall see, it became really serious.

Admiral Spruance gave Admiral Mitscher and his fast carriers a fresh accolade for their work in these pre-invasion strikes. They had, he said, surpassed their already high standards, and inflicted heavy damage on the enemy. The efficiency of C.A.P. was unsurpassed. Extraordinary energy and courage had been shown in repairing and saving badly damaged ships. And Admiral Nimitz, from his advance headquarters at Guam, also praised the endurance, teamwork and skill that Fifth Fleet had shown in the 18–21 March strikes.[31]

One week later, on 27 and 31 March, came the B–29 attacks on the Kyushu air bases which Admiral Nimitz had asked for. These closed down each field several days for repairs, and their minedropping operation in Shimonoseki Strait closed that vital supply artery for an entire week.

Thus, the burden of repelling the invasion fell upon the Japanese ground troops on Okinawa, numbering over 77,000. These constituted the Thirty-second Army, commanded by Lieutenant Gen-

[29] See Vol. XII Chap. VI.

[30] MacArthur *Historical Report* II 554.

[31] Com Fifth Fleet to CTF 58 2347 Mar. 23; Cincpac to Com Fifth Fleet 1340 Mar. 24.

eral Mitsuru Ushijima. This formidable garrison had not been rein-forced in 1945; it had in fact been reduced in December 1944 by sending replacements to Luzon. In addition, there were abou 20,000 Okinawan militia and labor troops.

Task Force 58 planes had taken numerous photographs of Oki nawa, on the basis of which Admiral Mitscher notified Admira Turner 26 March that the entire island was a honeycomb of caves tunnels and gun positions; that tanks and armored cars had bee observed popping into caves; that as tough a fight as on Iwo Jim should be anticipated. He assured Turner, however, that he woul give all possible air protection to the amphibious forces, day an night, and informed him that TF 58 planes were searching th Nansei Shoto daily as far north as the Osumi Gunto.[32]

5. *The Royal Navy's Participation*[33]

During the year 1944, the British government formed a plan t send the major part of the Royal Navy to the Pacific by June o 1945. Prime Minister Churchill had often and eloquently voice this intention, and by the summer of 1944 it had become his firn policy. By that time the situation in Europe had so improved tha the Admiralty believed it no longer needed to keep the Fleet i home waters. Having decided to create a British Pacific Fleet, th Admiralty sent for Commander Harry Hopkins RN, who had bee serving as British observer with Admiral Nimitz. He arrived a London in August 1944, gave the Admiralty the fruit of his ex perience for planning purposes; and charts of the Pacific Ocean, part of the world half forgotten in England, began to appear o bulkheads in the rambling Admiralty building in Whitehall.

[32] CTF 58 to CTF 51, 2155 Mar. 25.

[33] John Ehrman *Grand Strategy* VI 222–235 (*History of Second World Wa* U.K. Military Series, 1956); Capt. S. W. Roskill RN kindly allowed me to use th appropriate chapter in his *The War at Sea* III, a volume of this series, in advan of publication; story by correspondent Robert Trumbull, who was on board, i *New York Times* 16 Apr. 1945; Action Reports of Vice Adms. Rawlings, Via and Brind RN, and other restricted Admiralty sources.

At the OCTAGON Conference in Quebec in September 1944, where the Combined Chiefs of Staff met with President Roosevelt and Prime Minister Churchill, a leading issue was the participation of the Royal Navy in the Pacific War. Admiral King did not want it. He feared that a British Fleet's breaking into the Pacific at a time when the United States Navy was having a difficult time to supply itself would put an undue strain on logistics. But the British naval representatives and Mr. Churchill were so determined to have the Royal Navy fighting in the Pacific that they met this objection by promising to create a fleet train of their own, and on that basis the question was settled. The "approved report" of the C.C.S. to the President and Prime Minister, of 16 September, states: —

> We have agreed that the British Fleet should participate in the main operations against Japan in the Pacific, with the understanding that this Fleet will be balanced and self-supporting. The method of employment of the British Fleet in these main operations in the Pacific will be decided from time to time in accordance with the prevailing circumstances.[34]

On 22 November Admiral Sir Bruce Fraser RN, commanding the British Eastern Fleet in the Indian Ocean, was appointed Commander in Chief of the new British Pacific Fleet, and on 10 December he established his headquarters at Sydney. Six days later he and members of his staff arrived at Pearl Harbor to confer with Admirals Nimitz and Spruance and the Cincpac-Cincpoa staff. As a result of these meetings a "Memorandum of Understandings" between the two Navies was drawn up.[35] It was agreed that the Royal Navy's first contribution to the Pacific War should be a fast carrier task force, to operate in the Philippine Sea and approaches to Japan during Operation ICEBERG, separately from Admiral Mitscher's TF 58 but performing a similar mission on other targets.

The British Pacific Fleet, with its carrier commander Rear Ad-

[34] C.C.S. Report to President and P.M., 16 Sept. 1944, C.C.S. 680/2.

[35] "Memorandum Record of Understandings Reached in Conference 17–19 Dec. 1944 concerning employment of the British Pacific Fleet." Approved by Admiral King 2 Jan. 1945.

miral Sir Philip Vian as O.T.C., got under way from Ceylon 1
January 1945 for Australia. En route it managed to work in tw
successful strikes on Japanese-operated oil refineries at Palembang
Sumatra, and on 4 February reached Fremantle. Before returnin
to Sydney, Admiral Fraser sailed to Lingayen in U.S.S. *Ne
Mexico* and narrowly escaped death in the kamikaze attack o
6 January 1945.[86]

It was not yet settled what the main employment of this im
portant reinforcement would be during Operation ICEBERG. Th
J.C.S. were in favor of assigning Indonesia as the Royal Navy targe
area, with a base at Brunei Bay, Borneo. That was also what Genera
MacArthur and Admiral King wanted. But Admirals Nimitz an
Spruance wished to use the British carriers in their theater, to kee
the southern part of the Ryukyus pounded down. This exactly co
incided with the views of all British strategists from the Prime Min
ister down; no sideshow for them! After much discussion th
Cincpac-Churchill view prevailed in the J.C.S., and on 14 Marc
Admiral Fraser was directed to report to Admiral Nimitz with th
proviso that his Fleet could be withdrawn on seven days' notice
The reason for this condition was the desire of Admiral King t
use the British Fleet as a flexible strategic reserve in case a new
operation, such as the liberation of Indonesia, were decided upo
later.[87]

By mid-March Task Force 113, the combatant elements of th
British Pacific Fleet, was conducting training exercises near Manu
in the Admiralties. TF 112, the Royal Navy service squadron, ha
also come up to Seeadler Harbor, which had been agreed upon between Admirals Fraser and Nimitz as an intermediate British bas
between Australia and the combat theater. TF 113 was under th
tactical command of Vice Admiral Sir H. Bernard Rawlings RN
who also commanded the 1st Battle Squadron. It was organized a
follows: — [88]

[86] See Vol. XIII 105.
[87] Vol. XIII 257–258 and Ehrman VI 224.
[88] See end of Appendix I below for details and replacements. TF 113 was designated TF 57 when it came under U. S. Fifth Fleet.

1st Battle Squadron, Vice Admiral Rawlings RN
H.M.S. KING GEORGE V and HOWE

1st Carrier Squadron, Rear Admiral Sir Philip Vian RN
H.M.S. INDOMITABLE, VICTORIOUS, ILLUSTRIOUS and INDEFATIGABLE

4th Cruiser Squadron, Rear Admiral E. J. P. Brind RN
H.M.S. SWIFTSURE, BLACK PRINCE, ARGONAUT, EURYALUS, H.M.N.Z.S. GAMBIA

Fifteen destroyers, Rear Admiral J. H. Edelston RN

This was a well-balanced force. Three of the five cruisers were of the *Dido* antiaircraft class; the destroyers were new and fast. Two of these carriers were no strangers to the Pacific. H.M.S. *Indomitable,* at the approach of war with Japan, was sent to support Vice Admiral Sir Tom Phillips's ill-fated battle squadron, but owing to a mishap arrived too late. H.M.S. *Victorious* had been sent by the Admiralty in 1943 to the United States Pacific Fleet, which at that time, owing to the loss of *Wasp* and *Hornet,* had only two fleet carriers.[39] Sir Philip Vian's air groups, numbering over 200 units, used both United States Navy types such as the Corsair, Hellcat and Avenger, and British types, such as the Seafire (Navy version of the famous Spitfire fighter), and the Firefly, a heavy fighter. The service squadron (TF 112), commanded by Rear Admiral Douglas B. Fisher RN, comprised ten oil tankers, five replenishment-plane escort carriers and a large number of salvage and repair ships.

At sea, during the forenoon watch of 15 March 1945, Admiral Rawlings received the signal to report to Cincpac. He canceled all exercises, and after considering his logistic problem sent off this signal to Admiral Nimitz: —

I hereby report TF 113 and TF 112 for duty in accordance with orders received from C. in C. British Pacific Fleet. . . . Anticipate TF 113 with units of TF 112 be ready 1200 17th March to sail from Manus as you may direct. . . . It is with a feeling of great pride and pleasure that the British Pacific Force joins the U. S. Naval Forces under your command.

To which Admiral Nimitz replied: —

The United States Pacific Fleet welcomes the British Carrier Task Force and attached units which will greatly add to our power to strike

[39] Capt. Stephen Roskill RN *The War at Sea* II 229–231.

the enemy and will also show our unity of purpose in the war agains Japan.[40]

The Royal Navy task force sailed from Manus 18 March an arrived Ulithi on the 20th, where it fueled from United States Nav facilities. During the next two days plans were completed for sup porting Operation ICEBERG as TF 57, a part of Admiral Spruance' Fifth Fleet, but independent of TF 58. The mission assigned to Ad miral Rawlings was to cover the Sakishima Gunto, a group of is lands between Formosa and Okinawa.

Sailing from Ulithi 23 March, TF 57 rendezvoused with its flee train at a point east of Cape Engaño. The logistic group then pro ceeded to Leyte Gulf and set up a forward anchorage and suppl base in San Pedro Bay.

Upon joining Fifth Fleet the British Pacific Force accepte United States Navy tactical publications and communications pro cedures. Communication teams were provided for each combatan ship, and Captain E. C. Ewen USN, an experienced carrier skipper acted as liaison officer to Admiral Rawlings. The British found th transition easy. The Admiral reported that only one signal had to b added to the British general signal book in order to accommodat his Fleet to American tactical formations, and the appearance o American terms such as C.A.P., A/S and Dumbo in his ships' actior reports indicates that Senior Service sailors fell easily into new habits. Their fleet train proved to be adequate, since the U. S. Navy undertook to bring all black oil and avgas up to Ulithi; Admira Fraser informed the Admiralty that Service Force Pacific Fleet ha interpreted the "self-supporting" provision of the 16 Septembe memorandum very liberally.

After fueling at sea, TF 57 headed for its launching area 100 mile south of Miyako Retto, easternmost of the Sakishima Gunto. Begin ning at sunrise 26 March, fighter sweeps and bomber attacks were launched against airfields on Miyako in order to render them in operative. After the last strike of the day the task force withdrew southeasterly for the night. At sunrise it returned to the launching

[40] Vice Adm. Rawlings Action Report 9 May 1945.

area, where the first day's sweeps and strikes were repeated on airfields not before covered, and on coastal shipping. In the forenoon H.M. destroyer *Undine,* with fighter cover, was sent out to search for the crew of an Avenger which had ditched fifty-six miles from the launching point. She not only rescued this crew but picked up an American Corsair pilot who had been adrift for forty-eight hours. At 1805 lifeguard submarine U.S.S. *Kingfish* reported the rescue of a British Avenger pilot. Reports of a typhoon to the southward caused Admiral Rawlings to call off strikes planned for 28 March in order to fuel and replenish and be sure the task force would be in position to cover the Sakishima Gunto from 31 March through 2 April, the critical period at Okinawa. During its two days' absence, planes from the support carrier group of Rear Admiral Durgin USN took over its job.

Replenishment completed in the afternoon of 30 March, sweeps and strikes against Sakishima targets were resumed next day. Admiral Rawlings now borrowed another tactic from the American fast carrier book. Antiaircraft cruiser H.M.S. *Argonaut,* which mounted the latest radar, and H.M. destroyer *Wager,* were stationed 30 miles in advance of the task force to act as pickets and to prevent Japanese aircraft from returning with friendly strikes.

Having reached L-day minus 1 for Okinawa, we may break off the story of TF 57 until Operation ICEBERG really began. In that operation, the British carrier group became a flying buffer between the United States amphibious forces and the enemy airfields on Sakishima Gunto.

CHAPTER VII

Moving In on the Ryukyus[1]

18 March–1 April

1. *Sorties from Ulithi and Carrier Support*

HERE is a brief reminder of the principal elements of Vice Admiral Kelly Turner's Joint Expeditionary Force (TF 51) for Operation ICEBERG, the conquest of Okinawa: —[2]

TG 51.1 WESTERN ISLANDS ATTACK GROUP, Rear Admiral Kiland: One transport squadron and tractor flotilla, to land 77th Division on the Kerama Retto on L-day minus 6. Closely allied to this was TG 51.2, the Demonstration Group, Rear Admiral Jerauld Wright.

TF 52 AMPHIBIOUS SUPPORT FORCE, Rear Admiral Blandy: Escort carriers, minecraft, UDTs, LCI(G)s, etc.

TF 53 NORTHERN ATTACK FORCE, Rear Admiral Reifsnider: Two transport squadrons to land III 'Phib Corps, Major General Geiger USMC, on the northern group of Hagushi beaches, on L-day, 1 April.

TF 54 GUNFIRE AND COVERING FORCE, Rear Admiral Deyo.

TF 55 SOUTHERN ATTACK FORCE, Rear Admiral Hall: Two transport squadrons to land XXIV Army Corps on the southern group of Hagushi beaches on L-day.

The ships and craft employed in the amphibious phases of this operation numbered 1213, of 45 different classes and types, from 179 attack transports and cargo ships down, including 187 of the

[1] CTF 51 (Vice Adm. Turner) Action Report Capture of Okinawa Gunto Phases I and II 25 July; CTG 51.1 (Rear Adm. Kiland) Action Report 26 May 1945.

[2] For detailed breakdown see Appendix I.

handy, ubiquitous and greatly wanted LST. The over-all figure of 1213 does not include the 88 ships of Task Force 58, the 22 ships of the Royal Navy's TF 57, the 95 ships in Admiral Beary's logistic group or the service forces and fleet trains of both Navies, which together would add over 100 more. Assault troops numbered 2380 of the Navy, 81,165 of the Marine Corps and 98,567 of the Army.[3]

Routing so large a number of ships and groups to a single destination from widely spaced staging points, an old game for V 'Phib staff, now required more than usual dexterity. Leyte Gulf was ample for the Northern Attack Force, but even the big lagoon of Ulithi was insufficient to hold the Southern, in addition to the approximately 200 vessels of Service Squadron 6 and 10, which used it as a logistics base. Arrivals and departures had to be nicely calculated in order not to overtax berthing and shore facilities.

Ulithi was also the scene of intensive detailed planning. Rear Admiral Blandy arrived there 11 March from Leyte to find Vice Admiral Oldendorf, appointed to command the Gunfire and Covering Force, on the binnacle list.[4] Fortunately, Rear Admiral Morton L. Deyo, veteran gunfire support commander in Operation OVERLORD and DRAGOON, was available to relieve Admiral Oldendorf. The gunfire support plans promulgated by Admiral Turner, which had just arrived, had to be correlated with those of lower echelons. "Spike" Blandy's plan, appropriately ready on St. Patrick's Day, was promptly distributed to some 600 ships in Ulithi lagoon.

Task Force 58, Mitscher's fast carriers with the first echelon of their attendant service force, departed Ulithi 14 March.[5] On the 19th the minesweepers left. The Royal Navy contingent, with most of its fleet train, arrived that day from Manus and anchored in the southern part of the lagoon. Fire support ships straggled in by twos and threes, some from Pearl Harbor, some from Iwo Jima and others from the Solomons. Ships which had been engaged in

[3] Turner Action Report Part I.

[4] Admiral Oldendorf and his chief of staff, Capt. R. W. Bates, had been injured when the "skimmer" taking them from shore to flagship *Tennessee* rammed a mooring buoy.

[5] See Chap. VI for their strikes on Kyushu, 18–19 March.

the nervous business of fire support off Iwo for the past month were badly in need of rest, upkeep and refresher training – for which there was no time. On 18 March Admiral Blandy held a briefing conference of all group, unit and capital ship commanders on board his flagship *Estes*. Three days later he and they sortied, and next day transports which had lifted Marines from Guadalcanal, Tulagi and the Russell Islands, occupied their berths. It was "hot bunk" in Ulithi lagoon.[6]

Lagoon and atoll presented an astonishing appearance on 20 March. In addition to the 40 or 50 ships that flew British ensigns several hundred vessels of the United States Navy and Merchant Marine were present. Mogmog, the former seat of the king of Ulithi, transformed into a fleet recreation center, was so full of bluejackets in shoregoing whites that from a distance it looked like one of those Maine islands where seagulls breed; one could hardly walk a step ashore without kicking an empty beer can. On the headquarters island, Commodore O. O. ("Scrappy") Kessing, atoll commander, was dispensing characteristic hospitality at the crowded officers' club, to officers of the fleet and nurses from the three hospital ships present, *Solace*, *Relief* and *Comfort*. Some of these courageous ladies had their last dance on this occasion, except their dance of death with the kamikaze boys. A "boogie-woogie" band of colored Seabees gave out "hot" dance music, and in the brief intervals when they cooled their lips, another Seabee performed marvels on the harmonica. Press correspondents, profiting by free drinks, staggered about in imitation of the traditional sailor on liberty. A few Royal Navy officers, who had flown to Ulithi to join TF 57, relieved the drab American khaki by their white tropical uniform of shorts and sleeveless shirts with shoulder bars. Some of the United States Navy's most noted officers were present: Rear Admirals "Mort" Deyo, "Spike" Fahrion, "Turner" Joy and John H. ("Babe") Brown; destroyer squadron commanders such as Captains Roland Smoot, H. J. Martin and A. E. Jarrell; and a sprinkling of young reservists commanding destroyer escorts, such as "Charlie"

[6] For occupation and development of Ulithi, with chart, see Vol. XII 47–54.

Adams, son of a former Secretary of the Navy, and "Frank" Roose-elt, the President's son. Gene Tunney, former heavyweight boxing hampion, had just arrived to take charge of fleet recreation. This arty was a modern version of the famous Brussels ball before the attle of Waterloo; but no cry was raised of "They come! They ome!" since the enemy was conserving planes for ship targets earer home. Everyone was happy over a somewhat blown-up press elease on the fast carriers' strikes on Japan, and eager to start for he top-secret destination.

From Ulithi it was a run of only four days to the Ryukyus for he fire support ships. They arrived 25 March. Next day the North-rn Tractor Flotilla, which had come from Guadalcanal, preceded Transport Groups "Able" and "Baker" out of Ulithi lagoon. These, s well as the Southern Tractor Flotilla from Leyte, and the Demon-tration Group from Saipan, ran into a spell of foul weather.

From 25 through 30 March, heavy seas and wind of gale force rom the ENE reduced the normal 8-knot speed of advance of the STs, forced them occasionally to change course, and resulted in ome cargo shifting and damage.[7] Weather forecasts indicated a yphoon, but Admiral Turner stoutly held on. The tractor flotilla ust managed to meet target date and hour by displaying excellent eamanship and increasing speed at every opportunity.

The LCI gunboats which accompanied these tractor flotillas also ad a rough passage. Yet Mortar and Rocket Division 2 managed en oute to assemble and fuze all its rockets in the magazines.

The Southern Tractor Flotilla en route from Leyte took a similar uffeting, and Rear Admiral Jerauld Wright's Demonstration Group, which brought up the 2nd Marine Division from Saipan, nade schedule by a very narrow margin.

[7] CTG 53.3 (Capt. J. S. Laidlaw) Action Report 14 Apr. 1945 indicates for ve of 26 March a fresh ENE wind force 6 and a heavy beam sea, forcing change f course from 335° to 315°; same all day 27 March; man killed by tank that broke oose. Wind abated 28th to force 5–6, squally, heavy seas; *LST–268* lost pontoon arge; wind made up to force 8 early hours 30 March, heavy going, two men over-oard, both rescued; 20 miles behind schedule at noon. Capt. Laidlaw in *LCI–1080* as operated on that day for an infected hip by Lt.(jg) Wilbur C. Sumner USNR, ho had been transferred by breeches buoy from *LST–950* the day before.

On the last day of the approach, the Northern Tractor Flotill
was attacked from the air. It had just rounded Kerama Retto an
steadied on a northeasterly course at 0200 April 1 when a numbe
of torpedo-bombers began attacking destroyer *Hugh W. Hadley*
which was steaming ahead of the LSTs. She splashed one plane o
the twelfth successive try, and drove off the rest. One went for th
tractor flotilla and launched a torpedo which passed harmlessl
under the shoal-draft LSTs.

Task Force 58 was still out there, about 100 miles east of Oki
nawa. Between 23 March and 1 April Vice Admiral Mitsche
launched strikes on adjacent islands, including Kerama Retto, an
fighter sweeps over Okinawa, as part of his preparation for the im
pending landing. At least one task group was on station daily, an
those that needed replenishment were absent for one day only. I
the early hours of 23 March destroyer *Haggard* (Lieutenant Com
mander V. J. Soballe), in Admiral Radford's TG 58.4, depth
charged submarine *RO-41* on a sonar contact, forced it to the sur
face and rammed it, smashing her own bow so that she had to pu
out for repairs, but causing the submarine to roll over and sink wit
explosions of gratifying violence.

At 1300 March 24 Task Group 58.1 launched a strike of 11
planes to attack a Japanese convoy reported about 150 miles north
west of Okinawa. Postwar studies confirm the returning flyer
claim to have sunk an entire eight-ship convoy. The same day, bat
tleships *New Jersey*, *Wisconsin* and *Missouri* and five destroyer
under Rear Admiral L. E. Denfeld's command, were detached fron
the screen to bombard the southeast coast of Okinawa, while *Massa
chusetts*, *Indiana* and six destroyers threw 16-inch and 5-inch hard
ware at another section of the coast. The only attack on TF 58 dur
ing this period came from a single Jill torpedo bomber on 27 March
against destroyer *Murray*. The plane was splashed and the torped
passed through *Murray* from starboard to port, exploding clos
aboard and doing relatively little damage.

On 29 March, from a point about 120 miles south of Kyushu
three task groups launched fighter sweeps over airfields in souther

Kyushu. During the next two days, while TG 58.1 replenished, 58.3 and 58.4 launched sweeps and strikes against Okinawa and furnished C.A.P. for ships in the vicinity.

2. *The Minesweepers*[8]

"First to arrive and last to leave" might well have been the motto of Minecraft Pacific Fleet. The Okinawa campaign opened at 1720 March 22 when *Hambleton* encountered a floating mine on the approach, and sank it by gunfire. Next morning at 0630 *Adams* led in sweeping the outer approach areas, and from that time on the mine flotilla was doing business day and night, as well as beating off kamikazes. *Adams* sighted the peak of Kuba Shima in the Kerama Retto at 0749 March 24.

Except in certain waters of the Philippines, the Japanese had done little mining in the path of the United States Navy. But they were known to have purchased from us and the British thousands of mines at the end of World War I, and it had to be assumed that they would have acquired from Germany the formula for making those influence mines which were so fatally effective off the coast of Normandy. Fortunately they had not done so. Although their mining of Ryukyus waters was neither abundant nor technically good, there was enough of it to make a lot of trouble.

Rear Admiral Alexander Sharp's mine force (*Terror*, flag) was organized as a task group of Rear Admiral Blandy's Amphibious Support Force. It comprised 122 minecraft and patrol craft in addition to net and buoy tenders. Smallest and most numerous were the YMS (yard or motor minesweepers), diesel-powered vessels 138 feet long, fitted primarily for sweeping acoustic, magnetic or other influence mines in shoal waters. Backbone of the minecraft fleet were the 185-foot, 800-ton AMs of *Admirable* class, and the 221-

[8] CTG 52.2 (Rear Adm. Sharp) Action Report 23 July 1945; conversations in 1945 with him, and with Capt. R. D. Edwards of Administrative Command Minecraft Pacific at Pearl Harbor, and their publications *Mines Away* and *Mine Warfare Notes;* A. S. Lott *Most Dangerous Sea* (1959).

footers of the *Heed* class, which began coming out in 1942.[9] Next were the destroyer minesweepers (DMS), converted from destroyers either of the old four-piper World War I vintage (*Gamble*, for instance), or of the 1630-ton *Bristol* class. The four-pipers had borne the burden of minesweeping in previous invasions as well as minelaying up the Solomons' Slot in 1943; the *Bristol* class, converted in 1944, reached the Pacific in time for Okinawa. These 1630-ton high speed minesweepers had fire control radar, which none of the smaller classes at that time possessed, and they had sacrificed only one of their five 5-inch guns. They could sweep a 150-yard width of ocean when steaming 15 knots. Biggest of all were the DMs, destroyer minelayers. These were 2200-ton destroyers of the *Allen M. Sumner* class, converted to fast minelayers in the course of construction.[10] But fast minelayers are only wanted when enemy shipping lanes are so near our own that they can dash in, "lay eggs," and retire. So these big DMs were used off Okinawa as antiaircraft, mine disposal, buoy laying and fire support vessels for the sweeper groups, functions which they performed admirably. Each carried six dual-purpose 5-inch 38-caliber guns mounted in twin turrets, two 40-mm quads and two twins, and eight 20-mm machine guns; but no torpedo tubes. They were also employed as radar pickets after the kamikazes had whittled down our destroyer strength.

The destroyer minesweepers, organized as a group under Captain R. A. Larkin, were employed in units of four or five, with a supporting DM, to make fast exploratory sweeps outside the 10-fathom line. But the typical sweep unit for the Okinawa operation consisted of five AMs equipped with "O" gear[11] to sweep for

[9] Four of those at Okinawa – *Sheldrake, Skylark, Starling* and *Swallow* – and others which began coming out in June 1945 were named after birds, but they do not belong to the World War I "Bird" class, all the survivors of which had been converted to ATOs and other auxiliaries by 1945.

[10] The Navy in February 1944 decided that, in view of the falling-off in German U-boat activity, it was building too many destroyers. It asked various branches of the Fleet if they could use any of the 2200-tonners. The minecraft office in Washington at first declined, but finally and fortunately accepted.

[11] So named after H.M.S. *Oropesa*, which first used it.

moored contact mines at a depth of 10 to 20 fathoms, together with one 2200-ton DM as support and one PC or PGM to destroy floaters by machine-gun fire. Admiral Sharp had seven of these units, organized in two groups under Commanders T. F. Donohue and L. F. Freiburghouse. One of the commonest (and most welcome) sights off Okinawa in April was an AM unit with the ships in echelon, sweep gear streamed, steaming methodically at 5 to 8 knots, patrol craft peeling off to explode a floating mine. These ships were equipped for sweeping ground or influence mines, which the Japanese did not have, but they were equally efficient for cutting moored contact mines in depths of less than 100 fathoms.[12] The AMs took care of most areas off the western and southern coast of Okinawa, while four of the six YMS units entered Nakagusuku Wan and Kimmu Wan on the east coast to clear them for future military operations. The sweeping plan was largely drafted at Admiral Sharp's headquarters by Captains Ralph Moore and Robley D. Clark; the latter was killed by the kamikaze which crashed *Terror* on 1 May.

The importance of the minesweepers may be gauged from their slogan "No Sweep, No Invasion." The Okinawa operation could not begin without extensive preliminary sweeps, nor continue without constant re-sweeping. Up to L-day, 2500 square miles of ocean were swept, six enemy minefields were discovered, and 184 mines, including floaters, were destroyed.[13]

No influence mines were encountered, but the sweepers had to cope with mines moored in shoal waters off the landing beaches. On 26 March, near sunset, destroyer *Halligan* (Lieutenant Commander E. T. Grace) hit a mine when she ventured into unswept waters less than 50 fathoms deep, about three miles southeast of Maye Shima. The mine exploded her two forward magazines, sending smoke and debris 200 feet aloft, and the entire forward part

[12] The 100-fathom curve was at that time considered the limit of mineable waters, but Admiral Turner directed clearance sweeps up to the 200-fathom curve and exploratory sweeps up to the 500-fathom curve. Rear Adm. Sharp's Action Report shows that this was done.

[13] For the loss of *Skylark* on 28 March see Chap. VIII below.

of the ship down to No. 1 stack was blown off. Most of the survivors gathered on the fantail. *PC–1128* searched the area by moonlight, picked up six swimmers, and after the senior surviving officer, an ensign, had ordered Abandon Ship, the PC with the aid of *PC–584* and *LSM–194* took off the other survivors. During the night *Halligan* drifted ashore. She lost 153 killed and 39 wounded out of a total complement of about 325, a dreadful warning of what to expect from enemy mines.[14]

A day in the life of a destroyer minelayer may be gathered from the log of *Henry A. Wiley*, Commander P. H. Bjarnason. On 29 March, in the neighborhood of Kerama Retto, she splashed a Japanese plane half an hour after midnight. At 0355 the bridge received 40-mm fire from a nearby LSM that was under attack. Six minutes later a Jake from right overhead dropped a bomb that missed. At 0402, *Wiley* fired on another plane, which escaped. At 0519 she fired on another. Around six o'clock, when it was getting light, she joined two destroyers for mutual protection; within a few minutes they were under attack by three planes, one of which was splashed by the antiaircraft fire of a destroyer. At 0613 a sixth plane came in on a steep glide; *Wiley's* 5-inch fire caused it to veer, and a 40-mm hit exploded it. Another kamikaze, then starting to dive, was taken under fire. The forward 20-mm battery snipped one wing clean off and the plane exploded 75 yards on the starboard bow. This fight was hardly over when a plane from one of our escort carriers splashed astern of *Wiley*, which recovered the pilot. Now the real day's work began. "0700 commenced sweeping operations." These were interrupted only by a "submarine contact" (later evaluated as non-submarine) on which a depth-charge pattern was dropped at 1400. "1700, completed sweep." [15]

Wiley, *Tolman* and *Shea* shot down 15 enemy planes before 1 April while protecting minesweepers, and *Adams* was knocked out the same day by a kamikaze which crashed her well aft, whose

[14] Com 'Phib Group 7 (Rear Adm. Kiland) Report of Loss of *Halligan* 1 Apr. 1945, with endorsements.

[15] *Henry A. Wiley* Action Report 1 Apr. 1945.

two bombs exploded under her fantail. One of the subordinate duties of these DMs, which helped the transports and combatant ships to thread their way through swept channels in the open ocean, was to plant a series of buoy markers that radar could pick up at night. As the operation progressed, and numerous screen and radar picket destroyers were sunk or damaged by suicide planes, Admiral Turner detailed more and more of the larger minecraft for these duties. Their exploits will be recounted in the course of the narrative. As a result, practically all the sweeping after L-day had to be done by the YMS, and only four out of eleven new, and five out of twelve old destroyer minesweepers were operational on 21 June, the day when Okinawa was declared secured. Minecraft suffered more than 15 per cent of all naval casualties during Operation ICEBERG.[16]

3. *Kerama Retto Occupied*[17]

Moonset	1432	March 25
Sunrise	0627	March 26
Sunset	1842	March 26

Fifteen miles west of Naha in Southern Okinawa lies a group of mountainous, irregularly shaped islands known as the Kerama Retto. The capture of this small group, unsuitable for airfields, was decided upon as the geography of the Ryukyus was studied, and the need of some better place than open ocean for fueling and ammunition replenishment became clear. Admiral Turner was struck by the possibilities of the Kerama Retto for this purpose. The roadstead or Kerama Kaikyo, between the largest island of the group and five smaller ones to the westward, was capable of accommodating 75 large ships in 20- to 35-fathom anchorages, with good holding ground, and both entrances could be closed by nets; the smaller

[16] Rear Adm. Sharp Action Report pp. F–2, G–1.

[17] Rear Adm. Blandy "Report of Operations Against Okinawa Gunto including the Capture of Kerama Retto, March–April 1945," 1 May 1945; Rear Adm. Kiland Action Report; personal observations and conversations with Adm. Kiland and staff in *Mount McKinley* 31 March, and with Cdr. Draper Kauffman 13 Apr. 1945.

Aka roadstead offered sheltered anchorage for seaplanes and their tenders, with a two-mile runway for the takeoff. Thus an advanced naval base might be set up in these islands before the main airdromes on Okinawa were captured.

Admiral Turner's proposal that the Navy seize this group about a week ahead of the main attack on Okinawa is said to have been opposed at first by almost every officer whom he consulted. That is surprising, in view of the success of the Union Navy in the Civil War in holding Ship Island off Biloxi, and the islands off Port Royal, S.C. Probably the inability of the Royal Navy to hold islands off the coast of Norway in World War II was in everyone's mind. The bogy of land-based air was brought up, since the enemy would have five airfields within fifty miles of Kerama while we were engaged in occupying it. It was even predicted that the Fleet, after taking heavy losses in Kerama, would be forced to seek the open sea. But the Iwo operation, as it unrolled its bloody scroll, accented the need of a sheltered anchorage for replenishment. Admiral Turner figured that he could get away with it, and he did. Naval fire power, delivered by ships and planes, diverted the enemy's main forces while the pirate team of Blandy and Kiland "cut out" Kerama right under his nose.

Admiral Turner was willing to go into Kerama Retto with nothing more than a reconnaissance battalion, and could easily have taken it with that. But Rear Admiral Ingolf N. Kiland,[18] who, as CTG 51.1, was directly responsible for the Kerama phase, wished to take no chances. Instead of fighting fanatical rear-guard actions from island to island with a small force, he planned simultaneous landings on five of the six larger Keramas, and on 26 March (L-day minus 6), instead of two days later as originally planned. The Army provided the 77th (Statue of Liberty) Infantry Division commanded by Major General A. D. Bruce USA.

Admiral Kiland's Western Island Attack Group (TG 51.1) consisted of command ship *Mount McKinley* and 19 large transport types with a screen of destroyers and destroyer escorts, two de-

[18] For brief biography of Adm. Kiland see Vol. XIII 93–94.

stroyer transports carrying underwater demolition teams, a tractor flotilla of 18 LST and 11 LSM, a flock of LCI gunboats and patrol craft for control and close fire support, survey ship *Bowditch*, a service and salvage group of two tugs and two repair ships, a couple of tankers and seaplane tenders; two Victory ships as ammunition carriers, several units of the minecraft flotilla with their net and buoy group, a transport converted to a hospital ship and miscellaneous auxiliaries. This Western Islands Attack Group was covered from enemy air or surface interference by one of Admiral Durgin's escort carrier units and by Rear Admiral C. Turner Joy's fire support unit, both to arrive in Okinawan waters within twenty-four hours of the Kerama landings.

The Kerama Retto covers a space about 7 by 13 miles, most of it water. The ten principal islands are precipitous, broken, rocky, covered with scrubby vegetation, and with deeply scalloped shores. The highest point on the biggest island, Tokashiki Jima, is 787 feet above sea level. There are white sand beaches in many of the coves, closed in by bothersome coral reefs. The general aspect of the group might well have reminded Admiral Kiland of the land of his Viking ancestors. They were thinly populated by the poorer sort of Okinawans, who lived on fishing and from tiny gardens terraced into the rocky hillsides. The only industrial plant was a copper mine, no longer being worked, on Yakabi Shima. Intelligence estimated 1000 to 1500 Japanese troops to be present, in this instance an exaggeration. Air reconnaissance (originally by Luzon-based Army planes, latterly by TF 58) showed six beaches, one on each of the six westernmost islands, that looked good for landing.

The Western Islands Attack Force was mounted at Leyte where the 77th Division had recently played an important part in the fighting. Rear Admirals Blandy and Kiland, General Bruce of the 77th Division, and Captain Hanlon of the Underwater Demolition Teams worked out the detailed plan, dated 17 March.

In Commodore T. B. Brittain's Transport Squadron 17, newly formed in 1945, half of the ships had never seen action. Their landing craft crews were inexperienced and the task of finding the right beach on the right island in early morning was certain to be difficult. By good fortune, Hinunangan Bay on Leyte and the Cabugan Islands made possible a remarkably lifelike rehearsal of the Kerama landings, which was held on 13–15 March. Admiral Kiland, moreover, had an efficient intelligence officer, Lieutenant Commander Ellery Sedgwick USNR, whose section got out an illustrated "Coxswain's Guide to the Beaches." [19] This the lads studied so carefully during the five-day passage from Leyte that they made no false move. The tractor flotilla, with support craft and net tenders, sailed from Leyte 19 March; Admiral Kiland, with the transports and the rest of the attack force, two days later. In company steamed escort carriers *Marcus Island, Savo Island* and *Anzio*. The minecraft, as we have seen, were first to arrive and first to be hit.

At 0530 March 25, Palm Sunday, Admiral Joy with two cruisers and three destroyers peeled off from Admiral Deyo's main body some 22 miles southeast of Okinawa to deliver preliminary fires on the Kerama Retto. Five destroyer transports carrying the UDTs had earlier broken off arriving off Kerama about 0600. Commander Freiburghouse's minesweepers were already there. Before daylight, radar picket destroyers were stationed at points around the Retto to give warning of approaching planes. Joy bombarded the beaches and such strong points of the central island as had previously been noted by photo interpreters, and the minecraft joined their fellows from Leyte in scheduled sweeps.

The UDTs, which next went into action, had a strenuous program. Team 19 from *Knudson* (Lieutenant G. T. Marion USNR) reconnoitered Kuba, Aka, Geruma and Hokaji; Team 12 from *Bates* (Lieutenant Commander E. S. Hochuli USNR) took care of the Yakabi, Zamami and Amuro beaches; while Team 13 from *Barr* (Lieutenant Commander V. J. Moranz USNR) concentrated on Tokashiki. Following standard doctrine, each team proceeded to a point about 500 yards off its assigned beach in an LCVP. The landing craft then turned parallel to the reef, casting off a swimmer about

[19] Almost this entire section had been with the late Rear Admiral Moon in the invasion of France.

every 50 yards. Each man, clad only in trunks, goggles and rubber feet, was festooned with the gear of his trade. He carried a reel of marked line knotted every 25 yards, the bitter end of which he secured to the edge of the reef. He then turned toward the beach, uncoiling the line as he swam, halting every time he felt a knot to take soundings with a small lead line; or, if the depth were one fathom or less, with his own body which was conveniently painted with black rings at 12-inch intervals. The swimmer recorded his soundings with a stylus on a sheet of sandpapered plexiglass wrapped around his left forearm. After an hour or more of reconnaissance, depending on the width of the reef, each swimmer was picked up by his LCVP, which in the meantime had been planting little colored buoys on dangerous coral heads. The method of recovering swimmers was simple and effective. A sailor held out a stiff rope to the swimmer, who grasped the "monkey's fist" at the rope's end, while the boat was making three or four knots, and was hauled on board. Landing craft then returned to their APDs where the swimmers' data were correlated and entered on a chart. All this went on under gunfire support from destroyers and gunboats, and "really beautiful air support," as Commander Draper L. Kauffman USNR described it, from escort carrier planes. This kept the enemy so busy ashore that he never even fired on the underwater demolition teams.[20]

One could follow these "frogmen," as they were nicknamed, from the ships; and as they calmly waded about the beach they looked (as Admiral Deyo observed) more ursine than ranine – like shaggy Kodiak bears fishing for salmon in an Alaskan river.

The teams that took care of Kuba and Yakabi Shima ascertained that the beaches in these two outer islands were impracticable for landing craft, and could only be approached by amphtracs. After this had been reported to Admiral Kiland and General Bruce on board *Mount McKinley* at 1625 March 25, they decided, since there were not enough LVTs for all six beaches, to postpone these

[20] Conversation with Cdr. D. L. Kauffman USNR 12 Apr. 1945; UDT plan; Com UDTs Pacific (Capt. B. Hall Hanlon) Action Report 4 Apr. 1945.

two landings and take only Zamami Jima, Aka Shima, Geruma (also called Keruma) Shima and Hokaji (also called Fukashi) Shima on the 26th.

In the meantime the transports had made their last right turn and were approaching from the westward, with rising Altair as guide. It was a beautiful night under a moon only two days short of full, and few clouds in the sky. The sea was calm, ruffled only by light southerly airs; the temperature was 61° F. At 0430 March 26 the transports hove-to in their assigned area about six miles west of Kuba Shima, the southwestern island of the group. Soon after, Admiral Joy's fire support unit (cruisers *San Francisco* and *Minneapolis* augmented by battleship *Arkansas*) resumed bombardment of beaches and installations. The tractor flotilla divided into two groups, the smaller, of four LSTs, steaming into a designated area two miles north of Yakabi, and the larger, of 14 LST and LSM, to an area about two miles SSW of Kuba. When the sun rose at 0640 over a bank of mist that obscured Okinawa, thirty miles distant, troop-laden amphtracs from the southern group were already on their way in, and those of the northern group were boiling out of their LSTs.

Owing to the position of these islands each landing group had to make a "dog leg" approach. These are very apt to go wrong, but none did here. The northern group made a 45-degree turn to pass through the narrow channel between Zamami and two small, reef-ringed islets, then turned 90 degrees left for the half-mile run to Beach Violet in front of Zamami village. The southern group divided into three units. Two steamed in company for six and three-quarters miles on a straight course, then split and landed on Geruma (Beach Yellow) and Hokaji (Beach Blue). The third, steaming parallel to the others about a mile northward, had another half mile to go before hitting Beach Gold on Aka Shima. Excellent bomb, rocket and strafing support was rendered by planes from the escort carriers, directed by CASCU (Commander Air Support Control Unit) in *Mount McKinley*. All landings but one were effected on schedule, between 0800 and 0900, without the loss of a man or an

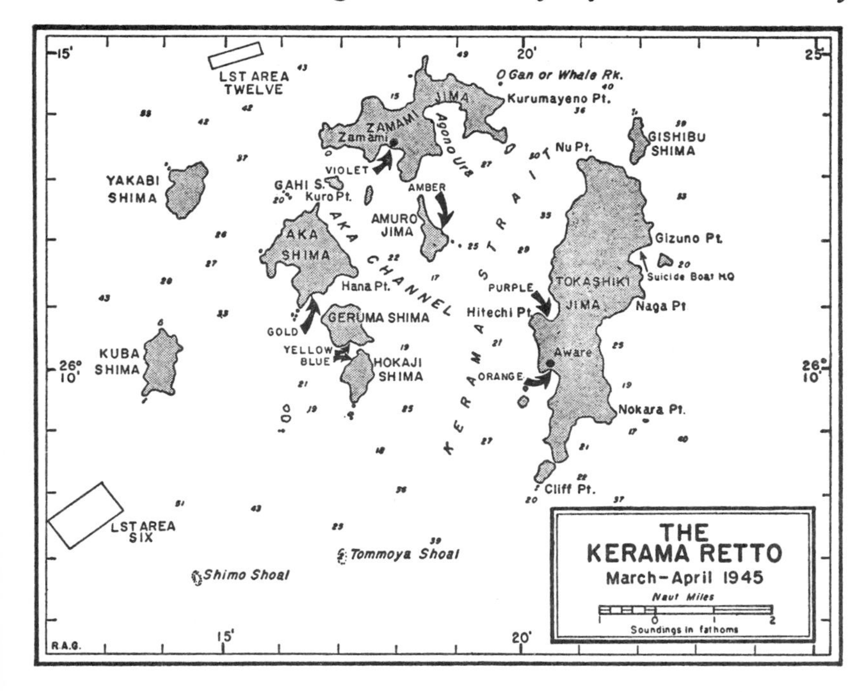

amphtrac; the Hokaji landing, delayed by congestion of landing craft, was made at 0921.

This neat though complicated landing took the Japanese completely by surprise; they had never imagined that the Kerama would interest us. The few hundred soldiers remaining there herded the natives into caves and tunnels and prepared to die fighting. On Zamami Jima the Japanese retired to the hills, leaving the invading troops to establish a beachhead almost unopposed. Two counterattacks were made during the following night, netting 106 Japanese dead. Resistance thereafter was individual and sporadic. The story at Aka Shima was similar. Five unoccupied pillboxes were found on the beach at Geruma, but there was no organized resistance. Twelve native women and a few children were found strangled in a cave by their own menfolk, who had been convinced by the Japanese that "fate worse than death" awaited them from the supposedly brutal and licentious Yanks. When the murderers, who were taken prisoner, found out what American troops were like, they begged their guards to allow them to "take it out" on the few Japanese prisoners. Civilians and Korean laborers generally surrendered easily, but most of the Japanese hid out in the hills.

All principal islands of the group except Kuba and Tokashiki were under American military control by the afternoon of 26 March. Net laying began at once and the first guide mooring buoys were set out before the close of that day.

Air opposition began at 1815 March 26, when nine kamikazes attempted unsuccessfully to crash ships of the Western Islands Attack Group and covering forces. At 0625 next morning two Vals attacked. *Gilmer's* galley deckhouse was hit by one that went over the side; she lost one man killed and three wounded. Destroyer *Kimberly*, on radar picket station about 20 miles southwest of Kuba Shima, was also attacked about the same time by two Vals of ancient vintage, one of which had a versatile pilot. He approached through the destroyer's full broadside, slipping, skidding, slow-rolling, zooming and weaving, until astern at 150 feet altitude. *Kimberly* maneuvered briskly, but Val stayed inside her wake and crashed a 40-mm mount, killing four men and wounding 57. The destroyer was not badly enough damaged to be taken off patrol until Kerama Retto was secured.

The only military use being made by the Japanese of Kerama Retto was to base Sea Raiding Units of "suicide boats," as we called them. Over 2300 troops had been brought in to set up and operate this base, but by 25 March their principal job had been completed and over half of them had pulled out. The rest were divided between Tokashiki, Zamami, Aka and Geruma. Immediately after our landings a careful search was made for the "suicide boats," and over 250 were discovered, mostly well hidden in camouflaged hangars and caves. They were only 18 feet long, each operated by one man, but carried two 250-pound depth-charges. On the night of 28 March net tender *Terebinth*, anchored 1000 yards off Hokaji, was surprised by one whose pilot seems to have had no stomach for

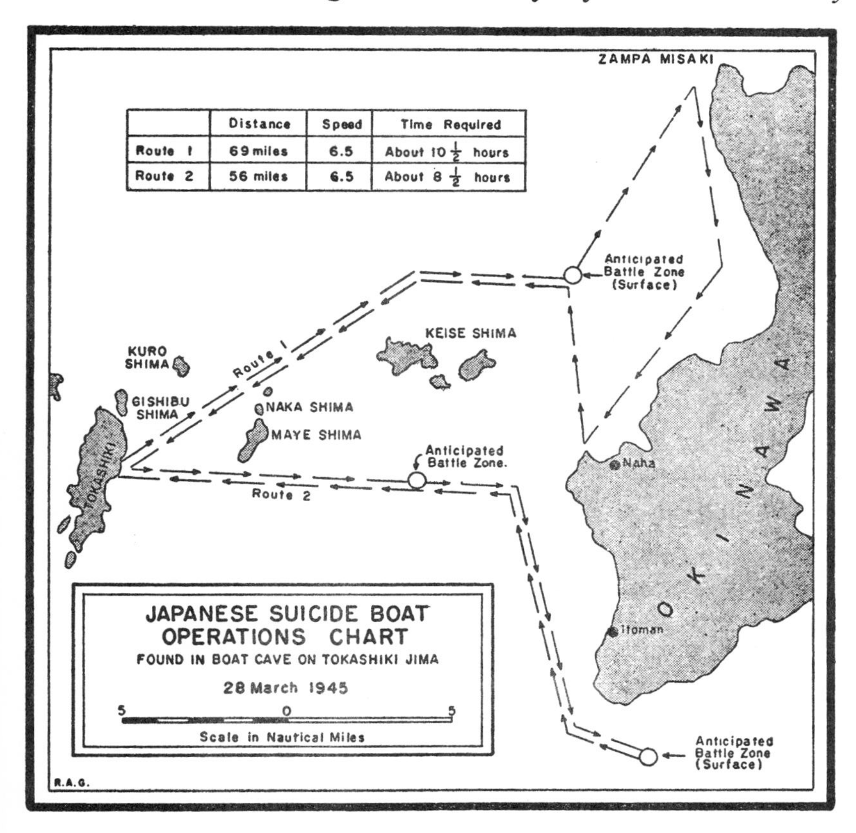

glory, as he dropped his depth charge 40 to 60 feet away and did no damage. That night three boats when attempting to retire from Tokashiki to Maye Shima were destroyed by patrolling LCIs; next morning *LSM(R)–189* destroyed three which attacked her. A talkative Japanese boat battalion commander who was taken prisoner told how they were to be employed in night attacks on the expeditionary force and produced the chart to guide them, which we have reproduced.

On 27 March the rest of Kerama Retto was secured. LCVPs from large transports, using channels through reefs blasted by UDTs, landed troops on Kuba Shima. No enemy being present, this island as well as Yakabi was soon evacuated. From Zamami as a base, a battalion landing team of the 77th Division, lifted across a bight of the roadstead to Beach Amber on Amuro Jima, secured that island. Two BLTs were staged via Geruma across Kerama Strait to Beaches Purple and Orange on the biggest island, Tokashiki Jima, which closed the roadstead on its eastern side. A shore battery there opened up on an LCI gunboat and killed one man – the only naval casualty in the Kerama landings. One company of Japanese put up a brief fight behind the beach, but resistance ended there. Since the Army made no attempt to control the whole of Tokashiki, about 300 Japanese troops remained in the hills until the end of the war. It was then discovered that they had at least one good coast defense gun on the western shore, literally looking down the throats of American ships anchored less than a mile away. Apparently awed by our show of overwhelming strength they lay doggo from 27 March to 23 August, when they surrendered. By late afternoon 28 March the entire group of eight islands was secured at the cost to 77th Division of 31 killed and 81 wounded; to the Navy, 124 killed or missing, 230 wounded. About 530 Japanese had been killed and 121 taken prisoner. Two battalions of the 77th were ashore on Zamami Jima and their supplies were 70 per cent unloaded; three battalions had been landed on Tokashiki, where two pontoon causeways were being set up on one of the beaches. The floating seaplane base had arrived.

Two 15-plane squadrons of Navy Mariners flew in next day, 29 March; they set up antisubmarine patrol near the island and began flying searches several hundred miles out.[21] Seven seaplane tenders under Captain G. A. McLean in *Hamlin* were anchored in Aka Channel, where they were soon joined by a fleet of auxiliaries. Fueling of combat ships had begun from two station oilers which refilled from a fleet tanker. Ammunition replenishment from specially equipped LSTs was about to begin; a boat pool was established and functioning. Japanese charts of the anchorage

[21] Michael G. Kammen *Operational History of the Flying Boat . . . World War II* (BuAer, 1959) p. 46.

were checked by survey ship *Bowditch*, and a new chart of the group, printed on board, was ready by 6 April.[22] Buoying of ship lanes was completed 28 March. Nets for the two entrances to Kerama Kaikyo, the principal roadstead, were then almost completed, and several of the little beaked net craft of the "tree" class (*Terebinth*, *Corkwood*, and the like) took up the boring but necessary task of net tending. All this, three days before Okinawa L-day. On 31 March when the writer entered Kerama Kaikyo on board *Tennessee*, the roadstead already had the appearance of a long-established base, and 35 vessels were anchored there.

Thus, the main objects of the Kerama operation were secured – the establishment of an advance logistics base and of a seaplane base for search and patrol. It also became home port for the minecraft and their tender *Mona Island*. A landing craft base and boat pool was established in Agono Ura, the eastern harbor of Zamami Jima. Tractors dragged equipment up the steep mountain paths of Tokashiki Jima to place antiaircraft batteries and search radars on the summit, in order to intercept enemy planes attempting to sneak in over the mountains. As early as 27 March, Admiral Kiland was "serving customers" of the fire support groups with oil and ammunition. Replenishment from his LSTs and LCTs with Hanson crawler cranes on deck proved to be much more expeditious than from the regular ammunition ships.[23] So popular was his "store" that on 2 April he asked Admiral Turner for pontoon units and ten more LCMs, and got them.

Kerama Retto also served as base for the occupation of Keise Shima, one of two island groups that lay between it and Okinawa.[24] Keise Shima consisted of four low, sandy islets, the largest only 900 yards long, between six and eight miles off the southernmost coast of Okinawa. As they commanded the town of Naha and vicinity,

[22] H. O. Field Chart No. 2055, "Japan-Nansei Islands Okinawa Group-Kerama Retto and Passages."

[23] Rear Adm. Kiland Action Report Sec. VII.

[24] The other group, Maye and Naka Shima, when reconnoitered, was found to contain neither Japanese nor installations.

where the enemy had numerous strong points, they were wanted as emplacements for XXIV Corps 155-mm artillery to support the advance of ground troops on the big island.[25] The Japanese command made no attempt to defend them. A careful UDT reconnaissance, on 27–28 March, found good beaches but drew sniper fire. On the 30th, after all approaches and surrounding waters had been minesswept, units of Captain Webb's tractor flotilla moved out from Kerama Strait to a position south of Keise and landed unopposed next morning on three of the four islets. The divisional artillery, promptly emplaced, was sited and ready for 1 April (L-day).

On 30 March the Western Islands Transport Group reëmbarked the 77th Division, excepting one battalion which was retained for the defense of Zamami Jima. The transports, under the command of Commodore Brittain, departed on the afternoon of 2 April and before nightfall were subjected to a heavy air attack.

Kerama roadstead became increasingly crowded with repair, service and ammunition ships, escort carriers fueling or bringing up replenishment planes, battleships, cruisers, destroyers and destroyer escorts taking on fuel, mail and ammunition; PBMs taking off and landing; mine and patrol craft enjoying a brief rest from their incessant labors; cripples from kamikaze attacks. The roadstead was not altogether free from air attack, but in general the kamikazes overlooked the plethora of profitable targets there. An occasional Japanese sniper troubled the troops ashore, and on the night of 1–2 April two bold fellows swam out to *LST–884*, anchored close to Zamami, climbed up the cargo net that she had carelessly left trailing, shot the deck sentry, and got away. Another climbed on board a damaged destroyer through the hole in her bow.

The natives soon lost their fear of Americans and went calmly about their simple occupations.

Between 28 March and 8 April, seven fleet tankers carrying 515,000 barrels of fuel oil and 121,000 barrels of diesel oil arrived at Kerama and the three station tankers issued 425,000 barrels of the

[25] Compare taking Wakde Is. in the New Guinea campaign (Vol. VIII 91) and Ukiangong Pt., Makin (Vol. VII 123).

ɔlack and 82,000 barrels of the diesel, together with large quantiies of lube oil and avgas, to 277 ships — an average of 23 per diem.[26]

Ships generally entered Kerama roadstead from the north, passing he isolated O Gan or Whale Rock, which shows a man's profile on one side and a woman's on the other. Inside the roadstead, despite requent air alerts, one had a feeling of security, like having a roof over your head in an air raid. As Rear Admiral Allan Smith wrote, Kerama "gave a firmness to the Okinawa tactical situation that was elt by all. We were there to stay, with a place to tow damaged hips, look after survivors, replenish and refuel, drop an anchor." [27]

Aye, drop an anchor! For that boon alone, sailors blessed Kelly Turner, whose bright thought made it possible.

Although several days elapsed before the enemy made any serious ffort to attack this concentration in the Kerama, he understood very well its significance. The aged Admiral Ito, in a Tokyo periodical of 1 April, said that America had stretched her supply line as ar as she dared; and, with reference to an athletic event in which he Japanese have long held the record, the Admiral guessed that he United States was endeavoring to reach Japan by a hop to Kerama, skip to Okinawa, and jump to Kyushu. "In the Ryukyus ve can best break the enemy's leg," the Admiral concluded. "He cannot continue his hop, skip and jump operations." [28]

[26] Memorandum from 'Phib Group 7 Logistics Officer to Rear Adm. Kiland, Apr. 1945. See Chap. X for Okinawa logistics in general.

[27] Comcrudiv 5 (Rear Adm. A. E. Smith) Action Report on Okinawa 26 May 945 p. viii–10.

[28] Broadcast by Radio Tokyo 2 April, translated by O.S.S. Honolulu. Admiral o also made the interesting remark that Kerama Retto was our substitute for mami O Shima, which in the naval disarmament negotiations of 1921 we tried to ersuade Japan not to fortify. In Article IX of the Treaty of Washington of 6 Feb. 922, Japan agreed that the Kuriles, Bonins, Amami O Shima, "Loochoo," Formosa nd the Pescadores should remain *in statu quo*, with no increase of naval facilities r coast defenses, and the United States made a similar agreement with respect ɔ the Philippines, Guam and Wake.

CHAPTER VIII

More Preliminaries[1]

25–31 March

1. *The Fire Support Group*

REAR ADMIRAL Morton L. Deyo, gray-haired with bushy black eyebrows, a wiry, taut officer nearing his fifty-eighth birthday, commanded the largest gunfire and covering force (TF 54)[2] that had yet been assembled for a Pacific operation. It did not include any of the newer battleships, which as usual were attached to Task Force 58, and would have nothing bigger than a plane to shoot at for the next two months. Not that TF 54 was weak. It included that consistent slugger *Tennessee* (14-inch main battery) as flagship, three 16-inchers of the *Maryland* class, two of the 14-inch *New Mexico* class, 14-inch *Nevada*, the elderly 14-inch *New York* and *Texas*, and that thirty-three-year-old patriarch of the battlewagons, 12-inch *Arkansas*. In addition, TF 54 had seven heavy cruisers, three light cruisers, 24 destroyers and eight destroyer escorts. The Advance Support Craft, a separate group under Blandy

[1] CTF 52 (Rear Adm. Blandy) Action Report 1 May 1945; CTF 54 (Rear Adm Deyo) Action Report 5 May; CTG 54.1 (Rear Adm. Rodgers) "Report of Gun fire Support Group 3, Fire Support Unit 3 and Crudiv 13 in Phases I and II o Okinawa Campaign, 21 Mar.–30 Apr. 1945" 30 Apr. 1945; Comcrudiv 5 (Rear Adm Allan E. Smith) Action Report 26 May. Also the writer's personal observations an dispatches collected on board *Tennessee*, and Rear Adm. Deyo's series of persona accounts entitled "Kamikaze."

[2] Although CTF 54 was his designation and title, strictly speaking Deyo com manded TF 54 only on night retirement and in the event of a surface action. I daytime he "loaned" the fire support ships to Blandy, under whom Rear Adm Rodgers became Com Fire Support Group. Deyo did not command gunfire on lan objectives. This curious command arrangement was originally made by Admira Turner because Oldendorf, the original CTF 54, was a Vice Admiral, and it wa kept because Deyo was senior to Blandy.

included 53 LCI and LSM, mostly rocket and mortar ships. For fire support purposes this force was divided into six units.[8]

Plans for the pre-landing bombardment were largely prepared by the staff of Rear Admiral Blandy, the top commander in Okinawan waters until Admiral Turner arrived on L-day. One could not expect to destroy all possible targets on so big an island before the troops landed.

Photographic interpretation showed few defensive installations immediately behind the landing beaches. Consequently the ships were enjoined to seek out profitable targets through the eyes of their aircraft spotters, and to fire from the closest possible ranges.

During the midwatch on Monday, 26 March, the principal units of Admiral Deyo's Fire Support Force (as we shall call TF 54) began steaming at 10 knots in four close columns through the ten-mile-wide channel between Tonaki and the Kerama Retto, which Admiral Sharp's minecraft had already swept and marked with radar-reflecting buoys. The moon, two days short of full, was setting over the port quarter, casting a golden sheen on the calm waters and a bright glow on the edges of the few clouds. There was a coolness in the air that contrasted pleasantly with the steaming tropics left behind. The dark profiles of Kuba, Yakabi and Zamami were plainly visible, and a grass fire was burning on one of them. With the familiar triangle of Vega, Altair and Deneb to steer for, there was nothing to suggest that one was in the East China Sea save for a "distant and random gun that the foe was sullenly firing," somewhere in the Kerama Retto. Encouraging reports of progress in Kerama came over radio, but veterans of the Pacific War knew very well that the enemy never showed his hand at the start of an operation.

At dawn the ships deployed for their several bombardment missions. Helped by air spot, the battleships and cruisers attempted at long range (since they dared not close unswept waters) to knock out known targets furnished by photographic interpreters. There was no reply from the shore, except antiaircraft fire that damaged

[8] See Appendix I for details.

one of *Portland's* planes. Submarines, however, were lying in wait. *Wichita* reported a torpedo wake at 0940 passing her ahead, and a second passing ahead of *St. Louis*. Both cruisers and *Biloxi* sighted others within the next hour. Since these fire support ships were just loafing along, the enemy missed a very good chance to make a kill.

2. *Air Support, Naval Bombardment and UDTs*

The air aspects of this preliminary bombardment and other operations prior to L-day must be kept in mind. We have already mentioned the seaplane searches from Kerama Retto.

No land-based aircraft were available. Air support came mainly from the fast carrier groups (TF 58) which had already struck Okinawa on 23, 24 and 25 March, and from Rear Admiral Durgin's escort carrier group (TG 52.1), most of which arrived in the area on 25–26 March. These comprised five units of 18 CVEs under Rear Admirals C.A.F. Sprague, Felix Stump and W. D. Sample, all heroes of the Battle off Samar.[4] Planes from both fast and escort carriers performed the following services in this phase of the operation: daily strikes on Okinawan targets, C.A.P. over the amphibious forces, spotting for naval gunfire (in conjunction with the battleships' and cruisers' own float planes), photographic missions, and antisubmarine patrol.

All air operations during this phase were supposed to be controlled as well as coördinated by CASCU (Commander Air Support Control Unit) of the Amphibious Support Force, Captain Elton Parker in flagship *Estes*. The same amphibious command ship was the center for photographic interpretation and distribution by a special naval intelligence unit. On L-day – when Admiral Blandy relinquished the over-all naval command to Admiral Turner – Captain Whitehead, CASCU on board TF 51 flagship *Eldorado*, re-

[4] See Vol. XII for their brief biographies and exploits, and Appendix I, this volume, for details of TG 52.1.

lieved Captain Parker. A great deal of the success of this operation depended on the training, intelligence and quick wit of CASCU.

This system of directing escort carrier planes worked splendidly. C.A.P. was not so important in this preliminary phase as it became on and after 6 April, when kamikazes came out in startling numbers. The escort carrier planes began providing C.A.P. on 26 March. They also made an excellent set of photographs for the gunfire ships, and flew the great majority of air bombing missions on Okinawa prior to L-day. Their pilots were assiduous in spying out new targets and bombing concealed defenses. The fast carrier planes flew an average of five daily strikes against Okinawa during the same period and supported the landings on 1 April. But their great service in this campaign, one for which they were blessed by every man afloat, was to furnish C.A.P. for the amphibious forces until land-based air was ready to take over. They shot down many more enemy planes than did ships' antiaircraft fire. Without their aid, losses of the expeditionary force might well have been insupportable.

All bombardment missions of 26 March were concluded at 1630 and Admiral Deyo's fire support ships retired. All went well that night, except that a snooping Betty severed one of *Porterfield's* radar antennas. But dawn came up like thunder with bogeys on the radar screen, and no C.A.P. overhead. Seven kamikazes attacked; one ignored the screen and aimed at the circle of big battleships and cruisers. Repeatedly hit by antiaircraft fire, it burst into flames directly over *Nevada*. The burning carcass crashed her main deck abreast turret No. 3, knocking out both 14-inch guns, with three 20-mm mounts besides, killing eleven men and wounding 49. Another splashed on the port beam of *Tennessee*, a third near *Biloxi*, and a fourth hit that cruiser at the waterline, making two big holes n the plating. Its 1100-pound bomb, which fortunately failed to letonate, entered one of the cruiser's flooded compartments. She had no casualties, and was soon repaired at Kerama Retto. Destroyer *O'Brien*, detached from the retirement group to provide star shell hat night over Kerama Retto, was severely damaged by a kamikaze n the dawn attack. She lost 28 men killed, 22 missing and 76 wounded, and had to return to the West Coast for repairs. Destroyer minesweeper *Dorsey* was crashed on her main deck but got off with minor damage and few casualties.

Naval bombardment on invisible targets is tedious enough, and even more tiresome to read about. For several hours, morning and afternoon, the fire support ships lay-to or steamed slowly as near shore as prior minesweeping permitted. They covered areas behind the Hagushi and the southern or demonstration beaches, firing deliberately with air spot. Between four and five in the afternoon, the different units assembled at a rendezvous 10 to 15 miles off Okinawa, formed a circular cruising disposition for antiaircraft protection, and retired seaward for the night, zigzagging in the light of the moon. A destroyer or two remained to help the patrolling LCI gunboats by delivering harassing fire and throwing up star shell. Before dawn the fire support ships returned to Okinawa, near which they usually sustained a routine early-morning kamikaze attack. The one on 28 March was ineffective, raising premature hopes that the self-sacrificing boys were going sour.

Since a minefield had been spotted off the Hagushi beaches, Lieutenant Commander Estep's Unit 7, *Skylark* leading, swept inside the fire support ships on the morning of 28 March. This observant "bird" had just signaled that she had seen 15 to 20 Japanese tanks scuttle out of a wood in order to avoid shellfire, when she ran smack into a mine. There was a great explosion, blowing out fuel oil which burned on the surface with bursts of flame and black smoke. Twenty minutes later she hit a second mine and took a heavy list. Within fifteen minutes her mast was under; her stern rose at a 90-degree angle and then plunged. Yet the rescue work by *Tolman* was so efficient that *Skylark* lost only five men, all killed by the explosions.

That night, enemy planes based on the Okinawa fields made a special go at small patrol craft. A dozen or so of these planes were destroyed, but one damaged *LSM(R)-188*, killing 15 men and wounding 32. From midnight to dawn 29 March, TF 54 was almost continuously snooped by enemy aircraft, ten of which were shot down. DMS *Ellyson,* when delivering short-range bombardment in the morning, saw what appeared to be a white man waving on the beach, and passed the word to *San Francisco,* which sent an SOC to the rescue. The man was Lieutenant F. M. Fox USNR of *Yorktown,* who after crashing had spent three days hiding near Kadena airfield. The SOC, piloted by Lieutenant (jg) R. W. Gabel USNR, damaged its float in the process but taxied out to *Ellyson* and delivered the rescued pilot.

On the same day the UDTs reconnoitered the Hagushi beaches, where the attack force proposed to land, and also those where they would pretend to land. The same technique was employed as at Kerama Retto. There was no enemy reaction except a little mortar and sniper fire. The swimmers reported that the reef was suitable for amphtracs, but only in a few places would there be enough water over it at high tide to float landing craft. The only artificial obstacles were about 2900 wooden posts driven into the coral.

From 29 March (L-day minus 3) battleships and cruisers delivered precision fire on the Okinawa airfields and other targets, the sweepers having enabled them to close the range. Special efforts were made by the escort carrier planes to interdict the Yontan and Kadena fields to the enemy by "intruder" missions. They caught a number of aircraft lining up to take off; and next morning there were no dawn attacks on the ships.

During the midwatch of 30 March, *Irwin, Hall, Tolman* and *LSM(R)-190,* on patrol off Okinawa, engaged two or three groups of Japanese motor torpedo boats which approached from the north. There was no damage to our ships, and at least one enemy boat was sunk.

Good Friday, 30 March, fifth day of bombardment, opened overcast and warm with a light southerly wind which later developed into a brisk breeze. This was the time for the UDTs to "blow the beaches," as they called the explosion of obstacles. From 1000 until noon the "frogmen" calmly worked along the wooden anti-boat stakes on the reef off Beaches Purple and Orange. Battleship sailors could see them placing their charges and being picked up on the run by LCVPs, while projectiles of the covering vessels screamed over their heads and exploded on the beach. The enemy did not reply with so much as a rifle shot.

So far as anyone could see, the entire island was depopulated. Not one human being was visible to ships, boats or even planes. The neatly tilled fields were completely deserted, even by cattle, and nobody moved abroad in the villages. If any military installations were there, they were deserted or effectively camouflaged. If the Japanese had been Christians, one might have assumed that they were all at church. As it was, everyone had the uncomfortable feeling that they were about to spring a very nasty surprise. Intelligence assured us that at least 60,000 troops were somewhere on the island, and actually there were many more. What were they up to, and where the hell were they?

Ie Shima, the little island with the big airfield off the dog's ear, was also reported by reconnaissance planes to be completely deserted, and a Japanese officer rescued from a sunk motor torpedo boat supported the delusion by insisting that it had been evacuated. Aircraft photos indicated that the airfield had been cratered, trenched and blasted to render it useless. No human being was visible, and no gun opened fire on our hedge-hopping planes. Two weeks later, the 77th Division had to kill about 3000 Japanese to secure Ie Shima.

When photo interpretation revealed a midget submarine nest in Unten Ko, a reef-fringed harbor on the east coast of the Motobu Peninsula (the Okinawa pup's upraised ear), escort carrier planes on 30 March bombed four of the pens and destroyed two loaded motor torpedo boats, expending two aircraft in the process. This attack wiped out the midgets; no more trouble from that source; but several Japanese fleet submarines were prowling about Okinawa. An hour before midnight 30 March, a night patrol plane sighted by moonlight a full-sized submarine on the surface about

30 miles southeast of Okinawa. Destroyer *Morrison* was ordered thither to conduct hunter-killer operations with the plane. *Stockton,* in the vicinity escorting an oiler to Kerama Retto, peeled off for this more congenial task. A coördinated depth-charge attack, at 0210 March 31, forced *I–8* to the surface, where the two destroyers opened fire and quickly sank it. They had the satisfaction of recovering one survivor.[5]

Despite the cumulative evidence of the enemy's having retired from the shoreline, reconnaissance pilots and officers who accompanied the UDTs ashore expected the landing to be resisted. The Hagushi beaches were bisected by the Bisha River, which was full of Japanese landing craft and motor torpedo boats, most of which (as they did not know) had been holed by our bombing planes. This river flowed into the sea between two outthrusting limestone bluffs, whose faces were honeycombed with caves and tunnels from which machine guns could enfilade the landing beaches. Like the installations at Iwo Jima and on Omaha Beach, they were inaccessible to naval gunfire or aërial bombardment. A similar limestone outcrop thrust down between and commanded the southernmost beaches, and a German-type concrete pillbox with stepped embrasures appeared ready to perform the same service for Beaches Yellow to the north of the river. Behind every beach was a thick six- to ten-foot-high sea wall of masonry and concrete, which had been very slightly breached by naval gunfire. Both airfields were dominated by tunneled and fortified hills. Only a few of these defenses, mainly new concrete emplacements, had been demolished by naval gunfire. It looked as if landing on the Hagushi beaches would be as bloody an affair as Tarawa, and that the three days allowed in the operation plan would be too little time for capturing Yontan and Kadena fields.

How wrong everyone was! What we thought to be difficult proved to be easy, and after the easy part was over the tough fighting began.

[5] Rear Adm. Blandy Action Report; the survivor's account is translated in M. Hashimoto *Sunk* (1954), p. 207.

3. *L-day minus One, 31 March*

At 0707 March 31 as Fire Support Unit 5 was proceeding to its station, four planes attacked. C.A.P. splashed two and *New Mexico* one; the third crashed Admiral Spruance's flagship, *Indianapolis*. The plane's wing struck an object on the port bulwark, twisting it so that it went overboard, but the bomb crashed through several decks and two messing and berthing compartments, killed nine men and wounded 20, and exploded in an oil bunker, damaging No. 4 shaft. *Indianapolis* could still steam at reduced speed and most of her guns could shoot; but the carelessness of a repair crew at Kerama Retto gave her damaged shaft the "deep six," and she had to go to Mare Island for major repairs. She was the first heavy ship in this operation to be knocked out by a kamikaze and, as we shall see, the last to be sunk in the war. Admiral Spruance transferred his flag to *New Mexico*.

All that day bombardment of the beaches continued at enhanced pace, with special attention to knocking breaches in the sea wall that ran behind them. Not many were made, and few in places whence vehicles could sortie. At 0830 the UDTs, covered by close gunfire from LCI and larger vessels, completed blowing the beaches.

XXIV Corps artillery now commenced landing on Keise Shima. By sundown half the artillery and rolling stock, and an antiaircraft battery, were ashore and ready to support troop landings.

During this Holy Week that preceded the landings, an enormous amount of ammunition was expended.[6] There was no want of bullets; only targets were wanting, and much ammunition was wasted on cratering the fields of the Okinawa peasantry. The bombardment was completely one-sided, since the Japanese shore and mobile batteries took care not to disclose their positions by firing. Planes and gunfire between them wrecked most of the enemy aircraft on the island, which was all to the good. Apart from this, the principal re-

[6] In rounds, 1033 16-inch, 3285 14-inch, 567 12-inch, 3750 8-inch, 4511 6-inch and 27,266 5-inch.

sults achieved by air bombing and naval bombardment were the destruction of villages and isolated farmhouses that had no strategic value.[7] The operation would probably have proceeded very much as it did from L-day on if there had been no preliminary naval bombardment whatsoever. Yet a bombardment there had to be, if only to cover the demolition teams, breach the sea wall and destroy beach obstacles.

General Ushijima had left only token forces behind the Hagushi beaches and on the two airfields. He concentrated east and south of Naha, and on the Motobu Peninsula. In view of the overwhelming strength that United States forces had displayed in earlier amphibious landings, this was his best bet for prolonging the defense and inflicting maximum casualties. But these tactics were unsuspected by Admiral Blandy's force on 31 March. It seemed inconceivable that the enemy would abandon two airfields without a fight. For aught we knew, the Japanese were holed up on and behind the beaches, ready to give the boys hell when they stepped ashore. Task Force 54 took no chances and prepared to afford Admiral Turner's amphibious force, when it landed next day, the most impressive gunfire support that any assault troops had ever had.

[7] The writer's personal observations behind the Hagushi beaches on 9 and 13 April.

CHAPTER IX

The Landings[1]

1 April 1945

Almanac for 1 April, Okinawa

Sunrise	0621
Sunset	1845
Moon rose (full 28 March)	2147

High water at 0900 (5.9 ft.) and 2140 (5.5 ft.)
Low water at 0246 (1.4 ft.) and 1508 (0.7 ft.)

1. *Organization of One Attack Group*

PRELIMINARIES ended and Phase I of Operation ICEBERG opened at 0600 Easter Sunday 1 April, when Vice Admiral Turner assumed command over all ships, groups and forces in Okinawan waters.[2] Rear Admiral Deyo retained command of the fire support ships to cover the main and demonstration landings and southern Okinawa.

It will be easier to comprehend the mechanics of this vast operation if we concentrate on a single transport group. Commodore Melton O. Carlson's Transport Group "Dog" formed half of Southern Attack Force commanded by Rear Admiral John L. Hall. This group, which had the duty of landing the 7th Infantry Division

[1] CTF 51 (Vice Adm. Turner), CTF 54 (Rear Adm. Deyo), CTF 53 (Rear Adm. Reifsnider), CTF 55 (Rear Adm. J. L. Hall), and CTG 55.1 (Commo. M. O. Carlson) Action Reports; the writer's personal observations in *Tennessee*.

[2] The Amphibious Support Force (TF 52) was now dissolved, and Rear Adm. Blandy as CTG 51.19 assumed command of Eastern Fire Support Group, with the job of coördinating fire and air support for the demonstration landing and other operations on the east coast of Okinawa, for which see Chap. XIV Sec. 2.

(Major General A. V. Arnold USA) on Beaches Purple and Orange, comprised four transport divisions and two tractor groups, with a total of 16 APA, 7 AKA, 1 LSD, 1 LSV, 30 LST and 22 LSM.[3] Multiply these numbers by four, and you will have a fair idea of the magnitude of the entire amphibious landing on the Hagushi beaches.

Group "Dog" began loading at Leyte 3 March, embarked troops on the 12th and 13th, rehearsed during the following week, topped off with fuel and provisions during the next few days, sailed in slow, intermediate and fast echelons between 25 and 27 March, and arrived off the Okinawa beaches during the early morning hours of 1 April. This was an unusually short troop lift for a Pacific amphibious operation. The 7th Division, old hands at amphibious work, had made a careful study of the initial landing. Besides the 23 combat-loaded transports and cargo ships and LSD *Epping Forest* and LSV *Ozark*,[4] Transport Group "Dog" included 30 LST. These handymen of the Navy were used in much greater numbers in Operation ICEBERG than in any previous Pacific operation. More had become available after the howls of the Atlantic Fleet and of our British allies for more and more LSTs had died in the Hitlerian twilight. Besides their primary employment for lifting tanks and amphtracs, LSTs had proved capable of discharging assault cargo much more rapidly than the big transports, and without transfer to landing craft. They could be used for general or specialized cargo, or specially equipped as hospital ships, and their young reserve officers were keen, intelligent and trained to cope with special demands and emergencies.

The landings followed the pattern which had been worked out during amphibious operations in the Central Pacific, from Guadalcanal through the Marianas. The landing diagram for Saipan, now standard amphibious doctrine for the Pacific Fleet, was adopted for Okinawa with only such changes as the different topography required.

[3] For names and other details see Appendix I below.
[4] A converted minelayer.

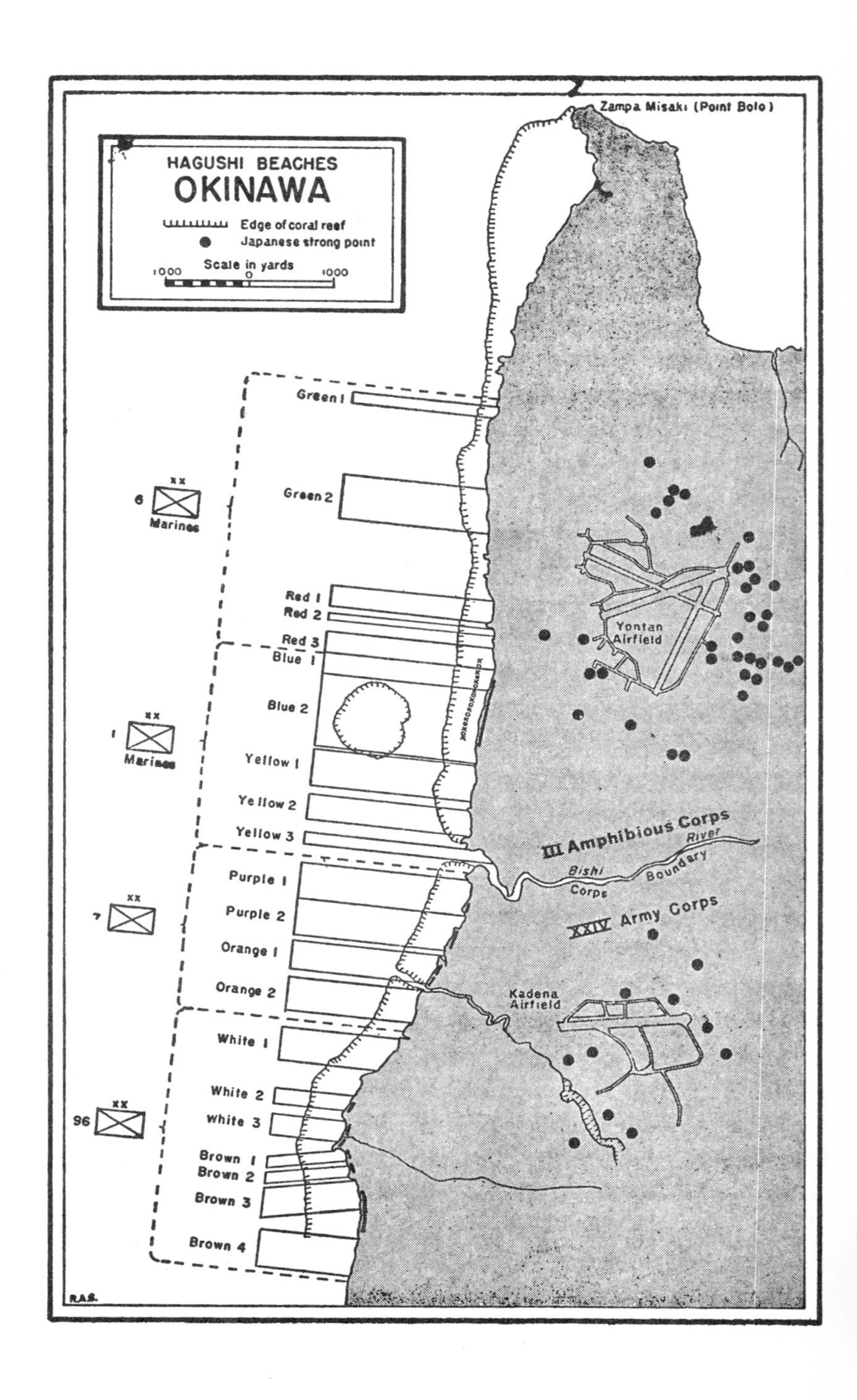
HAGUSHI BEACHES
OKINAWA
Edge of coral reef
Japanese strong point
Scale in yards
1000 0 1000
Zampa Misaki (Point Bolo)
Green 1
Green 2
6
Marines
Red 1
Red 2
Red 3
Blue 1
Blue 2
1
Marines
Yellow 1
Yellow 2
Yellow 3
Yontan Airfield
III Amphibious Corps
Bishi River
Corps Boundary
XXIV Army Corps
Purple 1
Purple 2
7
Orange 1
Orange 2
Kadena Airfield
White 1
White 2
White 3
96
Brown 1
Brown 2
Brown 3
Brown 4
R.A.S.

Experience had proved that a ship-to-shore movement involving several hundred landing craft of many different types required a well-trained control group as traffic policemen to oversee the forming, dispatch and movement of boat waves. Under Captain B. B. Adell, Commander Southern Attack Force Control Group in *PCE-877*, Lieutenant Commander J. M. Dundon USNR in *PCS-1452* acted as squadron control officer for our Group "Dog." He had two assistants, Control Purple in *PC-463* and Control Orange in *PC-469;* four division control officers in SC or PC; two LCC carrying the beachmaster of Transdiv 7 for the Orange, and of Transdiv 38 for the Purple beaches; four boat group commanders in landing craft, one for each beach; and four to eight wave guides in LCVPs for each boat wave.

The big transports caught up with the tractor and PC groups around midnight 31 March, and in the early hours of 1 April reached their respective unloading areas in the exact order of their stations. The APA and AKA hove-to in Transport Area Dog, with a front of 3000 yards and a depth of 7000 yards, about seven and a half miles from Beaches Purple and Orange. Twenty-three LST and 13 LSM proceeded to LST Area 2, which lay about three miles from the beach, while nine LSM, six specialist LST (supply, water, ammunition and gas, maintenance, hospital) and LSD *Epping Forest* with boated tanks, dropped off at the rear and occupied LST Area 5, a little further to seaward of the control vessels. *PCE-877* closed Admiral Hall's flagship *Teton* to pick up Captain Adell, who had concluded last-minute arrangements with the Admiral's staff, and then proceeded to a point midway between the 7th and 96th Division beaches. She flew the Zero ("five of clubs") flag.[5] Lieutenant Commander Dundon's *PCS-1452*, top control vessel for Group "Dog," flying a purple and orange banner to mark the boundary between the divisional beaches, took station broadside to

[5] *PCS-1402* closed Adm. Turner's flagship *Eldorado* to stand by for the use of Gen. Buckner and staff during the day; *PCS-1421* performed the same service for General Hodge, Commanding General XXIV Corps, alongside *Teton*, while *PCS-1402* and *PCS-1455* acted as tenders for the commanding generals of the 7th and 96th Divisions who were in transports *Harris* and *Mendocino* respectively.

Captain Adell's *PCE-877*, and slightly seaward of the Line of Departure. That line, about 4000 yards from the beaches, had been established by the five other control vessels, each displaying a banner corresponding to the colors of the beach she controlled. Thus, the Purple and Orange Beach Line of Departure was marked by five control craft, on station and anchored by 0700, an hour and a half before H-hour, as follows: —

SC-1060 Lieutenant (jg) J. B. Sneddon USNR: Purple banner with one stripe, marking northern edge of boat lane to Beach Purple 1.

PC-463 Lieutenant E. E. Boelhauf: Solid purple banner between the two beaches of that color.

SC-1049 Lieutenant W. B. Carter USNR: Orange banner with one black vertical stripe, marking northern edge of boat lane to Beach Orange 1.

PC-469 Lieutenant D. D. Baker: Solid orange banner, marking boundary between the boat lanes to Beaches Orange 1 and 2.

SC-1312 Lieutenant F. G. Carpenter USNR: Orange banner with two vertical black stripes, marking southern edge of lane to Beach Orange 2.

This color scheme was carried out consistently. Every wave's guide boat flew a pennant of similar color and design and every landing craft of the initial waves had the color of the beach for which she was destined painted on her topsides. First wave ashore set up corresponding beach markers about ten feet high, brightly painted on canvas. Each landing craft could recognize at a glance the place where she should cross the line of departure, and for what beach she should steer. The colors and flags also made it easy for beach parties and troops ashore to recognize their own boats. Captain Adell had under him two LCC (fast motor boats equipped with radio and radar) which, flying purple and orange pennants, preceded the boat waves to positions shoreward of Line of Departure, where they acted as floating fairway buoys.

At 0629 *Epping Forest*, a number of LSM, and 15 LST began discharging amphtracs and landing craft, flying the appropriate beach flag at the dip during the process and hoisting it two-blocks when completed. The LSTs carrying LCTs on deck then retired to an area slightly to the southwest and shed their burdens with a loud splash. LCTs thus activated hustled out to the big transports to be in readiness for lightering cargo in the afternoon. LSTs carrying pontoon barges and causeway units dropped them off in Area 2, where the pontoon sailors hastily clipped their units together and soon were chugging off, propelled by mammoth outboard motors, to await orders.

All assault-loaded LSTs had departed Leyte in the same order that they would be wanted off Okinawa. Thus, Nos. 11 through 24, carrying the LVT(A) armored tanks, found themselves in the two front ranks nearest shore; those carrying LVT-4 personnel amphtracs in the center; specialist LSTs in the rear. The LVTs did not waste time running around in circles (that picturesque feature of earlier amphibious operations, provoking unnecessary consumption of fuel and loss of breakfasts), but, led by guide boats flying the appropriate colored pennants, filed in column to positions a few hundred yards outside Line of Departure, ready to deploy from column into line when given the word to go.

In the meantime, the big ships in Transport Area "Dog" were lowering landing craft and boating troops for the ninth and subsequent waves that followed the initial assault. Those that carried dukws, the amphibious trucks that roll supplies over the reef, launched them promptly. Dukws had their own rendezvous area behind the first three ranks of transports, where they were met by guide boats which led them to *LST-734* in Area 2. There they loaded priority supplies for the shore. Other transports with landing craft which were not used to boat troops stood by to provide assault supplies on call. General unloading was to begin only when the beaches were clear enough to receive masses of supplies.

Certain designated landing craft and LCC boated the Navy's beach parties. These went in to stand by the reef and direct the negotiation of that hurdle after the tide fell and Line of Departure became obsolete. The assault waves were landed around high water, at 0900; hence, it was anticipated that by the time supplies began coming ashore, it would be necessary to transfer them from the landing craft to dukws and LVTs, which could climb over the reef. Floating barges with cranes were provided to help this transfer. Each control PC kept two circles of cargo-bearing landing craft orbiting about 1000 yards from the beach, ready to be sent in on signal from Army shore parties when there was room for them. Thus, beach congestion, the dam of matériel that had clogged earlier amphibious landings, was prevented.

In order to land the 16th and subsequent troop waves, a simple transfer plan was provided. Retracting LVTs formed circles on each flank of the "Dog" area. Each LCVP then went alongside an LVT and transferred her men. And as all amphtracs were of the latest type, LVT–4, they could accommodate as many men as an LCVP.

In order not to overwhelm the reader with more detail, yet do justice to the magnitude and complexity of this great amphibious operation, I shall now describe the landing of the 7th Division on the Purple and Orange beaches by boats and craft of Transport Squadron "Dog."

2. *A Landing on the Southern Beaches*

Easter Sunday and L-day, 1 April 1945, broke slightly overcast and cool, a pleasant change for GIs who were accustomed to fighting in the steaming heat of the Philippines. Many a member of the fighting 7th Division, as he wolfed a hearty breakfast, wondered whether he would be alive to enjoy another meal. His luck could not hold out much longer; Okinawa was "it." Recent casualty reports from Iwo did nothing to cheer him, especially as the shipboard briefing had stressed the fact that Okinawa was likely to prove a bigger and tougher Iwo. As soldiers and sailors peered over the rail, straining for a look at the top-secret objective, most of the lads were too intent watching the bombardment by fire support ships to indulge in conversation; but there was a considerable amount of assertion and denial respecting the immediate future. Imperial General Headquarters would have been interested in the exact and detailed knowledge of the "next operation," such as our gun-deck strategists pretended to possess, although they would have been astonished to learn how many GIs and Seamen 2nd class claimed to share the intimate thoughts of General Buckner and Admiral Turner.

At 0406 Kelly Turner signaled "Land the Landing Force." H-hour had been set for 0830, and at 0640 Admiral Hall confirmed it for Southern Attack Force. At about that time the sun rose over heavy, low-lying clouds and gave the amphibious forces their first real look at Okinawa through gaps in the smoke left by the bombing and naval bombardment. It was a beautiful morning, and a perfect day for an amphibious operation: calm sea, just enough offshore wind to blow the smoke away and to float the varicolored banners of the control craft. The morning sun cast a peach-like glow over the water and on the multitude of ships, some painted solid gray, some with striped Atlantic Ocean camouflage. This was the sort of weather one expected on Easter Sunday but seldom experienced. But the parade that was being prepared was a strange one for Easter, and left no time in its tight schedule for church. One could only pray that this tremendous effort might guarantee an infinite series of peaceful Easter morns in the future; that, as the Resurrection had promised eternal life to men of faith, the work this Easter might help to make faithful men free.

We may now shift to the viewpoint of the principal bombardment unit for Beaches Purple and Orange, battleship *Tennessee*, in which this writer was embarked. She packed a terrific fire power with her twelve 14-inch 50's, sixteen 5-inch 38's and forty 40-mm guns. Though scheduled to bombard the beach area from a range of 5000 to 6000 yards, which would have placed her astride the Line of Departure, her skipper, Captain John B. Heffernan, insisted on closing to 1900 yards from the beach, 3250 yards from her nearest target.[6] Since 0300 she and the other fire support ships had been cautiously threading their way through the tractor groups and control vessels, which required neat ship handling.

At 0620, when she was approaching with the rest of the fire support ships, a Val dive-bomber attacked the formation. After near-missing a destroyer-transport, it was shot down by one of the ships and splashed just astern cruiser *Birmingham*, which must have been surprised to have anything miss her. Ten minutes later the sun appeared, as if a signal for the bombardment to start. *Tennessee* lay-to about half a mile shoreward from the two control boats that marked the Orange sector of the Line of Departure. Destroyer *Paul Hamilton* lay close aboard, *Birmingham* took a fire support station to the southward, off the Brown beaches, and *Idaho* lay northward. It was clear overhead, but morning mist at water level obscured both the land and the big transports. Every visible expanse of water was covered with LSTs and landing and control craft, gently rocked by a slight ground swell.

As the bombardment progresses, more and more amphtracs issue from the LSTs and begin forming up in waves under the watchful eyes of their guide boats, taking station seaward of Line of Departure. *Tennessee* at 0722 concentrates on shattering the sea wall behind the beaches. At 0735 she checks fire while carrier-based planes fly parallel to the beach, bombing and launching rockets. The sound of naval cannon is stilled, but the air is filled with the drone of airplane motors, the rolling rumble of exploding bombs, and the sharp, unmistakable impact of rocket fire, which sounds like a giant lash being well laid on along the enemy coast by an almighty hand. One hears the swish almost at the same time as sharp flashes of the missiles exploding on the ground strike the eye; then a great backlash of smoke and dust whips into the sky accompanied by a loud c-r-r-rack from exploding rockets.

In a few moments the air strike is over and the ten battleships,

[6] She drifted out to about 3600 yards from the beach before the bombardment was over.

nine cruisers and 23 destroyers that are disposed along the ten-mile front resume close fire support. *Tennessee* fires her 5-inch 38 broadside at the rate of 54 rounds per minute, and throws in 40-mm fire for good measure. Then the hoarse roar of her main battery provides a bass to Amphibious Symphony No. 1 by maestro Kelly Turner. The yellow cordite smoke is blown back in our faces; Admiral Deyo sniffs it appreciatively from his catwalk outside flag plot and remarks, "That has a good, offensive smell!"

At 0800 the cry goes up, "Here they come!" In the van are the LCI gunboats, twelve for our four beaches alone, moving in perfect alignment at a deliberate 3 to 4 knots in order not to outdistance the LVTs. They pass around the battleships, and when about 1000 yards nearer the shore open fire with their 3-inch guns, crackling like old-time musketry. In the meantime the first wave of landing craft, the armored LVT(A), has swept around the battleship's bow and stern, reforming on her landward side directly under her guns, which are shooting 14-inch, 5-inch and 40-mm projectiles over the men's heads. The 40-mm bullets go out in clusters of white-hot balls which look as if they would fall among the boats, but their flat trajectory carries them clear to the beach.

In ten minutes' time three boat waves, one of LVT(A) and two of the ramped, troop-carrying LVT–4, each flanked by flag-flying guide boats, have passed the battleship. Each craft leaves a wake of white water which subsides into a smooth slick, and the slicks run parallel as railroad tracks. The alignment of the landing craft, while not exactly that of soldiers on parade, resembles that of a cavalry charge, each amphtrac having a personality like a horse. The men in green coveralls and camouflaged helmets gaze curiously at the battleships' flashing guns. They seem silent and grim as troops always do when about to land, for a soldier is never so helpless as in this situation. The LCI gunboats are now much nearer the shore; their gunfire sounds like a roll of drums. Just as the fourth wave passes the battleship, the planes come in for their last pre-landing strafing and rocket fire, making a noise like a gigantic cotton sheet being ripped apart. The fifth boat wave passes, troops standing on

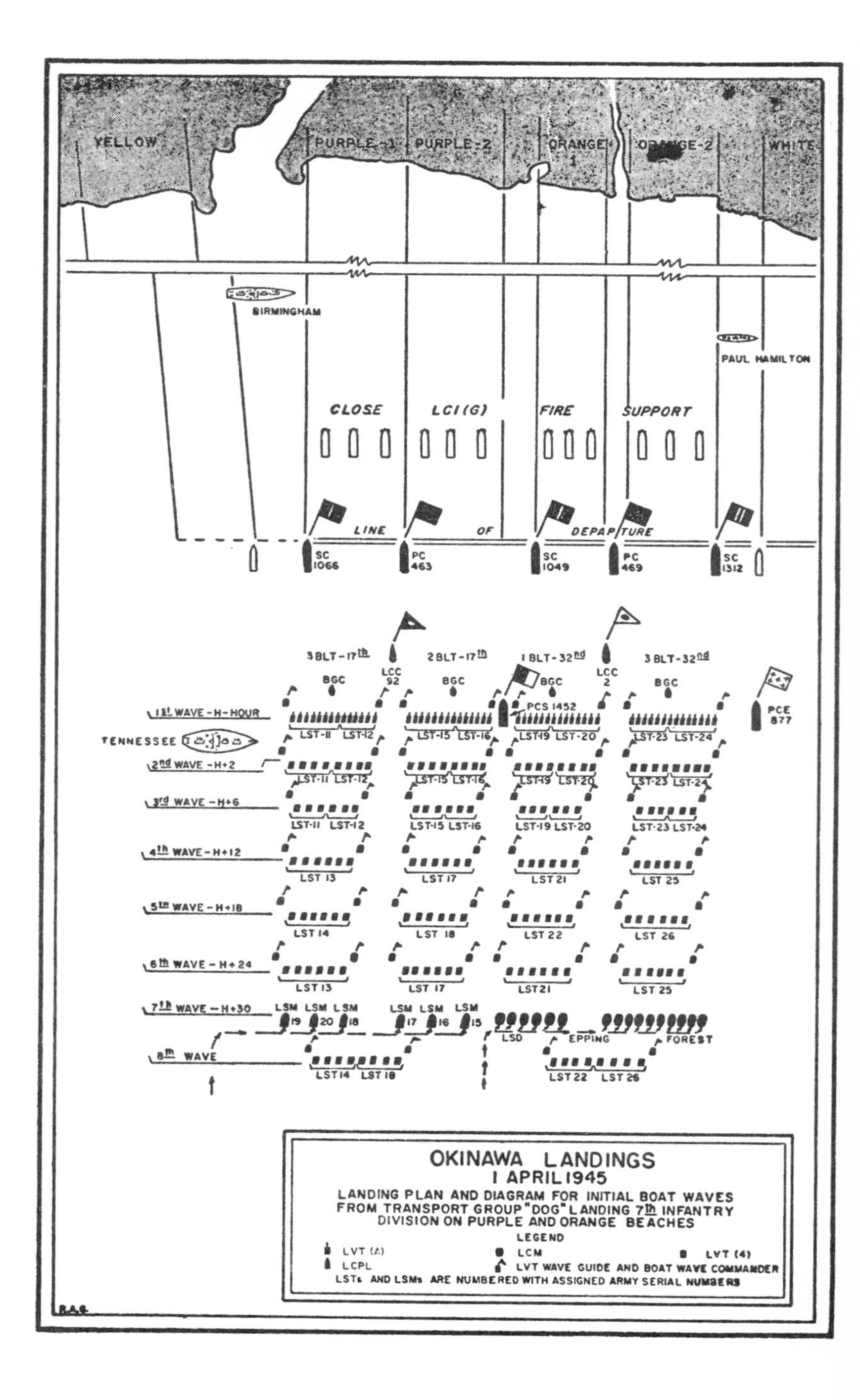

YELLOW
PURPLE-1
PURPLE-2
ORANGE 1
ORANGE-2
WHITE
BIRMINGHAM
PAUL HAMILTON
CLOSE LCI(G) FIRE SUPPORT
LINE OF DEPARTURE
SC 1066
PC 463
SC 1049
PC 469
SC 1312
3 BLT-17th
2 BLT-17th
1 BLT-32nd
3 BLT-32nd
LCC 92
LCC 2
BGC
PCS 1452
PCE 877
TENNESSEE
1st WAVE-H-HOUR
2nd WAVE-H+2
3rd WAVE-H+6
4th WAVE-H+12
5th WAVE-H+18
6th WAVE-H+24
7th WAVE-H+30
8th WAVE
LST-11 LST-12
LST-15 LST-16
LST-19 LST-20
LST-23 LST-24
LST 13
LST 17
LST 21
LST 25
LST 14
LST 18
LST 22
LST 26
LSM 19 LSM 20 LSM 18
LSM 17 LSM 16 LSM 15
LSD EPPING FOREST
LST 14 LST 18
LST 22 LST 26
OKINAWA LANDINGS
1 APRIL 1945
LANDING PLAN AND DIAGRAM FOR INITIAL BOAT WAVES
FROM TRANSPORT GROUP "DOG" LANDING 7th INFANTRY
DIVISION ON PURPLE AND ORANGE BEACHES
LEGEND
LVT (A)
LCPL
LCM
LVT WAVE GUIDE AND BOAT WAVE COMMANDER
LVT (4)
LSTs AND LSMs ARE NUMBERED WITH ASSIGNED ARMY SERIAL NUMBERS
R.A.C.

the after deck to see "what goes on." And a marvelous sight it is, these waves of landing craft extending parallel to the coast as far as the eye can see, all moving with a majestic, precise deliberation that well represents the stout though anxious hearts that they embark. No finer military spectacle could be seen in the entire war.

Over the radio at 0828 word arrives that the first wave is only 75 yards from the beach. From the bridge of *Tennessee* comes the order "Cease Fire." The LCI gunboats have halted outside the reef; amphtracs of Wave 2 are already crawling over the reef to begin their last dash through the lagoon. At 0832 comes the long-expected word, "First wave has hit the beach!" Waves 2 and 3 are on the reef, 5 and 6 take off from Line of Departure; others are forming up as far as you can view to seaward.

As *Tennessee* winds ship, in order to give her starboard secondary battery a chance to shoot, the first signs of enemy opposition appear. A plume of white water rises up between her and the beach, and then another, fortunately in spots not covered by landing craft. A mortar battery on the bluffs of the Bisha River tries to get the range but never makes a hit. Boat waves are now composed of LCVP, whose troops will have to be transferred to retracting LVT in order to cross the reef. Then comes the 7th wave, one of a very different composition: 17 LCM landing craft for the Orange beaches, six of the 200-foot landing ships medium (LSM) for the Purple. These LSM, little brothers to the LST, are built more like a ship than their elders. They are camouflaged in great blobs of green, yellow and brown paint, which light up to a modernist fantasy of color when seen in echelon; yet there is something curiously medieval about them. Nearly amidships rises a tall, cylindrical pilothouse with round ports like the turret of a castle, and the numerous alidades, peloruses and other gadgets which crown the turret have the effect of battlements protecting the helmeted sailors. Could our designers have consulted the famous tapestry at Bayeux depicting another successful invasion? Can it be a coincidence that the control craft for Purple 1 is numbered 1066? As the LSM formation passes, bow gates are already open, ready to disgorge the newest variety of amphibious vehicle, known as the "Tare-6, Swimming Tank," a medium Sherman tank supported by pontoons. Nine centuries of warfare and military architecture seem to come to a focus off the beaches of Okinawa.

Calmly proceed the LSMs, as enemy mortars drop another sequence of shells. Some fall perilously near *LSM–87*, but she does not concede an inch and is not hit. About a dozen LVT(A) are firing at this mortar battery from the water with their 75-mm guns, and presently silence it forever.

Nine o'clock. The sun has burned away the mist, disclosing an almost solid mass of transports to seaward, beaches swarming with amphtracs and men, troops moving through cornfields toward the tableland, an inexhaustible supply of landing craft forming waves, boats of the earlier waves beginning to retract. Now the medieval-and-modern LSMs pass again as on parade, having shed their floating tanks, and a spotting plane radios that our troops are already several hundred yards inland. Tanks can be seen swarming up the slope, orange and purple beach markers are clearly visible, landing craft bearing bulldozers and cranes pass; one labeled PRESS in large white letters darts by, bearing delighted correspondents who are going to "see it all," complete with typewriters to tap out the story. Wind and sea have made up; no whitecaps yet but enough chop so that landing craft pitch and throw spray.

At 0956 word reaches *Tennessee* from the flagship that the Marines in the northern sector are now on the edge of Yontan airfield, and have suffered no casualties.

Never was there a more pleasant surprise. All hands are stunned by the lack of opposition. Where are those 60,000 Japanese? What is wrong with their elaborate installations? Are they sucking us into a pocket, only to open up with a fierce attack later? No one knows the answer. Officers look at each other, smile and shake their heads. The big joke that morning was the word passed by some Corps humorist: "The Marines are going so fast that they have already contacted the Russians coming up the other side!"

Ten o'clock. *Tennessee's* shore fire control party is already in touch with her, but the troops fan out so fast that they have to break off. The battleship follows the word of her spotting plane by firing on several objects which to the pilot seem to be military installations – more likely they are family tombs. She then checks fire and nothing is heard for several moments but the drone of landing craft motors. My own rough count of landing craft within sight yields the incredible figure of 700.

At 1011, after two LCVP waves (the 17th and 18th) laden with regimental reserves have passed, *Tennessee* reopens fire. Shore fire control party offers no target, so she delivers deep support fire as spotted by her own planes. By 1035 assault troops have reached the edge of Kadena airfield. One can see with the naked eye the UDTs wading along the outer line of reef, now lifting above the ebbing tide, looking for likely places to blast a channel. At 1200 a message comes through that Kadena and Yontan airfields are already in our hands. In the operation plan, we were not supposed to capture them until L-day plus 3!

Throughout the afternoon unloading goes on without impediment from the enemy. A simple but effective scheme is employed to prevent landing craft being stranded by the falling tide. A salvage LCM fitted with extra towing gear is stationed off each beach. Whenever a landing craft coxswain is unable to retract with his own power, he calls for the salvage LCM, which yanks the craft off before it becomes hopelessly stranded.

Around 1345 Admiral Hall's aërologist predicts heavy surf for the afternoon of L-day plus 1, 2 April, a forecast which happily was not fulfilled. But, in anticipation of foul weather next day, Commander Southern Attack Force puts the heat on transport skippers, warning them to land "hot" cargo at once, and to stand in closer to the beach.

Throughout the afternoon the absence of opposition continues to astound sailors and soldiers alike. No enemy aircraft are sighted until dusk. The enemy behind the southern beaches offers but a few bursts of mortar fire, with some light artillery fire laid down on the right flank. On the northern beaches, nothing. Our aircraft can locate no troop concentrations; advancing troops meet only scattered snipers, and find a few enemy tanks in a cave. In the northern sector the Marines encounter only 15 Japanese soldiers, but they round up 675 Okinawa civilians, mostly old people and children, to be removed to a place of safety.

At 1400 Admiral Turner gives the order for general unloading which continues all night. There is a suppressed note of triumph in the laconic summary that he sends to Admirals Spruance and Nimitz at 1600 April 1: "Landings on all beaches continued, with good progress inland against light opposition. Beachhead has been secured. . . . Approximately 50,000 troops have landed over beaches. . . . 420th Field Artillery Group with two battalions 155-mm guns on Keise Shima in support ground troops. . . . Unloading supplies over Hagushi beaches commenced, using LVTs, dukws, LSMs and LSTs."

Retirement of all fire support ships, and of all but six transports with screen, begins in late afternoon. At that moment a few kamikazes come in. *West Virginia* was crashed at 1913, killing four men, wounding 23 and wrecking the galley and laundry, but leaving the ship fully operational. Fortunate indeed for the crowded amphibious forces that the depredations of TF 58 planes in March prevented any massed kamikaze attack on L-day, or until 6 April.

Rear Admiral Jerauld Wright's force, which simulated a landing on the south coast, received more attention from enemy air forces on L-day than did the real landings.[7] At 0549, while this demonstration group maneuvered for final approach, a kamikaze crashed the port quarter of *LST-884*, with 300 Marines on board. The LST burst into flames, ammunition exploded, and she had to be abandoned temporarily; but a fire and rescue party from *Van Valkenburgh* boarded her, and with the aid of hoses from four LCSs had the fire out by 1100. Twenty-four sailors and Marines were killed and 21 wounded. Another kamikaze managed to hole

[7] CTG 51.2 (Rear Adm. Wright) Action Report of Demonstration Group, 15 Apr. 1945; LSM Flot 5 (Cdr. W. H. Carpenter) Action Report 3 Apr. 1945.

transport *Hinsdale* in three different places, resulting in complete loss of power, 16 killed, and 39 wounded. Fleet tugs from Kerama Retto, *Yuma* and *ATR–80*, towed the stricken ships to safety.

The demonstration landings, which were repeated next day, did not deceive the enemy, but gave him the opportunity to claim that "Jerry" Wright and his men were "forced to withdraw . . . after being mowed down one after the other."

CHAPTER X

"Iceberg" Logistics[1]

March–June 1945

1. *The Logistic Support Group*

TO MOUNT so distant an operation, at a moment when the European war reached its final crisis, and supplies of every sort were being rushed to General Eisenhower's immense army groups, and when the Philippines were not yet completely liberated, required fresh efforts in American war production and logistic supply.

Even more troops had to be provided for an invasion of Okinawa than for the capture of Leyte, and they were poured into the Ryukyus much more quickly than they had been in the Philippines. Methods and procedures had been given a good test, and the command structure was simpler. Logistic plans have to be based on the organization and command relations of the forces to be supported and the forces rendering support.[2] When Admiral Nimitz moved to Guam in 1945 with part of his staff, he left the large Service Force Pacific staff, including Service Squadron 8 (Commodore Augustine Gray's oiler outfit), at Pearl Harbor.

Logistics planning for a big operation in the western Pacific began at Pearl Harbor well before the ice of Operation ICEBERG began

[1] Com Servron 6 (Rear Admiral D. B. Beary) War Diaries for 1945 and "Logistic Analysis Okinawa Operation" 31 May 1945; W. R. Carter *Beans, Bullets and Black Oil* chs. xxv–xxviii; Henry E. Eccles *Operational Naval Logistics* (published by Bupers 1950), "Pacific Logistics" (lecture at Naval War College 30 March 1946) and presentation of subject at Joint Army-Navy Staff College same month; also many conversations with him since his retirement as Rear Admiral.

[2] Eccles *Operational Naval Logistics* p. 32.

to freeze. In the late summer of 1944 Admiral Nimitz issued a general planning directive which started the ball rolling toward Iwo Jima and Okinawa. Around October the staffs of the assault and type commanders made preliminary plans which later became reconciled at a series of conferences at Schofield Barracks, Oahu, with Brigadier General Bertram Hayford USA, head of the logistics division of planning staff Pacific Ocean areas. In these conferences, which lasted through Christmas week, the major gears of the vast machine were meshed, and the staffs concerned were able to do most of the time-consuming paper work before the ICEBERG directive was issued.

Admiral Royal E. Ingersoll,[3] relieved as Cinclant on 15 November 1944, was then appointed Commander Western Sea Frontier. Admiral King felt that an officer of high rank and experience was needed to control the flow of logistic support and personnel into West Coast ports and the Pacific Ocean. Admiral Ingersoll was given ample authority to do that through two additional commands: Deputy Cominch under Admiral King, and Deputy Cincpac under his Annapolis classmate Admiral Nimitz.

At a logistics conference between Admiral Ingersoll's representatives and Service Force Pacific Fleet at Pearl Harbor on 22 February 1945, the keynote for the Okinawa operation was struck: "Every available facility on the West Coast should be prepared to operate at the maximum capacity."

A special problem for the Navy was the logistic support of the growing number of B-29s of the Strategic Air Force based at Tinian and Guam. Each of these Superfortresses flew an average of eight missions per month; each mission consumed 6400 gallons of aviation gasoline, and required eight tons of bombs. All this, together with "housekeeping" supplies for the ground crew, the Navy had to bring out to the Marianas bases. Combat Readiness section of Cincpac-Cincpoa staff estimated in June 1945 that over 100 ships were employed supporting the Superforts.[4]

[3] Brief biog. in Vol. I 206*n*; portrait is frontispiece Vol. X.
[4] Figures then obtained from Capt. E. M. Eller.

As in the Iwo campaign, all oilers and other auxiliaries that fed the Fleet in the battle area were placed under the operational command of Rear Admiral Donald B. Beary, Commander Service Squadron 6.[5] This Logistic Support Group, designated TG 50.8, had the mission "To furnish direct logistic support at sea to the Fifth Fleet in and near the combat zone, in order to maintain mobility and striking power." [6]

Beetle-browed Commodore Gray, "the oil king of the Pacific," had to provide for an estimated monthly consumption of over six million barrels of fuel oil, which had to be met by commercial tankers bringing oil from the West Coast to Ulithi. There a floating storage of 100,000 barrels was maintained and a shuttle service of 40 fleet tankers operated between it and the Ryukyus. In addition, there would be 900,000 barrels of reserve fuel, divided among Saipan, Guam, and Kwajalein, and a 5,000,000-barrel reserve at Pearl Harbor. During the three weeks 4–24 April, the peak of this operation, a daily average of 167,000 barrels of fuel oil and 385,000 gallons of avgas were issued to Fifth Fleet. The cumulative issue through 27 May was 8,745,000 barrels fuel oil, 259,000 gallons diesel oil and 21,477,000 gallons avgas.[7]

Four escort carriers converted for plane transport [8] were employed to bring replacement planes from Ulithi and Guam for all three classes of carriers; 17 more shuttled carrier planes between

[5] Donald B. Beary, b. Montana 1888, Naval Academy '10. Served in *Tennessee*, *Washington* and *Maryland;* M.S. Columbia 1917; C.O. *Remlik* and *Lamson* in World War I. Service in Bunav; C.O. *Talbot*, *Parrott* and *Sumner* 1921–23. Service in fleet training div. C.N.O. to 1925, navigator *New Mexico* to 1928. Instructor in electrical engineering Naval Academy to 1931. Assistant chief of staff to C. in C. Asiatic Fleet to 1934; fleet maintenance div. C.N.O. to 1936; senior course Naval War College; exec. *Colorado* 1937; C.O. *Richmond* 1938; duty at Naval Academy 1939–41, when became C.O. *Mount Vernon* (see Vol. I, 110–112). Com N.O.B. Iceland 1942–43, Com Atlantic Fleet operational training 1943; Comservron 6 from Nov. 1944. After V–J Day, as head of U.S. shipping control for Japanese merchant marine, took charge of repatriating several million Japanese troops. Com Twelve and Westseafron 1946; President Naval War College 1948; retired 1950.

[6] Rear Adm. Beary Op Plan 2–45, 9 Mar. 1945.

[7] Beary "Logistic Analysis" pp. 3–6. An oil barrel holds 42 gallons.

[8] Sometimes designated CVET, but this was not official. On return passages the CVETs carried 212 "flyable duds" back to the West Coast. In addition, TF 57, the Royal Navy carrier force, had five replenishment escort carriers in its logistics group.

West Coast and forward bases, just as the merchant tankers did with petroleum products; four CVEs brought up air units to be based on Okinawan airfields, and two constantly kept C.A.P. over the oilers. Altogether, 854 replacement planes and 207 pilots and crew members were issued to the Fleet at sea between 14 March and 27 May. The transport CVEs supplied aëronautical spare parts, including 3000 belly tanks, as best they could; but the enormous number of different items required, about 10,000 on a large carrier, made that service unusually difficult. Spare aircraft engines (weight 3500 pounds) and even jeeps to run on a carrier's deck, were transferred at sea by ammunition ship *Lassen*.

Fueling and provisioning at sea by now were an old story. Fueling was done by hose, but everything else had to be transferred on a line; and the principal limitation was a critical shortage of 3½- and 4-inch manila; for until the Philippines were liberated, manila line would not be back in production. Even so, the Logistic Support Group once managed to transfer 64,000 tons of cargo to Task Force 38 at sea in two days' time – which was more than the stevedores of a port like Boston then handled in a week.

Ammunition replenishment at sea had begun in the Iwo operation, and now two more floating services were added by Servron 6. Navy cargo vessel *Mercury* became a mobile general stores issue ship, a sort of floating variety store. In two days' time she delivered at sea to Rear Admiral Clark's carrier group 168 tons of dry and 84½ tons of fresh-frozen provisions, together with large quantities of general and miscellaneous stores. Among items delivered by *Mercury* at sea off Okinawa were uniform clothing and life jackets, blankets and steel helmets; signal flags, ship chandlery and electronics, rags, toilet paper, candy and cigarettes; copper tubing, valves, acetylene gas, chinaware, cooking utensils, gun sights and cartridges for line-throwing guns. *Mercury* also had refrigeration space for a limited amount of fresh and frozen foods, which were in such demand as to be all gone by the end of March, except for a few crates of apples and oranges. "Reefer" *Aldebaran*, a fresh-frozen provision ship, dispensed a chilled and frozen cargo at

Ulithi early in March and returned to San Francisco for more. *Virgo* helped by coming out with general stores, clothing and electronics. She also carried five civilian radar engineers, representing the major factories of that equipment, to service ships' radar. Thus, as Admiral Beary wrote, "This full logistic support of ships at sea wonderfully extended the endurance of the Fleet."

His Logistic Support Group (TG 50.8 or Servron 6) was organized at Ulithi in March into two replenishment units, comprising oilers, ammunition ships, provision ships and screen; a salvage unit of fleet tugs, and two carrier transport units of three CVETs each. Admiral Beary now had a suitable fast flagship, light cruiser *Detroit,* with sufficient space and communications for the complicated work that he and his staff had to perform. She led about 45 ships out of Ulithi on 13 March, ahead of the fast carriers, and proceeded to lat. 19°50′ N, long. 137°40′ E where all four carrier groups were replenished on 16 March. Two days later, when word came of the severe blow to carrier *Franklin,* four fleet tugs and two destroyers were dispatched to her aid, and assisted in saving her. All four carrier groups were again fueled on 23 March around lat. 22°23′ N, long. 131°38′ E. Floating mines were sighted almost daily, seven being destroyed on 22 March alone. No firm submarine contact was made until 14 May, when fleet tug *Sioux* destroyed a *kaiten* ("human torpedo") by 40-mm gunfire at lat. 23°43′ N, long. 132°07′ E.[9]

From 24 March, TG 50.8 remained within an ocean area comprised between lats. 22° and 24° N, longs. 128° and 132° E. This was about three days' steaming from Ulithi and less than two from Okinawa. Sometimes a fast carrier group closed for fueling, but usually a couple of oilers with screen were detached to seek out the thirsty ships. In either case the *ad hoc* fueling and service group was formed the previous evening and deployment completed at daybreak, so that the ships were ready to pass a line or a "tit" as soon as light permitted, and to finish early. Every few days empty oilers

[9] This may have been launched by *I-47,* which according to Capt. Ohmae's notes on Japanese submarine action reports, was then patrolling in the vicinity.

were sent back to Ulithi and full ones arrived. The weather became dirty on the 31st and all ships water-ballasted and battened down. Between 26 March and 1 April three oilers with escorts were sent into Kerama Retto, and at short intervals other units were sent there or to the Hagushi beaches; for TG 50.8 was taking care of Admiral Turner's amphibious force as well as Admiral Mitscher's fast carriers. For a time two full oilers were required at Okinawa every three days.

On 1 April Admiral Durgin's escort carriers, having borne the burden of close support and patrol during the first week of the Okinawa operation, were in need of replacement planes. Ferry pilots were brought up from a rear area in destroyer *Helm* and transferred to CVE *Windham Bay* at about lat. 23° N, long. 132° E. They then manned 13 replacement planes and took off for Kerama Retto. Hospital ship *Bountiful*, on account of her illumination, operated about 75 to 100 miles from TG 50.8, but occasionally was ordered by airplane message drop to rendezvous and receive patients from a fast carrier.

Every other fleet auxiliary service was strained to the utmost. Servron 10 (Commodore Worrall R. Carter) sent a selection of all classes of salvage and repair vessels to Kerama Retto, leaving the majority at Ulithi or Guam until 20 May when he moved most of them to Leyte. These ships rendered essential services to ships damaged by enemy air attack, and saved many of them from being sent to mainland yards for repairs.

As wells on Okinawa were supposed to be contaminated (an assumption which proved to be correct), troops ashore had to be provided with fresh water until the Army could set up distilling units. The exceptionally large number of beaching craft, gunboats and other small craft with no distilling apparatus on board meant an unprecedented demand. Four fleet oilers converted to water tankers, *Severn*, *Ocklawaha*, *Soubarissen* and *Ponaganset*, with millions of gallons and several H_2O experts on board, were sent out. Two new water boats, *Pasig* and *Abatan*, with a distilling capacity of 120,000 gallons per diem, were completed in time. But even these were not enough, because Eniwetok, Ulithi and Saipan also had to be provided with fresh water.

The Pacific Fleet fitted out a number of LST, designated LST(H), to receive wounded from the beach and give them treatment before transfer to regular hospital ships. As Okinawa had the reputation of being infested with snakes and all manner of vermin, Service Force obtained from the anti-snakebite laboratory at Calcutta a supply of the right kind of serum to counteract the particular variety of poison packed by Okinawan vipers. And it provided planes to sprinkle the area with DDT mosquito and vermin repellent.

More than 2,700,000 packages of cigarettes and 1,200,000 candy bars were issued between 14 March and 27 May. The oilers were the principal mail carriers; they and other ships in five weeks delivered 24,117,599 letters to ships engaged in the Okinawan operation and units ashore.

A vital factor in the success of Operation ICEBERG was the Navy shipping control system, which after much trial and error nearly reached perfection in 1945. This intricate network, starting at Washington and extending through Admirals Ingersoll, Nimitz and Spruance to the port directors at Eniwetok, Guam, Saipan, Ulithi and Okinawa, finally brought a close relationship between call-up and flow of resupply shipping, and beach unloading capacity in the combat area. Commander John Huntington, a key man in planning and operating this system, did an outstanding job, working from a converted LCI(L) as Port Director Okinawa. He and his group received a handsome tribute from Admiral Hall for their efficient work in shipping control, as well as hearty thanks for taking that onerous duty off the hands of the attack force commanders' staffs.[10]

[10] Com 'Phib Grp 12 (Rear Adm. Hall) Action Report 31 July 1945 p. (V) (G) 2. Unfortunately the lessons here learned were largely forgotten by both Army and Navy tactical commanders in the Korean War, leading to as bad a foul-up of shipping in 1950 as had happened in 1942–44. Letter of Rear Adm. Eccles 5 Jan. 1960.

2. *The Provisions Problem*

As in earlier operations, the Navy supplied fresh provisions for Army, Navy and Marine Corps, afloat or ashore, and dry provisions for these arms when afloat; the Army furnished dry provisions to all service personnel ashore.

Besides *Mercury* and *Aldebaran*, which belonged to TG 50.8, there were scores of provisions and general stores issue ships servicing the ships and men in this operation. First came the "reefers," carrying fresh and frozen provisions. On 1 March nine of these were issuing foodstuffs to combatant ships about to sail for Okinawa, at the Solomons, Ulithi, Leyte, the Marianas and Espiritu Santo. By 1 April they were loading or undergoing upkeep at Auckland or Pearl Harbor. On 1 May five of the new *Adria* class of reefers, loaded at Mobile, were beginning to discharge initial cargos in forward bases. *Bald Eagle* (a C-2) and *Antigua* (a converted banana boat), loaded respectively at San Francisco and Seattle, and three chartered Grace liners, were discharging provisions in the Marianas, and a fourth was doing the same at Ulithi. By 29 May all four vessels were on their way east, and six others, loaded in New Zealand, San Francisco and Norfolk, were also discharging at Guam and Saipan. Three of the *Adria* class with cargos from Mobile and Pearl Harbor were at Kerama Retto, and a merchant ship, San Francisco loaded, at Leyte.

There were good reasons for this tremendous movement of provisions to the Marianas. First, there were over 200,000 men of Army, Navy and Marine Corps ashore on Saipan, Tinian and Guam in January 1945 (and over 100,000 more by March),[11] and about 50,000 more men in ships in the harbors, who had to be fed. Second, although New Zealand furnished the Navy with large quantities of provisions, these were mostly fresh meat, so that ships which loaded "down under" were not prepared for fleet issue. They had to discharge into warehouses at Guam and reload with

[11] Cincpac Personnel Summary 14 Aug. 1945.

a balanced cargo for the ships. So as soon as a sufficient number of refrigerated warehouses had been constructed at Apra, Guam became the entrepot for fresh and frozen provisions for the Pacific Fleet. A shuttle service of reefers there took on balanced loads to be issued to TF 58, or at Kerama Retto, and in Japanese home waters after the surrender.

For issue of dry provisions, the Service Force had thirteen Navy cargo vessels and a number of War Shipping Administration ships, mostly of the C–1 type. By mid-March it was evident that too many WSA ships had been accepted. Certain loads already ordered were canceled, others were discharged into warehouses at Pearl Harbor, and five were offered to General MacArthur and Seventh Fleet. In spite of these diversions there was still an excess of dry provisions in forward areas all through the Okinawa operation. On 1 April, 15 dry provision ships were riding at anchor in Ulithi lagoon, doing very little business. *Azimech* and *Matar* were sent on to Kerama Retto, three others to Saipan and Guam, and ten went up to Leyte around 20 May, when Commodore Carter shifted base thither for his Service Squadron 10.[12] Yet *Ascella*, which arrived Ulithi 25 February, was still there 13 June. This long detention put Service Force "in the doghouse" with War Shipping Administration. It had indeed borrowed too many ships; but beyond its control were the main factors in this overestimate: –

(1) The Navy did much better in furnishing fresh provisions

[12] *Dry Provisions on Hand and Issued, in Units of 1000 rations, 1 Jan. to 1 June 1945*

On hand 1 Jan. in fleet issue ships, Central Pacific	3,130
Arrivals, 1 Jan. – 31 May, in 57 different ships	118,130
Total available	121,260
Issued, 1 Jan. – 31 May	55,760
On hand, 1 June	65,500

Fresh and Frozen Provisions Issued

Deliveries by 34 different reefers in forward area, in net tons, by month, 1945: –

January	18,150	April	28,500
February	17,050	May	35,200
March	23,550		

Data furnished by Provision and Supply Section of Servron 8 at Guam, June 1945.

than had been anticipated, and ships will seldom take dry when they can get fresh. (2) About one hundred ships which were sunk in the operation or returned to the West Coast for repairs, no longer had to be fed by Service Force Pacific Fleet.

3. *Ammunition — and Conclusion* [13]

Replenishment ammunition for a campaign over 4000 miles from Pearl Harbor and 6200 miles from San Francisco, respectively 17 and 26 days' steaming at 10 knots, was a problem that the Combat Readiness Section of Cincpac, the "Fun and Gun boys" headed by Captain Tom B. Hill, solved with their habitual cheerfulness. At least three times the amount used to reduce the Marianas had to be initially provided; and this estimate, based on consumption at Iwo Jima, was slightly exceeded before Okinawa was secured. Shortages developed of certain items for a few days, but none serious enough to affect gunfire support. The supply of reduced charges for 8-inch bombardment shells at one time became critical, but it did not run out.[14]

Replenishment at sea of the fast carrier forces by regular ammunition ships was much more extensively practiced than off Iwo, where this system was inaugurated. The carrier groups replenished while they refueled; one carrier while waiting to go alongside an oiler would close *Shasta*, *Wrangell* or one of the other AEs in TG 50.8, and take on ammunition by slings while she waited her turn to fuel.

The ships of TF 51 replenished in Kerama roadstead or off the Hagushi beaches by a new system. Victory ships converted to am-

[13] Data from Capt. Hill, Capt. E. M. Eller and Cdr. S. M. Archer, 1945.

[14] Beginning in the fall of 1944, conversion of the fire control system of heavy cruisers to accommodate charges of 2160 foot-seconds was started, as this reduced charge is better for close range bombardment and gives only one-sixth to one-seventh of wear on the gun as compared with the regular service powder charge of 2500 foot-seconds. Only one or two of the heavy cruisers were thus converted in time for Iwo, but all were ready for Okinawa. Reduced charges were not used for the light cruisers as their 6-inch guns wore so well as not to need them.

munition carriers brought powder, projectiles, bombs, demolition and pyrotechnics for the ground forces from the West Coast directly to Kerama Retto. There two of them, *Hobbs Victory* and *Logan Victory*, were sunk by kamikazes. This misfortune, together with unexpectedly heavy expenditure by the ground forces, caused a shortage of white phosphorus and 81-mm mortar shells. About 400 tons of the latter had to be flown up by plane from Guam. One or two converted Victory ships attended the fast carrier groups; but most of them discharged at Ulithi, Leyte or the Marianas into LSTs. Nine LST ammunition ships were used, and "type loaded"; i.e., they carried only ammunition used by one type of ship such as a cruiser or destroyer. With two hatches and a caterpillar crane working, these LSTs proved to be very quick and efficient at replenishment.

The following table of ammunition expenditures of 5-inch and upward during the Okinawa operation to 21 June, in round numbers, was furnished by Vice Admiral Hill when he took over the command of V Amphibious Force from Admiral Turner.[15]

OKINAWA OPERATION AMMUNITION EXPENDITURE IN ROUNDS

	Before 2 Apr.	*2–30 Apr.*	*1–10 May*	*10–20 May*	*Total through 20 May*	*On hand Kerama or en route 20 May*	*Expended 17 May–21 June*[17]
16" HC	1,500[16]	1,000[16]	400	800	3,700	2,000	510
14" HC	4,600	5,500	1,800	650	12,550	5,200	4,300
12" HC	750	1,600	350	0	2,700	0	0
8" HC	5,800	11,000	4,300	4,700	25,800	12,900	7,050
6" HC	7,200	18,000	6,400	5,100	36,700	19,000	11,650
5" 51 HC	5,000	9,000	2,000	1,600	17,600	11,500	2,000
5" 38 AAC	50,000	115,000	40,000	42,000	247,000	100,000	99,525
5" 38 Star	1,500	18,000	6,000	6,000	31,500	12,800	13,150
5" 25 AAC	9,000	27,000	9,000	11,100	56,100	20,000	14,925
5" 25 Star	500	8,870	3,000	3,200	15,570	6,000	4,500
EQUIVALENT IN TONS	7,417	11,870	4,052	3,651	26,990		

In addition to the above, ammunition ships issued to TF 58 at sea 77,582 5-inch 38 projectiles, 34,773 5-inch rockets, 19,297 500 pound General Purpose aircraft bombs, 18,579 100-lb G.P. bombs

[15] Com V 'Phib Speedletter to Cincpac 23 May 1945.
[16] Not including 16" fired by TF 58.
[17] This column from CTF 51 (Vice Adm. Hill) Action Report 4 July p. (V)-4

3671 250-pound G.P. aircraft bombs, 798 G.P., A.P. and S.A.P. bombs from 500 to 2000 pounds, 83 torpedoes and 810 depth charges.[18]

The five ammunition ships regularly employed with TG 50.8 issued at sea 15,169 tons of ammunition between 22 March and 27 May, a daily average of 143 tons; *Wrangell* on her top day dispensed 460 tons.[19] Their average turnaround period was 20 days. Transfer at sea offered no difficulties aside from the shortage of manila; trouble came from a different source. When one of these ships, carrying 150 different items of powder and bullets, was about half discharged, her load became unbalanced from the issue point of view; she could no longer furnish all ammunition requirements of a capital ship. In port under similar circumstances a ship would "shop around" until she got what she wanted, but you couldn't shop around on the high seas. Nor was it safe to consolidate cargos in the open ocean.

As an experiment, *Shasta*, after her load had become too unbalanced to be useful to TF 58, was sent to Kerama roadstead to dispose of "remnants"; but this so reduced her availability to the fast carriers that it was not repeated.

A comparative table of annual ammunition expenditure by heavy cruiser *Salt Lake City*, which had been dishing it out in the Pacific since early in the war, illuminates the amount and kinds of shooting that took place around Okinawa. Yet her 1945 expenditures in this table are through 5 May only, and were exceeded by the end of the Okinawa campaign.

AMMUNITION EXPENDITURE IN ACTION BY U.S.S. *Salt Lake City, 1942–1945*[20]

	8" AP	*8" HC*	*5" AAC*	*5" VT*	*5" Star*
1942	862	0	580	0	205
1943	1,031	711	483	118	100
1944	112	3,985	2,109	0	0
1945 1 Jan–5 May	32	10,613	8,478	79	1,756
TOTAL	2,037	15,309	11,650	197	2,061

[18] Beary "Logistic Analysis" p. 8.

[19] Same; the other AEs were *Shasta, Lassen, Mauna Loa* and *Vesuvius*. *Firedrake* issued rockets to the amount of 252 tons.

[20] Rear Admiral Allan E. Smith Action Report 26 May 1945.

The logistics aspect of the Okinawa operation was the most remarkable experiment ever tried of supplying a fleet at sea many thousands of miles from base. Admiral Beary, Commodore "Nick" Carter, Commodore "Gus" Gray and Vice Admiral W. W. ("Poco") Smith, who relieved Vice Admiral William L. ("Uncle Bill") Calhoun at the beginning of this operation as Commander Service Force Pacific Fleet, deserve the highest credit for so notably contributing to this capture of an important corner of the Japanese Empire. All regarded it only as a beginning, not a perfected system. As Admiral Beary modestly remarked in his Logistic Analysis of 31 May: –

"Many important requirements could not be completely supplied, but experience in the Okinawa operation has conclusively proved that full logistic support of a fleet at sea is entirely practicable, provided operations are being conducted in an area where reasonably satisfactory weather and sea conditions will be experienced."

Among the many tributes to Servron 10, that of Captain John B. Heffernan, C.O. of battleship *Tennessee*, stands out: – [21]

The *Tennessee* has been receiving supply services from Service Squadron 10 for more than fifteen months. The expansion and improvement in supply services during this period of time has been phenomenal, and has amazed experienced supply officers who understand the difficulties which had to be overcome. The actual achievement is indisputable evidence of the tireless energy, unceasing perseverance, and truly coöperative spirit of Commodore Worrall R. Carter, his hardworking staff, and the splendid personnel serving under him. Service Squadron 10 has labored under difficult climatic, living, and working conditions, without the compensation or personal satisfaction of combatant action, and in areas where typhoon danger was always present. Notwithstanding the difficulties inherent in their organization and situation, they have overcome the problems of communications; storage in large numbers of ships, barges, etc.; transportation between their wide-spread storage bottoms and the ships to be supplied; transportation from distant harbors and depots. Today their actual supply service compares very favorably with the service obtained from an efficient supply activity on shore in the continental United States. Their spirit of service and their help-

[21] Letter to Com Fifth Fleet 29 May 1945.

ful attitude is second to none. They made every conceivable effort to fill this ship to capacity, and they managed to "top-off" the ship in every instance when so requested.

The battle damage incurred on 12 April 1945, especially the damage to the after main battery director, was such that one competent and experienced maintenance officer who visited the ship expressed the opinion that she should go to a Navy yard. Commodore Carter, and Captain P. D. Gold, declared that Service Squadron 10 could do all the work, with some help from our ship's company, and the work was done in a most satisfactory manner, . . . thereby returning *Tennessee* to active combat duty with a minimum loss of time. Furthermore, these repairs were made while the ship was replenishing ammunition, supplies, fuel, etc., and carrying on routine upkeep.

Admiral Beary's group, while acting as mobile supply station in the open ocean about 200 miles south of Okinawa, was hardly ever attacked. Fleet ocean tug *Sioux*, as we have seen, destroyed a "human torpedo" that challenged her, and oiler *Taluga* "knocked down a Japanese plane with her bridge," as her action report humorously put it, but was promptly repaired and returned to duty. Admiral Clark, in his first action report for this operation, wrote, "the services received from CTG 50.8 were most excellent," and marked "a definite step forward in Fleet operations." They enabled the Fast Carrier Force to keep the sea for a period of over two months.

On 24 May Admiral Beary and staff held a conference with Admiral Halsey on board battleship *Missouri* at lat. 23°40′ N, long. 130°18′ E. Admiral Halsey took over command of the Fleet on the 27th when TF 58 became TF 38 and TG 50.8 became TG 30.8. The same organization was maintained and similar services were rendered.

CHAPTER XI

Feeling Each Other Out[1]

2–5 April 1945

1. *Where Is the Enemy?*

THE ASTOUNDING absence of enemy troops puzzled even Intelligence experts.[2] Some civilians who were interrogated said that the Japanese had withdrawn to the east, others said to the north, still others said to the south. In the amphibious forces it was generally believed that they had intrenched themselves in the rugged northern section of Okinawa.

Even without his hoped-for reinforcements, General Ushijima had about 100,000 troops, including the Okinawa home guard, which was greatly in excess of American Intelligence estimates. He used the tactics already laid down by Imperial General Headquarters for opposing a landing force of superior strength. There was no more wild talk of "annihilating" the enemy on the beach; on the contrary, he is to be allowed "to land in full" and "lured into a position where he cannot receive cover and support from the naval and aërial bombardment," and where the most effective fire power can be brought to bear. His force is then to be "wiped out." [3] These tactics were intelligent in that they gained time and inflicted maximum casualties; but the end product was the same,

[1] Action Reports already noted at head of Chap. IX; R. E. Appleman, James M Burns and others *Okinawa: The Last Battle* (U.S. Army in W. W. II series, 1948) chaps. iv, v; Maj. Charles S. Nichols USMC & Henry I. Shaw *Okinawa: Victory in the Pacific* (a Marine Corps Monograph, 1955), chaps. v–viii.

[2] III 'Phib Corps G–2 Report 1200 Apr. 2.

[3] Battle Instructions of 32nd Japanese Army, Okinawa, 8 Mar. 1945, Cincpac Cincpoa Translations, summarized in Cincpac *Weekly Intelligence* I No. 46 (2[illegible] May 1945) p. 5, and in Deyo "Kamikaze."

extermination of the Japanese garrison and total defeat of Japan. The General originally planned by thorough demolition to deny the Yontan and Kadena airfields to the invaders, but in the hurry of last-minute preparations he neglected this. Both airfields, as well as most of the hills that commanded them, were secured by Tenth Army on L-day. On the 2nd and 3rd, elements of the 7th Infantry Division and the 1st Marine Division reached the east coast. On 4 April the III 'Phib Corps (1st and 6th Marine Divisions) occupied the Katchin Peninsula and a good stretch of the east coast, putting a collar around the dog's neck several miles east of the Ishikawa Isthmus, which they had not expected to reach for twenty days. The Marines then rolled up into the northern half of Okinawa, meeting no serious resistance until they began fanning out into the dog's ear, the Motobu Peninsula.

Airfields were even more important than territorial gains. On 2 April the Kadena strip was operational for emergency landings, and next day two strips of the Yontan field could be used. One of the stories that went the rounds told of an enemy plane landing on the Yontan field the night of 1–2 April. The pilot taxied up to the filling station, hopped out and asked for gas in Japanese. A Marine sentry replied and the Emperor lost one pilot.

South of the Bisha River, in XXIV Corps territory, the 96th Division found stiffening resistance in rugged country on the afternoon of the second day. This resistance, by a rear guard covering the enemy withdrawal, was overcome on the 4th when the Japanese were reported to be falling back on Shuri, the ancient capital east of Naha. "Extensive reconnaissance and photographic flights see no sizable enemy concentrations, but report numerous targets for aircraft and ships," states Admiral Turner's summary at the close of 4 April. That night XXIV Corps was subjected to heavy artillery fire. On the 5th, cold and rainy, the soldiers advanced almost to the lines that they were destined to hold for the next two weeks.

The Allied assault on Okinawa could not have been better timed to hit the Japanese people where it hurt most; for 3 April, the day after they got the news, was Emperor Jimmu Day in Japan. Jimmu, some 2500 years earlier, had inaugurated Japanese expansion with the conquest of Yamato (whose namesake had but five days to live), and announced as his policy "I wish to make the universe our home." The Japanese government now admitted that a beachhead had been established and the situation was serious. Retired Admiral Takahashi pointed out in a broadcast on 2 April that the loss of Okinawa would cut Japan off from her southern conquests; he promised that the Japanese Navy would shortly take the offensive; and Premier Koiso blustered to the Diet that their heroes would drive the Americans off Okinawa, and then "retake Saipan and other points." But the sands were running out for Koiso. In a few days' time he resigned, and the aged Admiral Suzuki, chosen by the Emperor to find some honorable way for Japan to get out of the war, became Premier. Since any peace move would take time and require great circumspection and caution, to avoid a military *coup d'état*, there was no question but that Okinawa would be defended vigorously and to the last man. It is a sad reflection that this costly operation, and everything that followed until 16 August, was unnecessary from any point of view but that of keeping "face" for the military leaders who had started the war.

2. *Unloading* [4]

The Navy's main contribution to this rapid advance in Okinawa was unloading and fire support. The armored amphtracs (LVT-A), which were designed to get artillery ashore with the assault troops, had been used for the first time at Saipan, and had proved indispensable to fill the gap between the landing of assault waves and that of divisional artillery. Placed under the artillery

[4] The Action Reports already mentioned and personal observations. The Report of British Combined Operations liaison officer at Cincpac HQ (Col. G. I. Malcolm British Army) to the chief of his mission at Washington, 18 Apr. 1945, has been particularly valuable, as Col. Malcolm and the other two observers (Cdr. R. K Silcock RN and Grp. Capt. W. G. Tailyour RAF) are old Commando men who went ashore every day to see what went on.

regiment commander of each of the four assault divisions, they were used exactly like land tanks, and in the XXIV Corps area found plenty of targets.

Success in unloading an amphibious operation is dependent on everything both afloat and ashore working according to plan. Ships are combat-loaded with the expectation of so much ammunition, provisions, stores, and heavy equipment being needed at certain hours on definite days. If the enemy pins the attack force to the beach, as at Tarawa and Anzio, unloading gets fouled up; but an almost equal though less unhappy "snafu" occurs when the ground forces are unexpectedly successful and outrun their supplies. That is what happened at Okinawa. LVTs and dukws carrying "hot cargo" had to roll so far inland to reach the troops that their turn-around was delayed, and unloading consequently slowed down. This was particularly true of the northern beaches from which the Marines were distant twenty miles by 6 April. The Marines complained of Navy procedure on these beaches, but the Navy countered with the charge that the "leathernecks" used shore party as replacement troops, and withdrew almost all vehicles from the work of unloading. It made little difference in the end.

There were also difficulties on the southern beaches. LSTs of Captain J. S. Laidlaw's Northern Tractor Flotilla were overloaded with cargo, amphtracs, land tanks, dukws, wheeled vehicles, engineer equipment and naval ammunition. Twenty-nine LSTs carried pontoon barges or causeway sets secured alongside, 16 carried LCTs on their decks, and none of these could be unloaded promptly; vehicles stowed in an LCT, and naval ammunition stowed under them, had to be removed before the landing craft could be launched. LST stowage in this operation was something like those Chinese nests of boxes which must be unpacked in order, or not at all.[5]

Although each LST in the transport area discharged her men and amphtracs in time to land on schedule, the LSTs themselves were delayed coming into the northern beaches until L-day plus 1, when

[5] LST Flot 6 (Capt. Laidlaw) Action Report for Okinawa 1 Mar.–11 Apr.; LST Group 38 (Capt. J. R. Clark) Action Report 10 Apr. 1945.

eleven slots were ready for them on Beaches Blue 1 and Yellow 2. Unloading continued all night from 2 April on, with the aid of lights.

On Admiral Hall's southern group of beaches, below the Bisha River mouth, unloading ran very smoothly, probably because the shore parties there were composed of veterans of the Engineer Special Brigades. The Purple and Orange beaches lay behind made-to-order reefs of a uniform width (about 350 yards) and a smooth hard surface over which wheeled vehicles could run when the reef was bared at half tide. General unloading here began promptly at 1400 L-day. Bulldozers filled up holes in the reef with sand and thus made tracks by which trucks and jeeps could roll ashore from beaching craft. Any day after 3 April, the Orange and Purple beaches were lined solid with LST, LSM and LCT.

In an amphibious operation against a large island, where there must be a steady build-up by successive echelons, unloading never stops unless interrupted by weather or enemy action. On 4 April the north wind increased, a heavy surf built up on the beaches by midnight, all beaching craft that could retracted, and unloading was suspended by Admiral Turner's order. By 0400 April 5, the north wind had reached a velocity of 25 to 35 knots. Some 18 beaching craft were damaged that day, and the following night, by action of the surf. This suspension lasted until 6 April, when the wind changed to the regular NE monsoon and the sea moderated.[6] Admiral Turner sent every ship away as soon as she had discharged; the first departed 5 April. Very few casualties were suffered from enemy air attack in the transport areas and along the beaches. Landing craft crews were well trained, energetic and devoted. There were no complaints of their securing out of sight to "calk-off," or going souvenir hunting ashore. It was an inspiration to see these young boys and the winch crews swinging boats out smartly, and unhooking the lead-weighted welin davit blocks from the ringbolts of craft pitching and rolling alongside. Altogether, this was an operation for the amphibious forces to look back on with pride.

[6] CTF 51 Action Report p. (III)-16-22.

On 5 April, 29 empty attack transports and two LSV departed for Guam and Saipan with suitable escort. Admiral Wright's Demonstration Group had already gone. But several hundred transports, LSTs and smaller craft were left off Hagushi to receive the first serious enemy air attack, on 6 April.

After the 6th, XXIV Corps lines were stabilized for another two weeks. This gave Army engineers a good opportunity to enlarge beach exits, widen roads, and build a four-lane highway parallel to the shore front. The writer, who walked along the Purple and Orange beaches on 9 April when the 27th Division was coming ashore, and who also "thumbed" a series of rides inland, was impressed with the order and cleanliness of XXIV Corps sector.

3. *Retirement and Retaliation*

During the first two nights after L-day, Admiral Turner followed standard amphibious force practice in retiring his transports seaward for the night, in dispositions separate from the fire support ships. Twilight was the kamikazes' favorite hour for self-immolation; one at 1910 April 1 crashed transport *Alpine* about 15 minutes after she had got under way, blew two big holes in her side, killed 16 men and wounded 27. *Achernar*, in a different formation, was both crashed and bombed shortly after midnight, losing five killed and 41 wounded. Both transports discharged the undamaged part of their cargos before retiring for repairs. Transports of the Kerama Retto group were also attacked that night, but suffered no casualties.

Just as the Northern Force was getting under way, some trigger-happy gunner opened up on an imaginary enemy plane. Other ships in the formation commenced firing in the general direction of other ships' tracers or bursts, and the O.T.C. added to the confusion by giving the order "Make Smoke," so for the next half-hour the transports zigzagged under a cloud, in danger of collision as well as of their own gunfire.

Captain John W. McElroy USNR, C.O. of transport *Marathon*, thus described the confusion of that evening: —

For a radius of about fifty miles could be overheard on the voice radio every report made by every radar guard ship in the area of bogies here, there and everywhere. Regardless of whether the information originated five or fifty miles away, every word of this "hot" dope went over the J. A. sound-powered telephones into the ears of every gun crew and lookout. No one ever mentioned that fifty percent of the bogies turned out to be friendlies when interrogated; so the gun crews, like everyone else who was getting the dope, soon had the idea that the sky was full of enemy planes.

Ten minutes after the watch was relieved at midnight, this ship's C.I.C. passed the word "Bogey bearing 180° distant seven miles" — omitting to say that the report came from a radar picket ship about 17 miles away in the other direction. A gun captain, looking along that bearing, saw what he believed to be a low-flying enemy plane in the moonlight and promptly obtained permission to open fire. The skipper, clapping his binoculars on the reputed kamikaze, observed that it had a mast, two stacks and a set of torpedo tubes, dashed to the control station and managed to cancel the impending battle. In the meantime every ship in the column started blazing away. Fortunately nobody managed to hit the destroyer, one of their own screen.[7]

On 2 April the transports, which had reëmbarked part of the 77th Division from Kerama Retto, commenced retirement to a waiting position southward. At 1836, this group, when it had steamed only 16 miles, came under severe attack by ten or more kamikazes. One near-missed Commodore Brittain's flagship *Chilton*. A Nick crashed the bridge of destroyer transport *Dickerson*, killing her skipper, Lieutenant Commander Ralph E. Lounsbury USNR, the exec., Lieutenant A. G. McEwen, and 52 more officers and men, besides seriously wounding 15. She was towed back to Kerama

[7] Capt. McElroy informal "Reaction Report" 10 Apr. and letter to writer 16 Apr. 1945.

after the fires were out, but found unsalvageable, taken out to sea and scuttled.[8] *Goodhue* and *Telfair* of Transdiv 51 were attacked by three planes in rapid succession. One was exploded by gunfire in midair; a second, badly hit, bounced like a billiard ball from hell between the starboard and port kingposts of *Telfair*, hit her port bulwarks and toppled overboard, after killing one man and wounding 16. Next, a Nick headed for *Goodhue's* bridge. Her gunfire deflected its course sufficiently so that it clipped the mainmast at the yardarm and crashed an after 30-ton cargo boom, from which it slid into the after 20-mm gun tubs and finally into the sea. Five soldiers and 19 sailors were killed; 35 soldiers and 84 sailors wounded.

In this same dusk attack on 2 April, at 1838, a Fran came in unseen on *Henrico*, flagship of Transdiv 50, crashed the bridge and released two bombs which exploded. Captain Elmer Kiehl, the division commander; Captain W. C. France, the C.O.; Colonel Vincent Tanzola, commanding the 305th Infantry Regiment; and Colonel L. O. Williams, his exec., were killed, together with 21 other naval officers and men and eleven other Army officers and men. A dozen more sailors and one Marine were missing. The ship survived, but she was out of the war.

L-day plus 2, 3 April, broke beautifully clear for a dawn attack. When the Northern Group transports returned in formation to their anchorage off the Hagushi beaches, breakfast had to wait. In vain master-at-arms threatened that the cooks would "t'row it overboard"; every bluejacket on deck stayed there, hundreds of pairs of eyes scanning the heavens in hungry hope that "just one lousy Nip" would heave in sight. C.A.P. splashed every one that approached, but the ships at Kerama Retto were not so fortunate. There *LST-599*, carrying the gear for a Marine fighter squadron, took an attacking plane under fire at about 0715 and clipped off one wing, but the plane crashed and penetrated her main deck, where

[8] Lt.(jg) J. D. Ebert (gunnery officer and senior survivor) Interview 11 June 1945, Division of Naval History; *N.Y. Times* 12 July 1945.

it exploded and started fires. The Marine squadron lost most of its gear and 21 men were wounded, yet nobody but the kamikaze pilot was killed.[9]

As the big transports hauled in to their unloading stations off the Hagushi beaches they made smoke successfully. Admiral Turner, observing that the improvement of artificial smoking made the ships safer near shore than at sea, canceled night retirement thereafter.

Turner's screening plan for the protection of the expeditionary force in and around Okinawa was unusually comprehensive. He set up (1) a close antisubmarine screen of destroyers around the transport area; (2) a radar countermeasure screen of LCI inside it; (3) an outer antisubmarine screen, running from Motobu Peninsula around Kerama Retto to Abu Saki on the southeast coast; (4) an antimidget "flycatcher" screen, composed largely of LCI covered by a destroyer or light cruiser, patrolling in search of suicide boats, motor torpedo boats and enemy attempts to move troops and supplies by barge; (5) an anti-surface-craft patrol of five destroyer types, covering approaches by which the enemy might attempt a night raid; (6) and most important, the radar picket screen.

This last gave best protection against surprise air attack, and the radar picket stations were the posts of greatest danger. They were disposed around Okinawa at distances of between fifteen and one hundred miles from land, so as to pick up flights of approaching enemy planes and, with the aid of C.A.P., to intercept them. From 26 March on, each station was kept by a destroyer or DMS with a fighter-director team on board. This controlled the C.A.P. which was maintained overhead all day by Admiral Durgin's escort carrier planes. The picket vessel patrolled night and day within 5000 yards of her station, and when bogeys appeared on her radar screen, the fighter-director officer vectored out C.A.P. to intercept. By this means a large proportion of enemy planes approaching Okinawa were shot down before they reached the island, and our forces

[9] *LST–599* (Lt. R. P. Roney) Action Report 6 Apr. 1945.

engaged in landing, unloading or fire support were given timely warning of an air raid. Hundreds of sailors lost their lives and about a score of ships and craft were sunk rendering this service.

After L-day, as soon as the LCI gunboats, LCS support craft and LSM could be spared, Admiral Turner sent two or more of these to support the picket destroyers. They added punch to the anti-aircraft fire and proved a present and courageous help in time of trouble.

There was not much activity at radar picket stations before 3 April. Destroyer *Prichett* on station No. 1, directly north of Point Bolo, was under attack throughout the midwatch and until 0500 April 3. With the aid of a night fighter she splashed two. A bomb exploded under her counter, but the damage was quickly repaired at Kerama Retto. That afternoon *Mannert L. Abele*, a new 2200-ton destroyer, was patrolling radar picket station No. 4, on the northern approach, in company with *LCS–111* and *LCS–114*. The C.A.P. had just departed. The weak spot in air defense during the first ten days at Okinawa, before land-based night fighters were available, came at dusk. Planes could not land or take off from escort carrier decks in the dark, and TF 58 had no night fighters to spare for this service. Hence all picket stations and ships lost their air umbrella at dusk, children's hour for the kamikaze kids. At 1630 two Judys started diving on *Abele*, one after the other, while a third made figure-eights overhead. One was splashed by ship's gunfire; a second, already on fire, skimmed like a flying torch over her fantail and splashed; within a few seconds the third dropped a bomb which missed, and then flew away.[10] *Abele* was not damaged, but she had not much longer to live.

The escort carriers too were attacked on 3 April. *Wake Island* at 1744 picked up five planes on her starboard quarter. Two dived and missed, splashing close aboard, and the explosion of the second ripped a hole 18 by 45 feet in the carrier's side, all below the water-line. Casualties fortunately were not serious, but she had to go to Guam for repairs.

[10] *Mannert L. Abele* (Cdr. A. E. Parker) Action Report.

Wednesday, 4 April, when the weather made up, was relatively free from air attacks. "Be prepared for very heavy attacks by enemy aircraft from Kyushu throughout today," was the ominous opening message from Admiral Turner to his task force on the 5th.

The old formula, by which one could predict the first strong counterattack after an amphibious landing on D-day plus 4, still held good. As we have seen, the Japanese air forces were so depleted and their Kyushu fields so badly hit by the B–29 and TF 58 attacks before L-day that they needed four days before "throwing the book" at us. The kamikazes which had appeared so far were probably based on Okinawa itself or other airfields in the Nansei Shoto.

Rain and overcast on L-day plus 4, 5 April, gave Admiral Turner's ships another day's grace from air attack, but the battleships and cruisers supporting XXIV Corps drew return fire from a coastal battery near Naha. *Salt Lake City* was fired on, and then *Nevada*. At 1740 she took five hits of around 6- to 8-inch caliber, but this tough old battlewagon, which had survived the Pearl Harbor attack, remained operational and lost only two men killed and 16 wounded.[11] The 155-mm Army artillery on Keise Shima apparently silenced this battery, which was not heard from again.

[11] *Nevada* Action Report 19 Apr. 1945.

CHAPTER XII

"Ten-Go" Gets Going[1]

6–8 April

Almanac for 6 April at Okinawa

Last quarter moon rose	0030
Sunrise	0615
Sunset	1849

1. *The Gallant Fight of* Newcomb *and* Leutze

ADMIRAL TOYODA, commanding all Japanese air forces in the East China Sea sector, managed in the first week of April to effect a partial concentration on Kyushu and Formosa and to begin Operation TEN-GO in earnest. The numbers assembled fell short of his plan, which called for a total of 4500 aircraft, but the 699 (355 of them kamikazes) available for 6 and 7 April inflicted a distressing amount of damage. This was the first of ten massed kamikaze attacks to which the Japanese gave the name *kikusui*, "floating chrysanthemums." [2]

The wind on 6 April was NE, force 5 or 6, strong enough to raise whitecaps; the sky overcast, and the temperature unusually low – from 60° to 65°. Nothing happened until the afternoon. Admiral Deyo's fire support ships, as well as those supporting Admiral Blandy's operation off the east coast of Okinawa, were ordered to form up early, perform tactical exercises until dusk, and retire in

[1] CTF 51 (Vice Adm. Turner), CTF 53 (Rear Adm. Reifsnider) and CTF 55 (Rear Adm. Hall) Reports; writer's personal observations from *Tennessee;* MacArthur *Historical Report* II 555–56.

[2] A table of *kikusui* attacks will be found at head of Chap. XV.

company. Around 1635, as Deyo headed his formation toward the beach to pick up *Idaho* and Spruance's flagship *New Mexico*, the battleship sailors had the pleasure of seeing C.A.P. shoot down four planes which had been pursued from over Ie Shima. Up there a general air mêlée was going on, and minesweepers were catching it on the surface. By 1710 the transport area off the Hagushi beaches was ablaze with antiaircraft fire. About five enemy planes got through C.A.P. and four were shot down by ships. The transports' fire discipline was still poor, shooting on such bearings that the flak fell on their sister ships, and bringing friendly planes under fire.[3]

Admiral Deyo's night retirement disposition, still short of four heavy ships and six destroyers which had not got the word, consisted of nine battleships and cruisers steaming in circles respectively of 5000 and 12,000 yards' diameter, with a screen of seven destroyers 4000 yards outside. The disposition turned away towards Ie Shima. At 1753 destroyer *Leutze*, which had already been damaged off Iwo Jima, sighted a plane coming in eight miles distant and at 1800 opened fire. Within a few moments the clear evening air was spotted with black bursts from 5-inch gunfire, almost every ship was spouting red balls from her 40-mm quads, and the water was laced with spray from shorts. About twelve Kates and Oscars came in so low over the water that lookouts saw them before radar did. *Leutze* and *Newcomb* bore the brunt of this attack. In quick succession one kamikaze crashed *Newcomb's* after stack, a second was splashed, and at 1806 a third, carrying a large bomb or torpedo, crashed into her, amidships, gouging deep into the bowels of the ship with a tremendous explosion that cut off all remaining sources of power and blew "both engine rooms and the after fireroom into a mass of rubble." "With intentions of polishing us off," wrote Commander I. E. McMillian, "a fourth plane raced toward *Newcomb* from the port beam and although under fire by her forward batteries came through to crash into the forward stack, spraying the entire amidships section of *Newcomb*, which was a raging con-

[3] CTG 53.7 (Northern Defense Group, Capt. W. W. Weeden) Action Report.

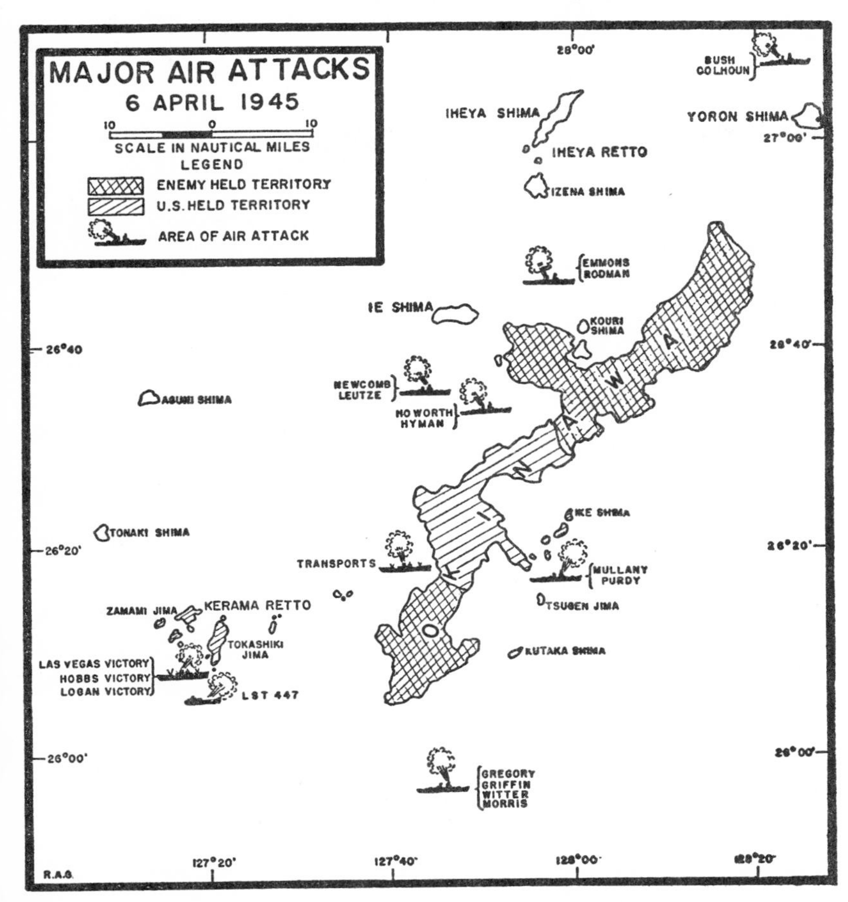

flagration, with a fresh supply of gasoline." [4] Flames shot up hundreds of feet, followed by a thick pall of smoke and spray which so completely covered the destroyer that sailors in nearby battleships (including the present writer) thought that she had gone down.

Destroyer *Leutze*, closing rapidly to render antiaircraft assistance to *Newcomb*, also assumed that she was sinking and swung out boats in preparation for rescue; but when close aboard she observed that McMillian's ship was still holding together. A solid mass of flame swept from bridge to No. 3 gun, but her valiant crew

[4] *Newcomb* Action Report 14 Apr. 1945; one of the best.

showed no intention of abandoning ship. Lieutenant Leon Grabowsky (Naval Academy 1941), C. O. of *Leutze,*[5] gallantly risked his ship to help her sister, closed her weather side at 1811 (only ten minutes after the first crash), passed hose lines on board to help fight fires; and then, at 1815, a fifth plane approached, heading for *Newcomb's* bridge. One of her 5-inch guns, fired in local control, made a hit which tilted the plane just enough so that it slid athwartship and on to *Leutze's* fantail, where it exploded.

Now *Leutze* too was in trouble. A fire sprang up in the after ammunition handling room. While one of her repair parties continued fighting fires on board *Newcomb,* the other two attempted to check flooding on their own ship and jettisoned topside weights. Steering control was lost with the rudder jammed hard right. Seventeen compartments laid open to the sea by the Japanese bomb let in so much water that *Leutze* began to settle. Destroyer *Beale,* with all fire hoses streaming, now closed the disengaged side of *Newcomb;* and not until then did *Leutze* signal "Am pulling away, in serious danger of sinking." At 1842 Lieutenant Grabowsky requested Admiral Deyo's permission to jettison torpedoes and depth charges. After permission had been granted *Leutze* signaled "Believe flooding under control." Minesweeper *Defense* (Lieutenant Commander Gordon Abbott USNR), which had been slightly damaged by two kamikaze hits shortly after 1800, took *Leutze* in tow at 2005. While making her slow way to Kerama Retto *Defense* sent this cocky message: "Sorry to be late, have scratched a kamikaze and taken two on board. Now have destroyer in tow." [6] She arrived off Kerama Retto and cast off her tow at 0230.

Newcomb, one of the "fightingest" destroyers in the Navy (she had led a torpedo attack in Surigao Strait), lost nothing in comparison with *Leutze;* Nelson's accolade to his sailors, "They fought as one man, and that man a hero," could well be applied to her crew.

[5] Her former C.O., Cdr. B. A. Robbins, had been wounded off Iwo Jima.

[6] George L. Batchelder letter of 23 Jan. 1960; *Defense* Action Report 15 Apr. 1945.

The exec., Lieutenant A. G. Capps, after being pulled out from under the tail of a crashed kamikaze, directed the local-control fire of the forward gun and then handled the firefighting; the surgeon, Lieutenant J. J. McNeil USNR, carried several severely injured men to a place of safety, operated on surgical cases in the wardroom in the midst of the uproar, and so continued all the following night; Lieutenant (jg) D. W. Owens USNR "by his personal direction and fearless leadership" quenched a magazine fire. Two out of 78 enlisted men singled out for special commendation in the Action Report may also be mentioned here: fireman Francis J. Nemeth was securing steam lines when burned to death by the spreading fires, and machinist's mate Richard C. Tacey was killed trying to reach some of the black gang who were trapped by the flames. All crews of guns that could shoot fired until they were blown overboard or killed.

Newcomb had all fires under control before fleet tug *Tekesta* towed her, too, into the calm waters of Kerama Retto. One marveled at the sight of them there next morning: scorched, scarred and half wrecked, *Leutze* alongside repair ship *Egeria*, with part of a kamikaze plane still resting on her fantail; *Newcomb* with No. 2 stack gone, No. 1 leaning crazily to starboard, her entire deck abaft the superstructure buckled into the contour of a roller coaster, and her fantail about six inches above the water. *Leutze* had lost only 7 men killed or missing and 34 wounded, but *Newcomb's* casualties were 40 killed or missing and 24 wounded. Both ships had to be beached or dry-docked and there was some question whether they were worth repairing, but repaired they were.

Captain Roland N. Smoot, the squadron commander, paid this tribute to *Leutze* in his endorsement to her Action Report: —

"Without hesitation, and in the face of continuing attacks, raging fires, and the grave possibility of further damaging explosions, she committed herself exclusively to her stricken sister ship until her own serious condition made it necessary to haul clear. Thence she proceeded to save herself against what appeared at first to be hopeless odds. This she accomplished in the most expeditious and effective manner possible."[7]

2. *Radar Pickets Blooded*

Two destroyers fared even worse that afternoon. *Bush* (Commander R. E. Westholm), on radar picket station No. 1, and *Colhoun* (Commander G. R. Wilson), on station No. 2, were the first to be encountered by "floating chrysanthemums" flying southwest along the Nansei Shoto. The ships had been out there since April 1 and 3 respectively, with "seldom a dull moment." Advance elements of the massed air attack heckled them all through the midwatch and *Colhoun* received eleven bombing attacks, all of which missed, between 0230 and 0600 April 6. The forenoon watch was fairly quiet. Around 1500, 40 to 50 planes flew down from the north, stacked at various altitudes between 500 and 20,000 feet, and began orbiting and attacking *Bush,* while about 12 others went after *Cassin Young* (Commander J. W. Artes) at station No. 3, next to the eastward.

Bush shot down two Vals and drove off two more, a few minutes before 1500. Thirteen minutes later a Jill was sighted heading low for her. Commander Westholm promptly swung ship to bring it abeam and unmask his main battery. Fire was opened at a range of 7000 to 8000 yards. The plane jinked and weaved at an altitude of 10 to 35 feet above the water, and although every gun on the destroyer was firing, it kept coming and crashed between the two stacks. The bomb exploded in the forward engine room, killing every man there, and most of those in the two fire rooms. Flooding started immediately and *Bush* took a 10-degree list, but escaping steam smothered the fires and power was regained as the auxiliary diesel generator cut in. Handy-billys were used to control the

[7] Action Reports of both ships; story by S. R. Linscott in *Boston Globe* 6 July 1945.

flooding, the wounded were treated on the fantail or in the wardroom and although the ship had gone dead, everyone expected to save her, and all hands cheered when a C.A.P. of four planes appeared overhead.

Colhoun at 1530, learning by radio that *Bush* was in need of help, began to close at 35 knots, bringing along her C.A.P. for the short time it could remain. The chief fighter-director commander in *Eldorado*, Admiral Turner's flagship, sent out another C.A.P. which encountered so many Japanese planes en route that a general mêlée developed some 15 miles south of *Colhoun's* course. This C.A.P. splashed bandits right and left, but ran out of fuel and ammunition before it could help the destroyers. At 1635 *Colhoun* closed *Bush*, then dead in the water, smoking badly and apparently sinking. She signaled a support craft, *LCS–64*, to rescue the crew and tried to interpose herself between the sinking ship and a flight of about 15 Japanese planes. They approached, and one went for *Bush* at 1700. Commander Westholm ordered about 150 of his men fighting fires topside to jump overboard for self-protection, and trailed knotted lines for them to climb on board again. All his 5-inch guns that would bear were jammed in train, but his 40-mm guns opened fire and frightened one Val away.

Colhoun in the meantime was shooting everything she had at an approaching Zeke, which missed and splashed midway between the two ships. "This left one down, eleven to go," remarked Commander Wilson. Another was hit by a 5-inch shell at 4000 yards, and its port wing caught fire. *Colhoun's* guns Nos. 1, 2 and 3 were quickly trained on a third Zeke diving at her starboard bow, and the first salvo hit him square on the nose; he splashed 50 yards abeam. Just then Wilson received a report that a fourth Zeke was about to crash his port bow. Too late he ordered full left rudder. The plane, already aflame, hit *Colhoun's* main deck, killing the gun crews of two 40-mm mounts. Its bomb exploded in the after fire room, killing everyone there and rupturing the main steamline in the forward engine room. Lieutenant (jg) John A. Kasel, the engineer officer, opened the cross-connection valve before diving for the bilge, so the after engine room had steam and a speed of 15 knots was maintained.

Colhoun was already getting her fires under control (despite loss of all handy-billys) when, at 1717, commenced the fifth attack on her within 15 minutes, by two Vals and a Zeke. The gunnery officer had the presence of mind and found the time to assign target sectors to his five-inch guns. One Val was splashed 200 yards on the port quarter. One missed *Colhoun* and was shot down by fire from *Bush* and *LCS–84*. The third plane crashed the forward fire room, where the bomb exploded, piercing both boilers, blowing a 4-by-20-foot hole below the waterline, and breaking the keel. *Colhoun* went dead in the water; all power and communications were lost. The indefatigable damage control party then applied CO_2 and foamite fire extinguisher. The gunnery officer reëstablished communication with guns 1, 2 and 4 of the main battery. The wounded were treated, fires brought under control; and the men had just begun to get rid of depth charges and torpedoes when at 1725 the sixth attack on *Colhoun* (and fourth on *Bush*) started.

Three planes dove on each bow and one on her quarter. All *Colhoun's* guns were now manned in local control; and it takes such strength and determination to point and train a 5-inch 38 without power, that the strong young bluejackets had to be relieved after two minutes. One Zeke was splashed 150 yards away. The other two were hit by 40-mm fire but only slightly damaged. One, a Val, caught its wing in the after stack, caromed on No. 3 gun, knocking off its gas tank which burst into flames, and then bounced off main deck into the water. There the bomb exploded, knocking a 3-foot-square hole below the water line and so deluging the after part of the ship with water that all fires were extinguished and everyone on the fantail was washed overboard. The third plane missed *Colhoun*, pulled out and started to dive on *Bush* against her 40-mm fire, the best she could now deliver. It missed the bridge, and crashed main deck between the stacks. The impact almost bisected *Bush;* only the keel held her together. Her men already overboard climbed back, the repair party threw water on the fire and

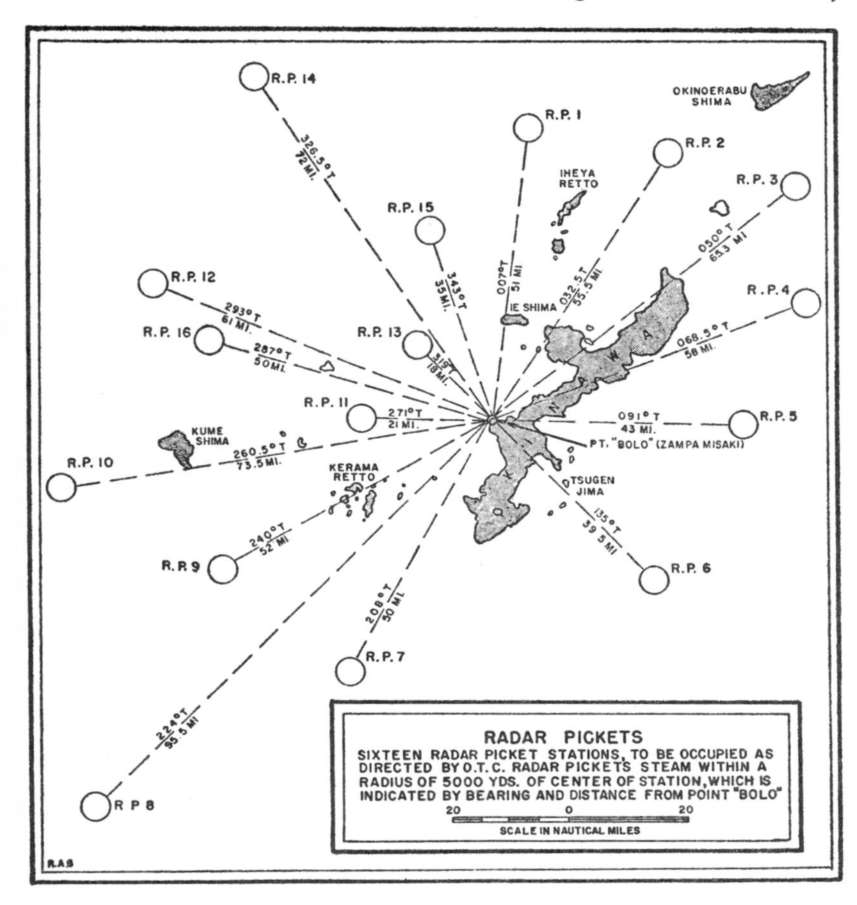

almost had it under control when, at 1740, a fourth plane, a Zeke, made a weaving dive. *Colhoun's* No. 4 fired at it but missed. For the last time the 20-mm and 40-mm guns of *Bush* spoke. The kamikaze cleared her by five feet, gained altitude, did a wingover, came in again, and crashed her port side at 1745, starting a terrible fire and killing or fatally burning all the wounded in the wardroom. A handy-billy, shifted to this fire, was no better than a garden hose on such a blaze; the entire forecastle was enveloped in flames, and ready ammunition began to explode.

Still neither crew would give up its ship. *Colhoun*, with only a bucket brigade operating, was taking water fast, but *Cassin Young* and a tug were coming in to assist. Commander Westholm counted on the fires in *Bush* above the main deck burning themselves out, as his ship was well buttoned up below; and although she could hardly fail to break in two in the heavy sea, he hoped that each half might be salvageable. Shortly before 1800 the bow began to settle. Suddenly a Hamp appeared "out of nowhere" and, evidently deciding that *Bush* was a goner, dived on *Colhoun*. Direct hits were scored on the plane at very close range. Already aflame, it hooked the pilothouse and crashed the port side. *Colhoun* was so badly damaged already that this additional hit did not make things much worse.

By that time daylight had begun to fade. Other Japanese planes were visible, but not another ship was within hailing distance. Damaged *LCS–64*, with many survivors on board, had cleared out. At 1830 a big swell rocked *Bush*. She caved in amidships, jackknifed until bow and stern sections were at a 135-degree angle, and quietly went down in a 350-fathom deep.

Commander Wilson of *Colhoun*, after consulting his exec. and heads of departments, decided to abandon ship. When *Cassin Young* closed at 1900, he begged her to search for *Bush* survivors. *LCS–84*, which also closed, commenced the arduous work of rescuing men in the rough sea. About 200 were transferred to *Cassin Young* between 2015 and 2100. *LCS–87* then came alongside and took over all who remained in *Colhoun* except a skeleton salvage crew of four officers and 17 men. Fires flared up again, and the men ran out of foamite and CO_2. When fleet tug *Pakana* arrived from Kerama Retto at 2320, *Colhoun* was listing 23 degrees and awash up to her No. 4 gun. The tug had no pumps to lend, so Commander Wilson ordered *LCS–87* to take off the skeleton crew, and, at his request, *Cassin Young* sank her by gunfire. She had lost 35 men killed or missing and 21 were wounded.

The plight of *Bush* survivors was desperate. To keep afloat they had one gig, a number of floater nets which were constantly breaking up and capsizing, and a few rubber life rafts inflated by CO_2 which were excellent – one supported 37 men. The seas were te to twelve feet high and whitecapped. Both air and water were cold. The men had taken a beating in the successive attacks on their ship and were suffering agonies from their burns. Many could stand no more, slipped out of their life jackets and went down. The gig finally attracted the attention of *LCS-64*, which commenced rescue operations at 2130; a fleet tug from Kerama and a PC arrived shortly after. They had to work in complete darkness as Japanese planes were still about. As the rescue vessels approached survivors some became excited and tried to swim to them, and drowned from exhaustion; or when alongside were broken against the hull, or caught in the propellers. Other men died after being taken from the water. Seven officers out of 26, including Comdesdiv 98, Commander J. S. Willis, and 87 men out of 307, were lost.[8]

3. *Attacks on Antisubmarine Screen and Minecraft*

There was air-surface action all around Okinawa on that bloody afternoon and evening of 6 April. Destroyer *Gregory*, Lieutenant Commander Bruce McCandless, was part of the outer antisubmarine screen off southern Okinawa, with APD *Daniel T. Griffin* and destroyer escort *Witter* in an adjoining station. Two Vals attacked at 1612. *Gregory* shot down one; the other went for *Witter*, nine miles distant, crashed her and killed six men. *Gregory* and fleet tug *Arikara*, escorting *Witter* to Kerama Retto, saw *Morris* in another patrol station under attack at 1815. She was crashed between her two forward turrets. *Griffin* and *R. P. Leary* closed with fire hoses ready; and although the kamikaze's gas tank had soaked compartments below deck, making a very hot and dangerous fire, they got it under control by 2030. *Morris* lost 13 men killed and 45 wounded; and, as in all these actions, many suffered ghastly burns.

Destroyer *Howorth* (Commander E. S. Burns) was steaming north off Zampa Misaki at 1600, with cruiser *St. Louis* about 1800

[8] Action Reports and conversations with the surviving exec., Lt. Malcolm G. Evans USNR.

yards away, when the air raid on the transport area approached. The kamikazes decided to attack the cruiser and the destroyer. Antiaircraft fire of both ships splashed one 25 yards astern of *St. Louis*. A Val dove on *Howorth* at 1623, passing between her stacks and splashing. At 1700, when patrolling her station between Nago Wan and Ie Shima, not far from the spot where *Newcomb* and *Leutze* were attacked, *Howorth* got word that *Hyman* on a nearby station had been hit, and went to her assistance. She had barely changed course when two groups of four Zekes each went for her. The first to attack, a slow glider, was knocked down 200 yards short. Two missed and splashed. The fourth, a steep diver, passed over her fantail with wing scraping the deck, and splashed. Another was shot down 250 yards away. The sixth to attack charged directly at the main battery director and crashed. Nine men were killed or missing and 14 wounded, but the fires were quickly brought under control; and while the damage control party was working another plane was shot down by her 40-mm fire, dead astern. Nevertheless, *Howorth* was able to make Kerama Retto unassisted.

Hyman (Commander R. N. Norgaard) had been attacked by four planes at 1612, when proceeding to a "flycatcher" picket station northeast of Ie Shima. She shot down three, but at 1627 was crashed by a Hamp on the torpedo tubes between the stacks. A tremendous explosion, to which torpedo warheads probably contributed, followed, and the flooded forward engine room had to be abandoned. *Hyman* was so severely damaged that destroyer *Rooks* was told off to escort her, and en route to Kerama the pair was attacked but not hit. Lucky *Rooks* (Commander J. A. McGoldrick) had already taken part in the destruction of five kamikazes in the course of the day. She was in the thick of things around Okinawa until 25 June, but suffered neither damage nor casualties — surely a record for good fortune.

On the east coast, destroyer *Purdy* (Commander Frank L. Johnson) was patrolling antisubmarine station A-2 off Kimmu Wan at 1730 when the word was passed that destroyer *Mullany* on a nearby station had been crashed by a kamikaze. Half an hour later Captain

Moosbrugger, commanding this east coast screen, ordered *Purdy* to go to *Mullany's* assistance, and she bent on 30 knots. At 1845 she found *Mullany* on fire, dead in the water and abandoned, with minesweepers collecting survivors from the water. Commander Johnson ordered the smaller minecraft to leave and destroyer minesweeper *Gherardi* to stand by, and requested a tug and a C.A.P. from Admiral Turner, while he started salvage operations. Presently the C.O. of *Mullany* boarded *Purdy* from his whaleboat and gave a gloomy report of the condition of his ship; but Johnson decided to persist in his efforts. At 1930 he closed *Mullany* with fire hoses rigged and played streams of water on her. When the fires began to die down, the C.O. boarded with his own salvage party, and was able to take *Mullany* to Kerama Retto under her own power.

Nor does this conclude the story of 6 April. A unit of six minecraft, *Ransom* flag, under Lieutenant Commander W. W. McMillen, supported by destroyer-minesweepers *Rodman* (Commander W. H. Kirvan) and *Emmons* (Lieutenant Commander Eugene N. Foss USNR) was sweeping the channel between Iheya Retto and Okinawa, when it suddenly became the target for a large flight of kamikazes. *Rodman* was surprised by the first of the gang. Diving out of the clouds it crashed her forward. Almost immediately thereafter its bomb exploded under her superstructure. Sixteen men were killed or missing and 20 wounded; but *Rodman's* engineering plant was still intact, and fires were under control by 1600, when she was crashed by two more kamikazes of the group that was after *Emmons*, and one that hit the skipper's cabin gutted the superstructure.

Emmons was about to go alongside *Rodman* to assist when her radar screen showed the air to be full of "bandits." She circled *Rodman* to provide antiaircraft support, and to such good purpose that six enemy planes were splashed by her gunfire. A large C.A.P. of Marine Corps Corsairs from one of the fast carriers went after these bandits like all-get-out; *Emmons* would put a 5-inch burst as near one as she could, and in a split second a Corsair would drop down from topside and splash the kamikaze. At least 20 victims of this C.A.P. were counted from the ship, which splashed six more before being hit herself. The Corsairs boldly pressed attacks right into the DMS's antiaircraft fire, but could not save her. In rapid succession *Emmons* was hit by five kamikazes as she was making 25 knots, and four others missed by yards. Two crashed her stern simultaneously, blowing off both fantail and rudder. A third crashed the forward gun and blew a large hole in the bow. A fourth hit under the bridge on the port side, slithering into the C.I.C. and killing the four officers and ten men who manned that brain center of the ship. Flames roared up through the pilot house, into which Lieutenant Commander Foss and most of the bridge personnel had ducked; they rushed out to take refuge on the bridge, but no bridge was there and overboard they went. The fifth kamikaze came in on a strafing run at 1833 which killed the machine-gun officer, then circled and crashed the wrecked superstructure.

With the wounded captain overboard, the executive killed and the first lieutenant wounded, the gunnery officer, Lieutenant J. J. Griffin USNR, took command.

Fires were raging in all spaces from the forward gun to frame 67, small fires were burning elsewhere, ready ammunition was exploding, the ship had a 10-degree list and appeared to be settling aft; but the sprinkling system in the handling rooms functioned, the engineering plant was little damaged, and the gun crews continued to fire in local control, No. 3 splashing a sixth kamikaze. Lieutenant Griffin had the less severely wounded removed to life rafts and ordered topside gear to be jettisoned. The fire in the superstructure was brought under control, but the fire forward could not be quenched owing to lack of water pressure, and the port engine conked out. At 1930, after a heavy explosion in the handling room, Lieutenant Griffin ordered Abandon Ship. *Emmons* might yet have been saved had she received assistance in fire-fighting and pumping; but *Rodman* had all she could do to reach Kerama Retto alive, the minesweepers under strafing fire fished from the water a number of survivors, including the skipper; and all fleet tugs were helping other cripples. *PGM–11*, a small mine-disposal vessel, bravely stood by. She boldly closed the burning and exploding ship and took of the 60-odd remaining men around 2000. Two hours later *Ellyson* closed the derelict, still burning but floating high; she was unable to put a rescue party on board, because of the rough sea, and, upon orders by Admiral Turner, sank her with gunfire lest she drift onto an enemy-held beach. Eight out of 19 officers and 53 out of 237 men were killed or missing, and three more officers died of their wounds.[9]

I doubt whether anyone could fully appreciate the results of this desperate fury of the Kamikaze Corps unless he were present, or in a hospital where wounded survivors were treated. Men wounded in these attacks were for the most part horribly burned. They suffered excruciating agony until given first aid; but if blown overboard, hours might elapse until a pharmacist's mate could relieve them. The medical officers did wonders if the wounded survived long enough to receive attention. And many men in rear hospitals, who looked like mummies under their bandages, breathing through a tube and being fed intravenously while their bodies healed, were cured by virtue of new methods of treating burns.

4. *Raid on Kerama*

Kerama roadstead, where many vulnerable ammunition and fuel ships were concentrated, had been largely neglected by enemy air until this great attack of 6 April, and not many planes got through to it then. At 1627 *LST-447* (Lieutenant Paul J. Schmitz), having discharged cargo at Okinawa, was proceeding to Kerama when at a point about a mile and a half below the southern entrance to the roadstead she sighted two planes 200 feet above the water, heading in. She opened fire on a Zeke and scored a hit at 3000 yards. The Japanese pilot, evidently figuring that he could not make the

[9] *Emmons* Action Report by Lt. Griffin; story in *New York Daily News* 19 June 1945; conversations at Aiea hospital with Lt. Cdr. Foss, who, badly burned, was picked up by *Recruit* after an hour in the water, went completely blind for two weeks, but eventually recovered both sight and health. My statement of casualties is that of Lt. Cdr. Foss.

crowded harbor, shifted target to the LST, and kept on coming, black smoke streaming out of his tail, despite more hits from her machine guns. He crashed the ship about two feet above the waterline and his bomb penetrated and exploded, completely gutting the LST and starting such fierce fires that within ten minutes Lieutenant Schmitz passed the word to abandon ship. Destroyer escort *Willmarth* and rescue tug *ATR–80* closed to fight fires, but, owing to the large amount of diesel oil on board, *LST–447* burned for about 24 hours, when she sank. Five men were missing and 17 wounded.

During this action, escort carrier *Tulagi* and three Victory ships converted to ammunition carriers – *Las Vegas Victory*, *Logan V.* and *Hobbs V.* – were moored just inside the southern entrance to Kerama roadstead. These received the full attention of other kamikazes which passed up the LST. One attempted to dive on *Tulagi* but swerved and crashed *Logan V.* as second choice. *Hobbs V.*, anchored nearby, weighed and stood out, but at 1845 another kamikaze crashed the after part of her bridge. Both ships were abandoned by their merchant marine crews. *Las Vegas V.*, Navy-manned, was discharging ammunition from both sides into an LCS, an LCT and two LCMs when this action began. She splashed a plane that picked on her, and most fortunately was not hit. The other two ammunition carriers, owing to their understandably prompt abandonment, sustained few losses – mostly to their Naval armed guard units; but the ships themselves were a total loss. They drifted, burning and exploding, for over a day, when they were sunk by gunfire.

A mile off Cape Zampa Misaki (Point Bolo) a number of LSTs of Lieutenant Commander J. R. Keeling's group 46, anchored and waiting their turn to beach, caught the eyes of kamikazes looking for meaty victims. At 1711 one dived on *LST–739*. Fired on by her and the other LSTs, it was splashed 200 yards from the group flagship; and between 1800 and 1815 five were shot down by the screen and by a group of minesweepers which were then returning to base.[10]

[10] Com LST Group 46 (Unit 4, Lt. Cdr. Keeling) Action Report.

Admiral Turner's staff estimated that 182 Japanese planes in 22 groups attacked the expeditionary force during the afternoon of 6 April; that 55 were destroyed by C.A.P., 35 by ships' antiaircraft fire, and 24 by crashing – a total of 108. On the same day, TF 38 claimed to have destroyed 249 attacking planes, *Essex* airmen alone splashing 65; and of the total, 136 were shot down over Okinawa. That these claims were not much exaggerated is proved by the fact that the Japanese themselves counted 355 kamikaze planes and 341 bombers committed to this, the first and greatest of their massed *kikusui* attacks; and kamikazes never returned home.

On the other hand, we had lost three destroyer types, one LST and two ammunition ships sunk; and ten ships, including eight destroyer types, a DE, and the minelayer *Defense*, suffered major damage and many casualties. This, however, fell far short of Japanese claims and expectations, which amounted to 60 vessels (including 2 battleships and 3 cruisers) sunk and 61 badly damaged. A comparison of our losses with the almost 700 enemy planes thrown into the battle indicated that the kamikazes planes were no longer so lethal, plane for plane, as they had been over Lingayen Gulf in January.

This particular blitz slipped over into Saturday 7 April, the day that *Yamato* was sunk. A kamikaze crashed *Maryland*, causing the loss of 16 men and wounding 37 more. Twenty planes approached the transport area, but did no damage; 12 were shot down, half by C.A.P. and half by ships. En route, one plane crashed radar picket destroyer *Bennett*, killing three men, wounding 18 and causing severe damage in the engineering spaces; she was escorted to Kerama by *Sterett*. Destroyer escort *Wesson*, in a screening station north of Ie Shima, was crashed by a plane which dove out of the clouds while she was engaged in firing on three others. Fires sprang up, engineering spaces flooded, and power was lost for a time; but she made Kerama on one shaft.

Radar picket stations Nos. 1, 2 and 3, where *Bush* and *Colhoun* were sunk, received more attention on 8 April, but no more damage was done to the ships. *Gregory* on station No. 3 was attacked by a

Sonia that evening. Although pieces were shot off it by machine-gun fire, it kept coming, and crashed amidships, abreast of the forward fire room. Then a second and a third came in, and were shot down close aboard. Commander McCandless got his fires out in short order, and *Gregory* steamed into Kerama roadstead under her own power.[11]

At the conclusion of these three days Admiral Spruance congratulated the escort carriers, and the search and reconnaissance planes operating from Kerama, for their outstanding performance and fine teamwork. At the same time he notified Admiral Nimitz that the situation respecting pilots and planes was not good, and might become critical if enemy air attacks continued. He requested that replacement pilots and planes be expedited by the transport CVEs of Service Squadron 6, even if our obligations in other Pacific areas had to be reduced. Everyone realized that the situation was serious for the destroyers and other screening ships, and might even get out of hand.

[11] *Gregory* Action Report. She proceeded to San Diego for repairs.

Official U.S. Army Photo

Liberator over Iwo Jima, 15 December 1944

Planning for Invasion

Left to right: Rear Admiral W. H. P. Blandy, Rear Admiral Harry W. Hill, Lieutenant General H. M. Smith USMC, Vice Admiral Richmond K. Turner

The Invasion of Iwo Jima

Courtesy Admiral Deyo

LCIs Moving In, 17 February 1945

One of the Damaged LCIs

The Invasion of Iwo Jima

H-hour, D-day

Boat Waves Forming

The Invasion of Iwo Jima

Marine Corps Photo

Fifth Marine Division Advancing near Mount Suribachi, D-day

Marine Corps Photo

Fourth Marine Division Moving up the Beach

The Invasion of Iwo Jima

Marine Corps Photo

Marines Moving In on a Cave

Marine Corps Photo

Fifth Division Command Post
Left to right in Foreground: Brigadier General Leo D. Hermle, Major General K. E. Rockey, Colonel James F. Shaw

The farthest LST is carrying a pontoon causeway, and the next one, an LCT. The nearest craft is an LSM; the wreck in the foreground is Japanese

Beaching Craft Unloading under Mount Suribachi, 24 February

Marine Corps Photo

A Marine-Navy JASCO in Position

Effect of Naval Gunfire on a Japanese Pillbox

On Iwo Jima

Views from Mount Suribachi, 21 April 1945

Courtesy Lt. Cdr. G. C. Waldo

Kure, 19 March

Courtesy Lt. Cdr. G. C. Waldo

Midget Submarine Pen, Okinawa, 27 March

Spring Bombing by U.S.S. Essex *Planes*

The Ordeal of U.S.S. Franklin, *19 March*

Photos Courtesy Lt. Cdr. Ellery Sedgwick, Jr.

General View of the Roadstead

Landing on Aka Shima, 26 March

Kerama Retto

Baka Bomb

Suicide Boat, Zamami Jima

Deadly Japanese Midgets

Avengers over the Beaches
Kadena Airfield under No. 57

LVTs Passing U.S.S. *Tennessee*

L-day at Okinawa

LVT(A)s of First Wave with Control Craft

Photos Courtesy of Cdr. R. A. Silcock RN

LSMs Going In

L-day at Okinawa

Official Coast Guard Photo

Unloading on Beach Yellow 3 – at Mouth of Bisha River
No. 1000 is an LST, No. 220 an LSM, and the four at the beach are LCTs

Destroyer *Ault* Fueling in Heavy Weather

Okinawa and Off Shore

Commodore Augustine H. Gray USN

Rear Admiral Bertram J. Rodgers USN

Vice Admiral John S. McCain USN

Vice Admiral Marc A. Mitscher USN in U.S.S. *Randolph*

CTF 38 and CTF 58

Portrait by Hugh Cabot

Rear Admiral C. Turner Joy USN

Rear Admiral Donald B. Beary USN

From portrait by J. J. Capolino at U. S. Naval War College

Commander Leon Grabowsky USN

Commander I. E. McMillian USN

Twilight Air Attack on Transport Area

U.S.S. *Newcomb* after Kamikaze Crash

Operation TEN-GO *Gets Going*

U.S.S. *Zellars* after Kamikaze Crash

U.S.S. *Tennessee*, after Splashing One on Each Bow, About to Be Crashed by a Third

U.S.S. *Tennessee* Fighting Fires

The Air Attack of 12 April

The Last of Battleship Yamato

The Black Spots Are Heads of Swimmers

Going, Going, Gone! (The Last of Light Cruiser Yahagi)

U.S.S. *Laffey*, after Hits on 16 April

U.S.S. *Aaron Ward*, after Hits on 3 May

Kamikaze Victims off Okinawa

U.S.S. *Hazelwood*, after Hits on 29 April

Hazelwood Restored, with Helicopter Deck, 1959

A Kamikaze Victim Survives

U.S.S. *Enterprise* Crashed off Kyushu, 14 May

Deck Crew Preparing to Catapult Planes, CVE *Mission Bay*

Aircraft Carriers

The Angry Sea – from U.S.S. *Pittsburgh* during the Typhoon

U.S.S. *Pittsburgh* minus her Bow

June Typhoon

Congratulations: Fleet Admiral King, Mr. Secretary Forrestal, Admiral Halsey, Fleet Admiral Nimitz

Ships of Third Fleet in Sagami Wan, 27 August – Mount Fuji in the Background

Victory

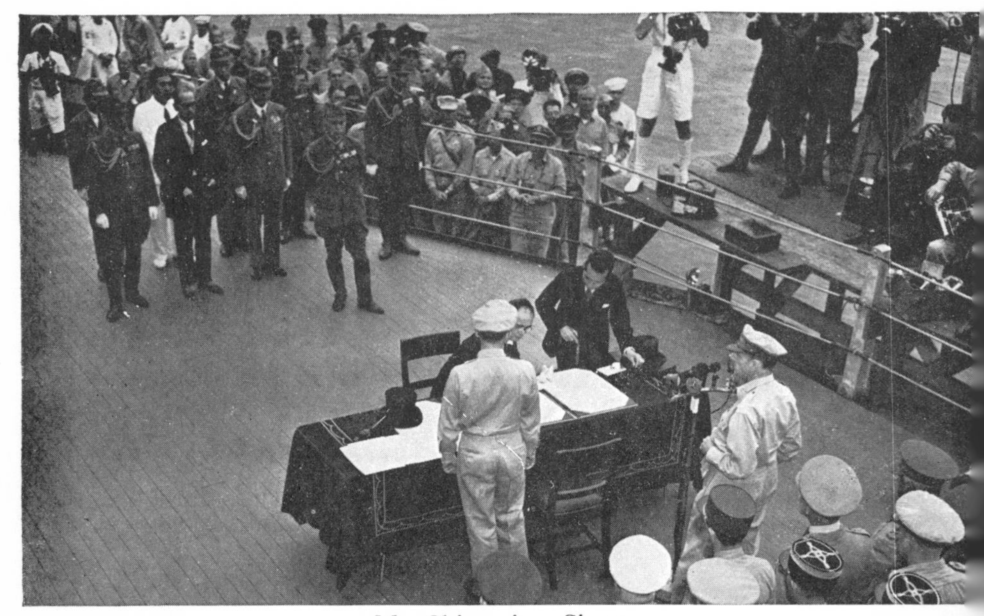

Mr. Shigemitsu Signs

Mr. Kase is standing by. General Sutherland has back to camera; General MacArthur is at right, General Umezu at head of Japanese delegation

General MacArthur Signs

Behind him, standing, left to right: General Wainwright, General Sir Arthur Percival, General Sutherland, Rear Admiral John F. Shafroth. Commodore Perry's flag is behind them

The Surrender on board U.S.S. Missouri, *2 S tember 1945*

The Japanese Delegation Departs

Wings over U.S.S. *Iowa*

Immediately after the Surrender

U.S. Submarine *Sand Lance* Flying Presidential Unit Citation Flag below her Battle Ensign

Homeward Bound

CHAPTER XIII

Fast Carrier Support[1]

1–12 April 1945

1. *The End of* Yamato, *7 April*

ON 6 APRIL, the day when Operation TEN-GO was unleashed, two groups of Task Force 58, "Jocko" Clark's 58.1 and "Ted" Sherman's 58.3, were operating some 70 miles east of the Okinawa dog's forelegs, the Katchin Peninsula. C.A.P. and a radar picket unit of six destroyers were thrown out 30 miles northeastward. *Cabot* had a very close shave from a kamikaze that skimmed over her deck but missed; three carriers, two cruisers and two destroyers were also near-missed, and about 30 planes were shot down over or near the disposition. It seems that the pilots who attacked TF 58 that day were second-string kamikazes. One even bailed out when his plane was shot down by C.A.P. He was picked up, as Admiral Mitscher signaled, "from a fancy red life raft, wearing silk scarf with Nip inscription 'Kamikaze Special Attack Unit 3.' Says he flew from Kikai Jima. Graduated from Kisarazu late 1944 and is a flight instructor. Now matriculating in *Hornet*."

Throughout this day, and for many days preceding and following, TF 58 also maintained C.A.P. over the amphibious forces around Okinawa; the importance of their work, in concert with the

[1] CTF 58 (Vice Adm. Mitscher) Action Report 17 July 1945 pp. 8–11, and Action Reports of CTG 58.1, 58.2, 58.3 and 58.4; Mitsuru Yoshida "The End of *Yamato*" U.S. Naval Institute *Proceedings* LXVIII (Feb. 1952) 117–130, translated by M. Chikuami and edited by Roger Pineau (copyright 1952 by the Institute); Combined Fleet Notice No. 24, 30 July 1945, trans. by Robert S. Schwantes; *Yamato* War Diary, and Desron 2 Action Report, translation in *Campaigns of Pacific War* 334–338; Naval Technical Mission to Japan "*Yamato* and *Musashi*" O.N.I. *Review* I No. 8 (June 1946) 3–17.

ships, we have already seen. *Essex* claimed that her planes alone shot down 65 of the enemy's on 6 April, and total TF 58 claims added up to 249 – a mighty achievement, even if discounted 50 per cent. And only two planes were lost by the Task Force.[2]

At 1745 April 6, Pacific Fleet submarine *Threadfin,* patrolling off the Bungo Suido entrance to the Inland Sea, picked up a surface contact of two large and about six smaller ships, moving southwest at 25 knots. In accordance with her orders she passed up a chance to attack in order to get off her contact report, which was promptly received by Task Force 58. *Hackleback* also sighted this group and sent off four contact reports.

This last-gasp effort of the Japanese Combined Fleet comprised super-battleship *Yamato,* light cruiser *Yahagi* and eight destroyers. As an integral part of Operation TEN-GO, their objective was the Hagushi roadstead off Okinawa, to attack "survivors" of the day's air blitz, at daylight 9 April. The sacrificial nature of this sortie is indicated by the fact that *Yamato* was given only enough fuel for a one-way trip to Okinawa.[3]

Yamato and her sister ship *Musashi,* the world's biggest battlewagons, were the pride of the Imperial Japanese Navy. The remains of *Musashi* were already on the bottom of the Sibuyan Sea, whither Avengers of the Fast Carrier Forces had consigned her on 24 October 1944.[4] But *Yamato* had come through the Battle off Samar and the subsequent air pursuit with relatively little damage, and was theoretically capable of outshooting any ship of the United States Navy.

Laid down in 1937 and completed in December 1941, *Yamato* displaced 68,000 tons on trials and 72,809 tons fully laden. Her main battery consisted of nine 460-mm (18.1-inch) guns. These enormous cannon threw a projectile weighing 3200 pounds, as compared with the 2700-pound shell of our 16-inchers, and had a maxi-

[2] CTF 58 (Vice Adm. Mitscher) Action Report p. 8.

[3] Rear Adm. Yokoi in U.S. Naval Institute *Proceedings* LXXX 509.

[4] See Vol. XII 162, 186, and air photo of *Yamato* in that battle facing p. 190. For sinking of aircraft carrier *Shinano,* which was converted from a similar BB hull, see Vol. XII 410–411.

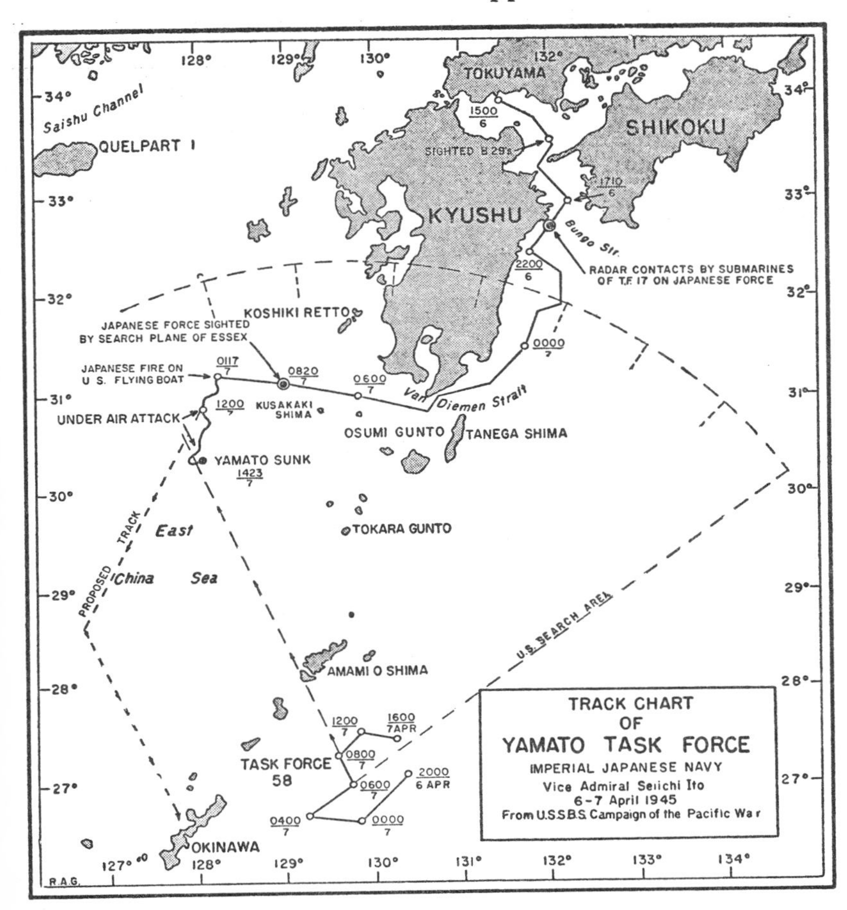

mum range of 42,000 meters (22½ miles), the flight time being a little over one minute and three quarters. Her planned complement of 2200 officers and men had been increased to 2767 on account of radar and additional antiaircraft guns, of which she possessed about 100. She measured 863 feet over all and drew 35 feet with full load. Her engine rooms were protected by 16.1-inch vertical and 7.9-inch horizontal armor plate. Her propulsion came from four turbine engines developing 150,000 horsepower; and in spite of her great weight she was capable of a maximum speed of 27.5 knots and a standard cruising speed of 25 knots. This ratio of speed to armor and weight was attained by electrical welding and a unique hull design, the principal feature being a gigantic bulbous bow to reduce hull resistance. *Yamato,* moreover, was a singularly beautiful ship, with a graceful sheer to her flush deck, unbroken from stem to stern, and a streamlined mast and stack. She was built at the Kure navy yard under conditions of extreme secrecy, and special dry docks to accommodate her and *Musashi* had been constructed at Sasebo and Yokosuka.[5]

The *Yamato* task force was set up by Admiral Ozawa, Commander Third Fleet, as "Surface Special Attack Force" (also called "First Diversion Attack Force"), with the objective to "destroy the enemy convoy and task force around Okinawa," in coöperation with the Japanese Air Forces and Army.[6] The task organization follows: —

Surface Special Attack Force, *Vice Admiral Seiichi Ito
Battleship *YAMATO, *Rear Admiral Kosaku Ariga
Comdesron 2 Rear Admiral Keizo Komura in light cruiser *YAHAGI, Captain Tameichi Hara
Comdesdiv 41 Captain M. Yoshida in FUYUTSUKI, with SUZUTSUKI
Comdesdiv 17 *Captain K. Shintani in *ISOKAZE, with *HAMAKAZE and YUKIKAZE
Comdesdiv 21 *Captain H. Kotaki in *ASASHIMO, with *KASUMI and HATSUSHIMO

* Sunk or killed in this action.

This forlorn hope of the Japanese Navy was rendered hopeless for want of air cover. According to one account, two fighter planes were over *Yamato* as late as 1000 April 7 but retired before the fighting began. In view of what had happened to another naked fleet, Admiral Kurita's in the Battle for Leyte Gulf, it seems inexplicable that the now unified Japanese air command should have hurled all its available fighters against TF 58 and the amphibious forces on 6 and 7 April, instead of covering these ships.

[5] Capt. K. Matsumoto and Capt. M. Chihaya (who took part in her construction) "Design and Construction of the *Yamato* and *Musashi,*" U.S. Nav. Inst. *Proceedings* LXXIX (Oct. 1953) 1103–14; U.S. Naval Technical Mission, Japan Summary Report 1 Nov. 1946 p. 9; data from Capt. T. Ohmae, 1959.

[6] Combined Fleet Notice No. 24. The 32nd Army on Okinawa, according to this, "was to open a general attack and wipe out the enemy landing party."

Admiral Ito's force got under way from off Tokuyama at 1520 April 6 and sortied from the Inland Sea by Bungo Suido at 2000. The crew of *Yamato* were assembled at 1800, when the exec. delivered a message from Admiral Ozawa, "Render this operation the turning point of the war." The crew sang the national anthem and gave three banzais for the Emperor. At 2020 a U.S. submarine was sighted "and repulsed," according to a subsequent Combined Fleet release. *Hackleback* reported that a destroyer peeled off three times in pursuit, but never came near enough to force her to submerge.

Special Attack Force skirted the eastern shores of Kyushu, turned west through Osumi Kaikyo (Van Diemen Strait), passed Sata Misaki, the southernmost point of Kyushu, and steered about WNW, leaving the big lighthouse on Kusakaki Shima well on the port beam, with the idea of circling around as far from TF 58 as possible and pouncing on Okinawa during the evening of 7 April.

Admiral Mitscher was expecting this, and made every possible preparation to see that *Yamato* and her consorts did not get very far. After receiving the two submarine contacts he ordered all four of his task groups to a suitable launching position northeast of Okinawa. Rear Admiral Radford's TG 58.4, which had been fueling on 6 April, managed to rejoin TF 58 during the night; only Rear Admiral Davison's TG 58.2, fueling, failed to get into the fight. Searches were flown by TGs 58.1 and 58.3 at daybreak 7 April. All strike planes were held on carriers' flight decks until results of the search were known.

At 0823 April 7 an *Essex* plane flushed the *Yamato* group southwest of Koshiki Retto. Nine minutes later the pilot sent an amplifying report giving the enemy course at 300°, speed 12 knots. The big battlewagon was actually making 22 knots, at the center of a diamond-shaped formation screened by the destroyers, with light cruiser *Yahagi* in the rear.

Admiral Spruance promptly transmitted these contacts to Rear Admiral Deyo of the gunfire and bombardment force off Okinawa, indicating that the *Yamato* group was fair game for him. Deyo held a conference of flag and commanding officers on board Admiral Turner's flagship *Eldorado* at 1030 April 7, as a result of which a battle plan was drawn up for six battleships, seven cruisers and 21 destroyers. Deyo planned to keep his ships between the Japanese and Okinawa, to prevent their getting at the transports. TF 54 sortied from the roadstead at 1530 and performed exercises and battle maneuvers, during which *Maryland* was hit by a Japanese aërial bomb on turret No. 3, which was temporarily knocked out. An eagerly anxious evening followed for TF 54. Staff officers familiar with range tables took care to remind others that *Yamato's* 18.1-inch guns should have a maximum range of 45,000 yards, as against 42,000 for the 16-inch gunned battleships in Deyo's force and 37,000 for *Tennessee;* and that her speed should enable her to make an "end run" and thrust at the transports. They were cheered by a signal from Turner to Deyo, "Hope you will bring back a nice fish for breakfast"; and just as Deyo had begun to write his answer on a signal blank, "Many thanks, will try to . . ." an intercepted message, to the effect that Mitscher's scouts had already picked up the enemy, suggested the conclusion, ". . . if the pelicans haven't caught them all!" – which is what they did.[7]

Of great assistance in reaching this much desired consummation were two amphibious Mariners belonging to VPB 21 based at Kerama Retto, piloted by Lieutenant James R. Young USNR and Lieutenant (jg) R. L. Simms USNR. These made contact on the *Yamato* force and shadowed it for the next five hours. Ito fired at them in vain; they sent out regular reports and homed carrier strikes onto the target. They also made a notable air-sea rescue, as we shall see.

From lat. 31°22′ N, long. 129°14′ E, where the *Essex* plane picked up *Yamato* at 0823, she and her consorts made frequent radical changes of course and evasive maneuvering, but the general trend of the disposition was south.

Admiral Mitscher, as soon as he received definite reports of the

[7] CTF 54 (Rear Adm. Deyo) Action Report pp. 38–41, and his Ms. "Many Sparrows."

enemy force and its location at sea, launched a tracking and covering group of 16 fighter planes at 0915. At 1000 the main strikes from TGs 58.1 and 58.3 commenced launching. These consisted of 280 planes, 98 of them torpedo-bombers. *Hancock's* contingent (53 planes) was 15 minutes late in launching and failed to find the target. Admiral Radford's TG 58.4, which could contribute only 106 units, as it had C.A.P. duty over Okinawa, did not reach launching position until 0945 and its planes were late reaching the target.

The approach of the first strike was spotted by *Yamato* at 1232. Rear Admiral Ariga ordered Open Fire, and scores of guns in the flagship "burst forth simultaneously," according to Ensign Yoshida. At 1241 she received two bomb hits near the mainmast, and, four minutes later, her first torpedo hit. (Carrier *Bennington* claims both for her boys.) *San Jacinto* planes at the same time got a bomb and a torpedo into destroyer *Hamakaze*, which plunged to the bottom bow first. Light cruiser *Yahagi* was also hit by a bomb and a torpedo at this time and went dead in the water.

Between 1300 and 1417 the force was under almost continuous attack. Ensign Yoshida gives a graphic picture of the big battleship's predicament, and what it felt like to be on board a mighty ship, helpless under an expertly delivered air onslaught. Her antiaircraft gunners, for want of practice on live targets, were unable to hit anything. After five torpedo hits on her port side between 1337 and 1344 had created serious flooding, Rear Admiral Ariga ordered the starboard engine and boiler rooms, as the largest and lowest compartments in the ship, to be counter-flooded. Yoshida phoned the occupants to warn them, but it was too late. "Water, both from torpedo hits and the flood valves rushed into these compartments and snuffed out the lives of the men at their posts, several hundred in all. Caught between cold sea water and steam and boiling water from the damaged boilers, they simply melted away." This sacrifice failed to correct the list, and with only one screw working, *Yamato* lost speed rapidly.

Now came in the fourth major attack wave. Aërial torpedoes blew more holes in the port side and at least ten bombs exploded on the decks. The wireless room, supposedly watertight, flooded so completely that thenceforth *Yamato* had to rely entirely on flag and light signals. From 1345 she enjoyed a precious 15 minutes free from attack, but it availed her nothing. As Yoshida relates, bombs, bullets and torpedoes had reduced the mighty battleship "to a state of complete confusion. . . . The desolate decks were reduced to shambles, with nothing but cracked and twisted steel plates remaining. . . . Big guns were inoperable because of the increasing list, and only a few machine guns were intact. . . . One devastating blast in the emergency dispensary had killed all its occupants including the medical officers and corpsmen. . . ."

At 1400 began the final air attack. Hellcats and Avengers were able to make selective runs on the slowly moving, almost helpless ship. A terrific torpedo detonation aft reverberated throughout the ship and ended all communications from the bridge. The distress flag was hoisted, steering room flooded, rudder jammed hard left, and the list increased to 35 degrees. "As though awaiting this moment, the enemy came plunging through the clouds to deliver the *coup de grâce*. . . . It was impossible to evade. . . . I could hear the Captain vainly shouting, 'Hold on, men! Hold on, men!' . . . I heard the Executive Officer report to the Captain in a heartbroken voice, 'Correction of list hopeless!' . . . Men were jumbled together in disorder on the deck, but a group of staff officers squirmed out of the pile and crawled over to the Commander in Chief for a final conference." Admiral Ito "struggled to his feet. His chief of staff then arose and saluted. A prolonged silence followed during which they regarded each other solemnly." Ito "looked around, shook hands deliberately with his staff officers, and then went resolutely into his cabin." The Captain concerned himself with saving the Emperor's portrait.

It was now 1420. "The deck was nearly vertical and *Yamato's* battle flag was almost touching the billowing waves. . . . Shells of the big guns skidded and bumped across the deck of the ammunition

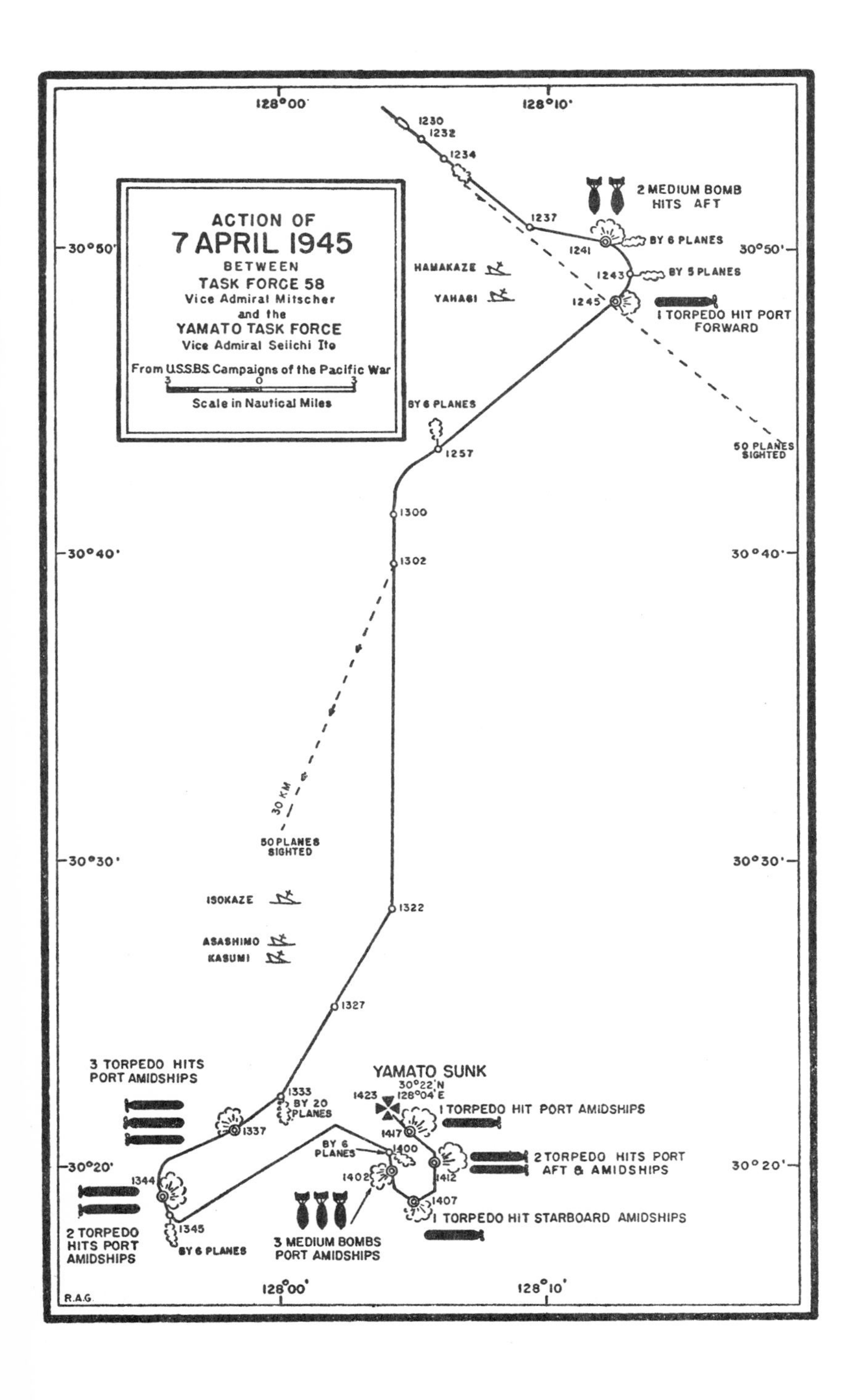
ACTION OF
7 APRIL 1945
BETWEEN
TASK FORCE 58
Vice Admiral Mitscher
and the
YAMATO TASK FORCE
Vice Admiral Seiichi Ito
From U.S.S.B.S. Campaigns of the Pacific War
Scale in Nautical Miles
128°00'
128°10'
30°50'
30°40'
30°30'
30°20'
1230
1232
1234
1237
1241
1243
1245
1257
1300
1302
1322
1327
1333
1337
1344
1345
1400
1402
1407
1412
1417
1423
2 MEDIUM BOMB HITS AFT
BY 6 PLANES
BY 5 PLANES
1 TORPEDO HIT PORT FORWARD
HAMAKAZE
YAHAGI
BY 6 PLANES
50 PLANES SIGHTED
30 KM
50 PLANES SIGHTED
ISOKAZE
ASASHIMO
KASUMI
3 TORPEDO HITS PORT AMIDSHIPS
BY 20 PLANES
YAMATO SUNK
30°22'N
128°04'E
1 TORPEDO HIT PORT AMIDSHIPS
BY 6 PLANES
2 TORPEDO HITS PORT AFT & AMIDSHIPS
1 TORPEDO HIT STARBOARD AMIDSHIPS
2 TORPEDO HITS PORT AMIDSHIPS
BY 6 PLANES
3 MEDIUM BOMBS PORT AMIDSHIPS
R.A.G.

room, crashing against the bulkhead and kindling the first of a series of explosions." At 1423 "the ship slid under completely," followed by "the blast, rumble, and shock of compartments bursting from air pressure and exploding magazines already submerged."

One American had a grandstand seat for seeing this queen of the battlewagons go down. He was Lieutenant (jg) W. E. Delaney USNR from carrier *Belleau Wood*. His Avenger had made bomb hits on *Yamato* from so low an altitude that the explosion set him afire and all had to bail out. The two crewmen had parachute trouble and were drowned, but Delaney managed to get into his rubber raft, from which he witnessed the death throes of *Yamato*. There he was spotted by Lieutenants Young and Simms who had been following the battle in their PBMs. While Simms acted as decoy to attract enemy gunfire, Young made a neat water landing, taxied toward the pilot, whose raft was in the midst of floating Japanese survivors, took him on board, made a jet-assisted takeoff, and subsequently landed him safe and sound at Yontan airfield.[8]

About two hours later another PBM, observing a mass of wreckage and many floating survivors, made a water landing and took prisoner some survivors, who admitted that *Yamato* was no more. At 1701 Admiral Mitscher sent a signal to Admiral Spruance, "We attacked *Yamato, Agano*, one light cruiser and seven or eight destroyers. Sank first three, two others burning badly, three got away. . . . We lost about seven planes."

Light cruiser *Yahagi*, which the pilots had wrongly identified as *Agano*, proved almost as tough as the battleship, taking 12 bomb and seven torpedo hits before going down. Besides *Hamakaze*, sunk early in the fight, three other destroyers were so heavily damaged that they had to be scuttled. The four destroyers remaining were damaged in varying degrees, but managed to get back to Sasebo. *Yamato* lost all but 23 officers and 246 men of her complement of 2767; *Yahagi* lost 446; *Asashimo* lost 330; the seven destroyers, 391

[8] *Belleau Wood* Action Report 14 Mar.–28 Apr., 4 May; VPB 21 War Diary for April; Delaney's story in *N.Y. Times* 11 Apr. 1945.

officers and men. Among the survivors were 209 wounded.[9] Losses on our side were 10 planes and 12 men.[10]

As we have seen in Chapter XII, the Kamikaze Corps was far from idle during this attack. It not only pulled off the first massed *kikusui* assault on the amphibious forces, but struck back at Task Force 58. At 1212 April 7 *Hancock* opened fire on an enemy plane at 3000 feet. It crossed her bows, then turned and headed for the ship, sharp on her starboard bow. After dropping a bomb that hit the flight deck forward it crashed the same deck aft, setting fire to parked planes. The bomb explosion holed and damaged the flight deck, set fire to nearby planes and to the forward part of the hangar deck. By 1230 damage control party reported the fires under control, and by 1300 only an occasional wisp of smoke could be seen from other ships as evidence of the attack. *Hancock* recovered her own strike group at 1630 and was able to handle aircraft on an emergency basis, but she lost 72 men killed and 82 wounded.

2. *Task Force 58 Operations, 11 April*

On 8 April Task Force 58 resumed routine support of Operation ICEBERG, and that day TG 58.2 rejoined.

Since the P.O.W. whom *Hornet* picked up on 6 April conveniently boasted that 11 April would bring another massed attack, Admiral Mitscher canceled all support missions over Okinawa for that day, and had all dive-bombers and torpedo planes debombed and degassed and parked on their hangar decks. C.A.P. was increased to 12 aircraft over the TF 58 picket destroyers and 24 over each of the two carrier task groups present. The other two were fueling.

[9] Information from Capt. Ohmae.

[10] Mitscher Report p. 9. Of the 386 carrier planes engaged, TG 58.1 contributed 113, TG 58.3, 167, TG 58.4, 106. By types they were 180 VF, 75 VB and 131 VT. CTF 58 Action Report p. 8. Each VF carried three 500-lb. bombs and each VB one 1000-lb semi-armor piercing or GP bomb, and two 250-lb. bombs.

The expected attacks began to develop at 1330 April 11 and continued throughout the afternoon watch. At 1443 a kamikaze crashed battleship *Missouri* near her starboard quarter about three feet below main deck level. Parts of the plane and the mutilated body of the pilot were strewn over the after part of the ship, but the resulting fire was brought under control within three minutes and damage was confined to scorched paint. *Enterprise,* now back with TG 58.3, caught it again. At 1410, just as she was in a port evasive turn, a Judy sideswiped her port quarter and struck the shields of two 40-mm mounts. Parts of the plane were left in the gun tubs and the bomb continued into the water, exploding under the carrier and causing minor damage. At 1510 another Judy crashed close under her starboard bow, raising a shock wave and causing more damage. Parts of the Judy were hurled onto the flight deck where a plane on the starboard catapult caught fire; it was catapulted free, still burning, and the fire on the flight deck was quickly quenched. But "Big E" had to curtail her flight operations for 48 hours.

Destroyers on picket duty for TF 58 had a rough time on 11 April. At 1357 a plane was observed by *Kidd* to dive out of the sun onto *Bullard,* which took it under fire and splashed it about 50 yards astern. Eleven minutes later *Kidd* took a second aircraft under fire about 5000 yards on the port bow. This one passed ahead and out of range. Two enemy planes were next seen indulging in a mock dogfight (apparently to convey the idea that one was friendly) on the other side of the destroyer *Black,* which was about 1500 yards on *Kidd's* port beam. One dog-fighter peeled off and made a low-level run on *Black* in such a direction that *Kidd* could not bring her batteries to bear. As it reached *Black* the plane pulled over that ship and continued low over the water toward *Kidd.* Although already smoking from hits, it crashed the destroyer's forward fire room at the waterline. The skipper, Commander H. G. Moore, was seriously wounded by the bomb, which passed through the ship and exploded on the port side. In less than five minutes the forward fire room was isolated from the engineering system, while the ship was still making 22 knots. She had 38 killed or missing and 55 wounded. Most of the enemy plane was carried back to Ulithi in the fire room. It was found not to be a kamikaze but a fully equipped fighter with instrument panel and self-sealing tanks.

At 1507 April 11 *Essex* took a near-miss on the port side from a bomb which caused extensive damage to fuel tanks and in the engineering plant. She lost 28 wounded but remained in action. *Hale* was jolted by a near-miss bomb while maneuvering to put her surgeon on board *Kidd. Hank* had three killed or missing and one wounded when a kamikaze crashed close aboard, causing minor damage to the ship.

All this belongs to the second *kikusui* assault, involving 185 kamikazes.[11] Next day the "floating chrysanthemums" concentrated on radar pickets and ships off Okinawa. April 12 proved to be one of the most trying days for the Navy in this campaign.

3. *Royal Navy off Sakishima Gunto, 1–12 April*[12]

As we have already seen, Vice Admiral Rawlings RN in H.M.S. *King George V* brought all combatant elements of the British Pacific Fleet, including four fast carriers, up to the Sakishima Gunto, where their planes struck airfields and installations on 26, 27 and 31 March. Still designated Task Force 57, these ships contributed to the success of Operation ICEBERG by neutralizing airfields in the southern group of the Nansei Shoto and, to some extent, those on Formosa. Their efforts were neatly dovetailed with those of Rear Admiral Durgin's escort carrier support group (TG 51.2), so that Sakishima Gunto had no respite.

The Japanese air forces first counterattacked TF 57 on Okinawa L-day, 1 April. Rear Admiral Sir Philip Vian's carriers sent off first fighter sweep at 0640. Ten minutes later bogeys, 75 miles westward, registered on radar screens. The sweep was recalled to intercept and

[11] See table at head of Chap. XV.

[12] See footnote to Chap. VI Sec. 5 for authorities, and end of Appendix I for task organization.

additional fighters were launched. Interception took place about 40 miles from the task force and four aircraft were shot down. This failed to break up the Japanese formation. On it pressed, pursued by Hellcats, Corsairs and Seafires, and reached the carriers shortly after 0705. One plane made a low-level strafing run on H.M.S. *Indomitable*, killing one man and wounding six, then turned its attention to *King George V* but did no damage there. Next, a kamikaze crashed the base of the island of H.M.S. *Indefatigable*, killing 14 men and wounding 16. Her steel flight deck was out of action only briefly and she continued to launch and recover on a somewhat reduced scale. H. M. destroyer *Ulster* received a near-miss from a 500-pound bomb, which ruptured the bulkhead between the engine room and after fire room. She had to be towed to Leyte by H.M.N.Z.S. *Gambia*.

At 1215 the carriers launched a strike against Ishigaki airfield and runways in the Sakishima Gunto, and destroyed a few more grounded aircraft. At 1730 a low-flying bogey was picked up 15 miles to the northwest and Hellcats were sent to intercept. The bogey, which proved to be two planes, evaded them in the clouds, and one dived on H.M.S. *Illustrious*, which evaded by use of full rudder; one wing touched the edge of the flight deck and the plane splashed in the sea, where its bomb exploded harmlessly. The Japanese pilot's instructions, listing the priority of kamikaze targets, were blown on board by the explosion and made very interesting reading for Captain Lambe and staff, and for Fifth Fleet Intelligence.

Inferring from his experience on L-day that the enemy was launching planes from Sakishima airfields at first light, Sir Philip Vian sent off two aircraft at 0510 by moonlight to cover Ishigaki, and two more for Miyako, but they had to return owing to radio failure. No activity was noted and at daylight 2 April a fighter sweep was launched to cover all airfields in the Sakishima Gunto. The task force then retired for fueling and was relieved, during its absence, by planes from Admiral Durgin's escort carrier group.

Bad weather prevented the fueling scheduled for 3 April and it was not completed until the 5th. On 6 April pairs of aircraft were launched to be over the Miyako and Ishigaki airfields at daybreak, but no enemy planes were there to be found. At about 1700 bogeys were picked up by radar and the fighter intercept shot down one Judy. One kamikaze out of four dived on *Illustrious*. Again this carrier successfully took radical evasive action. The wing tip hit the island and the plane spun into the sea; there were no casualties and but slight damage.

During the day a message was received from Admiral Nimitz indicating that in his opinion all-out enemy reaction to Okinawa by kamikazes was under way; and he was only too right. Consequently, TF 57 canceled a bombardment of Ishigaki planned for 7 April. Fighter cover was maintained over Sakishima Gunto all that day, and when it appeared that craters previously blown in the airfields had been filled, three bomber strikes were sent to re-hole them. Admiral Rawlings's task force was enjoying a peaceful sail; sailors were reading, playing chequers and shooting darts, and a Royal Marine barber was cutting hair on the deck of *King George V*, when the Stand-to was sounded and everyone jumped to battle stations. The fleet chaplain, Canon J. T. Bezzant (survivor from the sinking of H.M.S. *Repulse* on 10 December 1941), explained over loudspeaker that enemy planes were flying about. One Judy was splashed by Seafires close aboard *Illustrious;* Seafires shot down a second at a safe distance, and the only air attack of the day was over.[13]

That evening TF 57 retired to fuel, while a veteran U.S. escort carrier division – *Sangamon, Suwannee, Chenango* and *Santee*, with Rear Admiral Sample as O.T.C. – took over the job of pounding targets in the Sakishima Gunto.

Fueling completed 9 April, Sir Philip Vian's carriers had already started back to their launching area when a message was intercepted from Commander Fifth Fleet to Cincpac, recommending that TF 57 strike the northernmost airfields of Formosa on 11 and 12 April, while Luzon-based aircraft of the Southwest Pacific command took care of those in southern Formosa, and Admiral Durgin's escort

[13] Trumbull in *N.Y. Times* 16 Apr. 1945.

carriers covered Sakishima Gunto. Admiral Nimitz approved this diversion and the Royal Navy carriers reached launching position 30 miles off Formosa at 0600 April 11. Weather conditions were so unfavorable that the strikes were postponed to the 12th. Warned by Admiral Spruance that heavy air attacks were to be expected, Sir Philip Vian put up an unusually heavy C.A.P. when reaching his launching position. But no planes molested the four carriers as they sliced off 48 bombers, accompanied by 41 fighters, in two waves to hit Formosan airfields. The first wave well performed its mission. The second, impeded by weather, shifted attention to Kiirun and attacked a chemical plant, docks and shipping. Strikes were repeated next day, after which TF 57 withdrew for another drink of oil. Very few enemy aircraft were seen in or over Formosa, but the British carriers' C.A.P. had to deal with strikes from the Sakishima Gunto. Consequently, on Admiral Rawlings's advice, Admiral Spruance decided to leave Formosa to the Southwest Pacific command and let TF 57 concentrate on the smaller islands which were giving trouble.

CHAPTER XIV

The Second Week at Okinawa

7–13 April 1945

1. *The Situation Ashore, 8–11 April* [1]

ON 8 APRIL, first Sunday after Easter, when the second week of the assault on Okinawa opened, the ground situation was about as follows. In the north the rapid advance of the 6th Marine Division across the neck of the Motobu Peninsula came to an end. On Monday morning it began to meet stiff opposition. In the south, XXIV Corps had already encountered stubborn resistance from strong defensive positions, implemented by massed artillery fire of a quality never hitherto received from the Japanese Army. By Sunday the Corps was stopped cold. Shore fire control parties and planes were having trouble locating targets in this southern area that could be reached by naval gunfire. But these difficulties did not then seem serious. Hope sprang up that all might be over by Whitsuntide, so rapidly had the troops advanced.

Kamikaze attacks, especially that of 6–7 April, were disquieting. But Admiral Turner expressed the general sentiment when he signaled at noon 7 April, "If this is the best the enemy can throw against us, we shall move forward." Next day, in view of the sinking of *Yamato* and the favorable situation on Okinawa, Turner sent this jocular message to Admiral Nimitz: "I may be crazy but it looks like the Japs have quit the war, at least in this section." To

[1] Books and Action Reports mentioned at heads of Chaps. IX and XI; Robert Sherrod *History of Marine Corps Aviation* (1952) chap. xxv; the writer's personal observations and field notes. The Japanese version of the *baka* bomb attacks is in Inoguchi & Nakajima *The Divine Wind* (1958) chap. xvi.

which Commander in Chief Pacific Fleet made the succinct reply: "Delete all after 'crazy'!"

Overconfidence prevailed in many quarters. "Old hands" of the Luzon campaign insisted that the present crop of kamikazes was inferior to the one encountered off Lingayen. That was correct, but there was a lot more of them. Intelligence, after many estimates and much figuring, reached the comfortable conclusion that the Imperial Air Forces were scraping the barrel, and that the 6 April performance could not be repeated more than once.

Pessimism there was, too. Some destroyer officers insisted that a pilot bent on crashing could not be stopped by anything smaller than 5-inch shell, and that with the existing system of gunfire control, it was impossible to knock down planes in one-two-three order. Radar picket duty could be as suicidal for the picketing sailors as for the attacking Japanese, unless two or more destroyers were placed at each station and C.A.P. provided at dawn and dusk. A summary of battle damage issued by Admiral Turner 10 April, adding up the Navy, Army and Marine Corps casualties through the 9th, indicated that the taking of Okinawa was going to be very costly: — [2]

	Killed	*Missing*	*Wounded*
Army & Marine Corps	650	129	3010
Task Force 51	246	330	737

The most encouraging factor was the early capture of airfields and prompt building-up of a land-based air force. Yontan and Kadena fields were no beds of roses for tired airmen. Japanese artillery shelled them daily; strafers and bombers paid frequent visits. Yet, by the evening of 8 April, 82 Marine Air Wing Corsairs and seven night fighters were based on Yontan field, and more were brought up within a day or two by escort carriers. Of this number, 41 were already available for C.A.P.; in another week if all went well these would be increased to 144. But the land-based night fight-

[2] CTF 51 Action Report and Admiral Turner's 20th summary for 1800 Apr. 10. These figures do not include the casualties in TF 58. For Navy casualties Lingayen see Vol. XIII 325–326.

ers could not be used for C.A.P. before 14 April as their radar and calibration gear had not yet been unloaded. So the holes in the Fleet's air cover, at dawn and dusk, were not yet covered. If Admiral Spruance hoped soon to release TF 58 from close support duties, he was disappointed. Close support duties for Operation ICEBERG tied it down until well into June; it got away only to sink *Yamato* and strike Kyushu airfields.

The Japanese made Sunday night 8–9 April a rough one for the troops ashore. Turner assigned five battleships, five cruisers and 17 destroyers for night support of Tenth Army, whose "gratitude for our silencing rocket and mortar emplacement was almost heart-rending." [3] Every night thereafter, naval vessels stood by off southern Okinawa to deliver call fire and illumination, as requested by shore fire control parties. Star shell, the best way to uncover Japanese attempts at infiltration, was expended liberally, and its quality had greatly improved during the past year. "Up the Slot" in 1943 one expected half the star shell to be duds or fizz-outs; but off Okinawa a 100 per cent performance was not unusual.

Commodore McGovern's transports lifting the floating reserve arrived 9 April. Landing the 27th Division was completed next day; there were now some 160,000 American troops ashore on Okinawa.[4] In order to relieve shipping congestion, the 2nd Marine Division, still part of the floating reserve, was ordered by Admiral Turner to return to Guam, a move which turned out to be unwise. To shorten the supply line to the Marines on Motobu Peninsula, a secondary beachhead was established on the shores of Nago Wan.

In the early morning hours of 9 April the enemy delivered out of Naha Harbor his first successful suicide-boat attack. One 18-foot stinger hit destroyer *Charles J. Badger* off the Brown beaches and knocked out both engines temporarily, but hurt nobody. A second boat was detected by destroyer *Purdy*, and, when fired upon, dropped its depth charge and fled. In the transport area, assault

[3] Destroyer *Zellars* (Cdr. L. S. Kintberger) Action Report.

[4] Estimate by General Bruce at the time. Tenth Army G-1 Report says 175,000 landed by 21 April.

cargo ship *Starr*, target of a third, was conveniently protected by an LSM moored alongside which took the hit, not a lethal one except for the Japanese boat crew. At least three other boats and 15 swimmers carrying hand grenades were detected and destroyed in this attack. Thereafter "flycatcher" patrol was intensified, with one heavy ship and two destroyers assigned nightly to illuminate the mouth of Naha Harbor with star shell. But there were midgets also on the east coast, where *LCI(G)-82* had been sunk in the early hours of 4 April.

During the rest of this week the Marines were engaged in isolated actions against enemy strong points on the Motobu Peninsula; XXIV Corps was consolidating positions, getting ready for a big push in southern Okinawa. The soldiers were now up against the lines that the enemy intended to defend, the edge of a complicated and heavily fortified region across the three-mile-wide waist of the dog, from a point south of the Brown beaches to the Nakagusuku Wan. This area included pillboxes with steel doors impervious to flame-throwers. And Japanese artillery fire on our troops was increasing in volume and accuracy.

2. *East Side* [5]

One reason why Okinawa was chosen as the final springboard for Japan was the prospect of creating an advanced naval base on the shores of Nakagusuku Wan and Kimmu Wan. The one bay is located between the Okinawa dog's legs, and the other in the bend of his neck. Both lie directly across the island from the Hagushi landing beaches. Each is partly protected from the sea by a cluster of small islands and barrier reefs.

Before either bay could be used, the waters and their approaches had to be swept for mines, and the enemy removed from his vantage points on the offshore islands. This section of the Okinawa operation was called for short "East Side," and Rear Admiral Blandy

[5] CTG 51.19 (Rear Adm. Blandy) Action Report 1 May 1945.

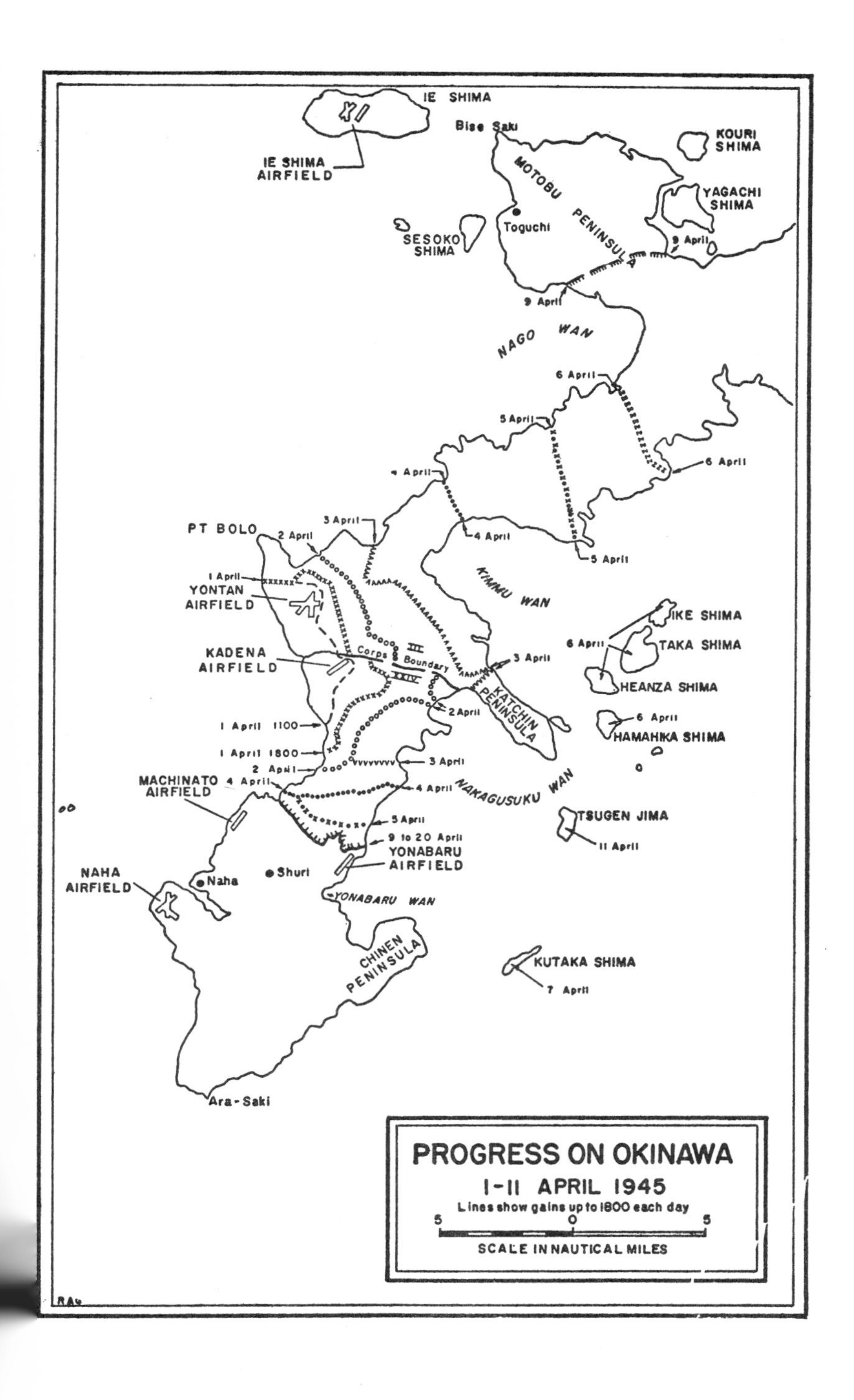
IE SHIMA
IE SHIMA AIRFIELD
Bise Saki
KOURI SHIMA
MOTOBU PENINSULA
YAGACHI SHIMA
Toguchi
SESOKO SHIMA
9 April
9 April
NAGO WAN
6 April
5 April
6 April
4 April
3 April
4 April
PT BOLO
2 April
5 April
1 April
YONTAN AIRFIELD
KIMMU WAN
IKE SHIMA
6 April
TAKA SHIMA
KADENA AIRFIELD
III Corps Boundary XXIV
3 April
HEANZA SHIMA
KATCHIN PENINSULA
2 April
6 April
1 April 1100
HAMAHIKA SHIMA
1 April 1800
2 April
3 April
MACHINATO AIRFIELD
4 April
4 April
NAKAGUSUKU WAN
5 April
TSUGEN JIMA
9 to 20 April
11 April
YONABARU AIRFIELD
NAHA AIRFIELD
Naha
Shuri
YONABARU WAN
CHINEN PENINSULA
KUTAKA SHIMA
7 April
Ara-Saki
PROGRESS ON OKINAWA
1-11 APRIL 1945
Lines show gains up to 1800 each day
5
0
5
SCALE IN NAUTICAL MILES
RA

who was given the job, earned a new nickname, "King of the Bowery."

Minesweeping the approaches to the two bays began 3 April and lasted six days. Commander E. D. McEathron had charge of these sweeps, and as depths in the bays were under 30 fathoms, his group was composed largely of small diesel-powered YMS. By the end of the second day's sweep, fire support ships were able to close the entrance to Nakagusuku Wan. On the 5th Admiral Deyo sent over three battleships, two cruisers and several destroyers to bombard East Side and islands, and that evening a Marine Corps reconnaissance battalion was landed on Tsugen Jima, which had to be secured before the bay could be developed. The Marine raiders were embarked in destroyer-transports *Scribner* and *Kinzer*, screened against possible attack of suicide boats by a "flycatcher" unit composed of an LCI gunboat and six LCS(L) support craft. After the landing, the Japanese garrison of Tsugen Jima came to life and the Marines, although not really run off the island (as they intended only to reconnoiter), had their departure expedited by a shower of machine-gun and mortar fire.

The casualties to Admiral Blandy's task group, during the eventful day of 6 April, we have already noted.[6] Minecraft worked all day clearing the East Side approaches and swept good sections of both bays. On the 7th *PGM-17* was sunk by a mine.

That night the Marine raiders reconnoitered three small islands of Kimmu Wan and found no military present. It was now clear that Tsugen Jima was the only East Side island that had to be taken, since it commanded the main channel to Nakagusuku Wan; and taken it was, on 10 April, by a battalion of the 105th Regiment, 27th Division, lifted from Kerama Retto in two transports and two LST covered by *Pensacola* and two or three destroyers. The Japanese were entrenched in a village at the center of the island and let go a soon as the troops approached. With plenty of naval gunfire support the battalion had overrun the island on the afternoon of 1 April. Of the Japanese defenders, 234 were killed; about 50 mor

[6] See Chap. XII: *Witter, Morris, Purdy* and *Mullany*.

fled, but were rooted out a few days later. All enemy installations, including three 6-inch guns, were captured or destroyed. Losses on our side to Army and Navy were 24 killed and about 100 wounded. The troops were reëmbarked to join the rest of the 27th Division in reinforcing XXIV Corps, and another unit had to mop up.

Every day through 11 April, assigned fire support battleships, cruisers and destroyers bombarded East Side targets designated by air spotters, and delivered call fire for the Marines and XXIV Corps.

3. *Air Battles of 9 and 12 April*[7]

Almanac for 12 April

Sunrise 0609	Sunset 1851
New moon rose 0354	Set 1838

Destroyer *Sterett* (Commander G. B. Williams), after successfully driving off kamikazes on 6–7 April and rendering aid to others not so lucky, now caught one herself. In company with *LCS–36* and *LCS–24*, she was patrolling No. 4 radar picket station northeast of Okinawa, on the evening of the 9th. Five Vals approached in loose V formation. The first, when taken under fire, waggled wings and turned away. The second started a gliding attack. Main battery took it under fire so close that it exploded and splashed on *Sterett's* starboard beam. The third then began its run, and in spite of many hits, retained sufficient control to crash the destroyer at her waterline. When the smoke had cleared, the fourth Val was seen to be coming in on the starboard bow. It was immediately taken under fire by two 5-inch guns in local control and by the machine-gun battery. When 1000 yards distant, 40-mm fire sheared off one wing, which splashed 20 feet on the starboard bow, while the Val turned belly-up, then righted itself and continued over the destroyer. It splashed, after a landing wheel had near-missed the gunnery officer's head and the Japanese pilot's body had hurtled over No. 2 gun. As *Sterett* was making 32 knots when hit by the third Val, the in-

[7] CTF 54 (Rear Adm. Deyo) Action Report 5 May 1945.

rush of salt water put the fires out automatically, but the destroyer received enough structural damage to be sent to a rear area. By good fortune she suffered no loss of life.

The weather on 10 April was too foul for kamikazes, and there was only one air attack, on destroyer escort *Samuel S. Miles*. The plane nicked a gun shield, killing one man, and then splashed alongside, showering the ship with bomb fragments and debris. The following night a Japanese attempt at a counter-amphibious landing against the northern sector was detected steaming northward in Yonabaru Harbor. Destroyers *Anthony* and *Morrison* were summoned, and took the barge completely apart with a direct hit.

On Thursday 12 April the weather was gorgeous, as clear and cool as a summer day in Maine when the wind blows off shore. But there was blood on the new moon. The Japanese chose this day for a second *kikusui* attack of 185 kamikazes, together with 150 fighters and 45 torpedo planes. Early that morning Admiral Turner warned all hands to expect strong air attacks and added, "Don't let any return." Some did return; but ships of TF 51 with the aid of C.A.P. shot down about 147, and TF 58 claimed an additional bag of 15

As usual radar picket ships were the first to catch it. At 060 about 25 planes in ten groups approached from the north. A nigh C.A.P. from damaged *Enterprise* and a few shore-based planes we on duty, but shot down only four of the enemy. Three of th groups flew on to the Hagushi beaches, whence they were drive off, largely by ships' antiaircraft fire, without doing any damag *LCI(R)-356* splashed one with her 40-mm. In the afternoon abo 30 Vals concentrated on station No. 1, manned by destroyers *Pur* and *Cassin Young* and four 158-foot support craft. At 1340 o kamikaze was splashed only 15 feet on *Cassin Young's* port quart a second was shot down at a safe distance, and at 1346 a third stru her port yardarm and disintegrated, knocking out the destroye forward fire room, killing one man and wounding 59. While t was going on, a second plane dived on *Purdy* out of the sun. S fired everything she had and splashed it 2500 yards away.

Damaged *Cassin Young* now retired to Kerama Retto and on